Latin American Cultural Objects and Episodes

Viewpoints/Puntos de Vista
Themes and Interpretations in Latin American History

Series editor: Jürgen Buchenau

The books in this series will introduce students to the most significant themes and topics in Latin American history. They represent a novel approach to designing supplementary texts for this growing market. Intended as supplementary textbooks, the books will also discuss the ways in which historians have interpreted these themes and topics, thus demonstrating to students that our understanding of our past is constantly changing, through the emergence of new sources, methodologies, and historical theories. Unlike monographs, the books in this series will be broad in scope and written in a style accessible to undergraduates.

Published

Beyond Borders: A History of Mexican Migration to the United States
Timothy J. Henderson

Bartolomé de las Casas and the Conquest of the Americas
Lawrence A. Clayton

A Concise History of the Haitian Revolution
Jeremy Popkin

The Last Caudillo: Alvaro Obregón and the Mexican Revolution
Jürgen Buchenau

Spaniards in the Colonial Empire: Creoles vs. Peninsulars?
Mark A. Burkholder

Dictatorship in South America
Jerry Dávila

Mothers Making Latin America
Erin E. O'Connor

A History of the Cuban Revolution, Second Edition
Aviva Chomsky

A Short History of U.S. Interventions in Latin America and the Caribbean
Alan McPherson

Latin American Cultural Objects and Episodes
William H. Beezley

Forthcoming

Emancipations: Latin American Independence
Karen Racine

Mexico Since 1960
Stephen E. Lewis

Latin American Cultural Objects and Episodes

William H. Beezley

WILEY Blackwell

This edition first published 2021

Registered Office
John Wiley & Sons, Inc., 111 River Street, Hoboken, NJ 07030, USA

Editorial Office
111 River Street, Hoboken, NJ 07030, USA

For details of our global editorial offices, customer services, and more information about Wiley products visit us at www.wiley.com.

Wiley also publishes its books in a variety of electronic formats and by print-on-demand. Some content that appears in standard print versions of this book may not be available in other formats.

Library of Congress Cataloging-in-Publication Data

Names: Beezley, William H., author.
Title: Latin American cultural objects and episodes / William H. Beezley.
Description: Hoboken, NJ : Wiley-Blackwell, 2021. | Series: Viewpoints/Puntos de vista : themes and interpretations in Latin American history | Includes bibliographical references and index.
Identifiers: LCCN 2020030563 (print) | LCCN 2020030564 (ebook) | ISBN 9781119078265 (paperback) | ISBN 9781119078142 (adobe pdf) | ISBN 9781119078074 (epub)
Subjects: LCSH: Material culture–Latin America. | Popular culture–Latin America. | Mass media–Social aspects–Latin America. | Latin America–Social life and customs. | Latin America–Civilization.
Classification: LCC GN562 .B44 2021 (print) | LCC GN562 (ebook) | DDC 306.098–dc23
LC record available at https://lccn.loc.gov/2020030563
LC ebook record available at https://lccn.loc.gov/2020030564

Cover Design: Wiley
Cover Image: © Gabriel Perez/Getty Images

Set in 10.5/13.5pt Minion by SPi Global, Pondicherry, India
Printed and bound by CPI Group (UK) Ltd, Croydon, CR0 4YY

10 9 8 7 6 5 4 3 2 1

Contents

Series Editor's Preface

Each book in the "Viewpoints/Puntos de Vista" series introduces students to a significant theme or topic in Latin American history. In an age in which student and faculty interest in the Global South increasingly challenges the old focus on the history of Europe and North America, Latin American history has assumed a prominent position in undergraduate curricula. At a time when immigration restrictions, a growing income gap, and a pandemic have combined to problematize globalization under the aegis of neoliberalism, knowledge of Latin American history is also important for the public at large.

Some of the books in this series discuss the ways in which historians have interpreted these themes and topics, thus demonstrating that our understanding of our past is constantly changing, through the emergence of new sources, methodologies, and historical theories. Others offer an introduction to a particular theme by means of a case study or biography in a manner easily understood by the contemporary, non-specialist reader. Yet others give an overview of a major theme that might serve as the foundation of an upper-level course.

What is common to all of these books is their goal of historical synthesis. They draw on the insights of generations of scholarship on the most enduring and fascinating issues in Latin American history, while also making use of primary sources as appropriate. Each book is written by a first-rate scholar and specialist in Latin American history committed to bringing their expertise into the undergraduate classroom and to a public audience.

The books in this series can be used in a variety of ways, recognizing the differences in teaching conditions at small liberal arts colleges, large public universities, and research-oriented institutions with doctoral programs. Faculty have particular needs depending on whether they teach large lectures with discussion sections, small lecture or discussion-oriented classes, or large lectures with no discussion sections, and whether they teach on a semester or trimester system. The format adopted for this series fits all of these different parameters, as well as the needs of a general public interested in learning more about Latin American history without prior academic preparation.

This volume celebrates a milestone as the tenth book in the "Viewpoints/Puntos de Vista" series, and the first edited and published with the assistance of Jennifer Manias, Wiley's Acquisitions Editor in History. In *Latin American Cultural Objects and Episodes*, William H. Beezley provides a compelling and fascinating analysis of Latin America's rich cultural history, using as its point of departure the history of objects. Drawing on historical literature and primary sources from Latin America, Europe, and the United States, the author takes the reader on a historical tour de force that uses a vast array of objects, from coffee beans to bowler hats, cartoons, and roasted chicken, as gateways to understanding major themes in cultural history, and most importantly, the complex art of survival and resistance in a world region buffeted by conquest, colonialism, exploitation, imperialism, and social inequality. Written by one of the pioneers in Latin American cultural history whose 1987 book, *Judas at the Jockey Club and Other Episodes of Porfirian Mexico*, helped spark intense interest in this field, the book also brings objects to life as mementos to everyday life and material culture – aspects of history that a more traditional or textual analysis illuminates only with great difficulty. I am most pleased to present this important work to what I hope will be a wide readership.

Jürgen Buchenau
University of North Carolina
Charlotte, USA

Call...cry...shout...yell

"Ooo-wa-ooo-aaooaaooaa-ooo!" or "Taaar-maan-ganiii"

The call to action, the cry for attention, the shout for followers, or the yell for adventure – the expression of much of Latin America's history comes through these declarations of political battles, alerts to domestic or foreign dangers, rallies of like-minded individuals, and introductions of the first step to challenges. These outcries also signal identification of real and imagined communities, built through the appropriation of cultural items in Latin America and the mass media creation of cosmopolitan popular culture. Calls, or *gritos*, serve a major role in Latin American, for example Mexican, politics and culture. The best known surely is Padre Miguel Hidalgo's "Grito de Dolores" that in 1810 launched the struggle for Mexican independence. The Catholic rebellion beginning in 1927 against the Mexican revolution leaders featured the iconic cry, "¡Viva Cristo Rey!" Moreover, groups and institutions adopt yells that identify those who shout, such as the National Autonomous University of Mexico students who chant approval, "¡Goya!, ¡Goya!" Searching out these cries for different organizations and different Latin American countries provides an intriguing scavenger hunt that reveals a different dimension of both global and national cultures.

No shout, sounding across Latin America and most of the rest of the globe's comic strip pages, radio airwaves, and movie soundtracks, has ever equaled Tarzan's signature roar. When Edgar Rice Burroughs created his fictional hero slightly over a century ago, he described the shout as "the victory cry of the bull ape." Whatever it sounded like, it called together a global following for the syndicated comic strip that by 1935 appeared in 278 newspapers worldwide. When Tarzan appeared in movies and on radio, fans heard it for the first time. The initial version premiered in the partial sound movie serial *Tarzan the Tiger* (1929) as a "Nee-Yah!" noise and then on the first radio serial in 1932 James Pierce as Tarzan yelled something like "Taaar-maan-ganiii" (still common in Cuba and other parts of Latin America) that, according to the novels, meant in simian language "White Ape." For the first full sound movie, the producer wanted a distinctive cry that fans across the Americas and the world could recognize. The movie shout succeeded so well it was adopted and used by young Tarzan fans, called Tarzanistas throughout Latin America.

The newspaper comic strip, radio programs, and subtitled movies attracted great popularity. In Argentina, it resulted in the writing and publication of *el nieto de TARZAN* (the grandson of Tarzan), by an apocryphal author in 1932 and in 1950 the filming of the unauthorized *el Hijo de Tarzan* (the son of Tarzan) with Eugene Burns, Johny Colloug, and Mae Comont. Argentina's first International Comics Convention held in 1968 at the Torcuarto Di Tella Institute featured as its International Guest of Honor Burne Hogarth, the illustrator of the comic strip "Tarzan." A later parody was done in one of Latin America's most famous comic strips, Chile's "El Condorito," using a Tarzan character called "*Condorzán*."

The prominence of the yell suggested using a button like a musical Hallmark greeting card in this prologue. Such a button proved to be prohibitively expensive for the book, but anyone can go to this link: https://www.mentalfloss.com/article/12328/disputed-history-tarzan-yell to hear it[1] or search videos of Tarzan's yell in any search engine. Moreover, the objects in this book serve as yells, calling for action, celebration, or adventure expressed in episodes that are linked, however thinly, to the things in each chapter title.

Note

1 Bill Demain, "The Disputed History of the Tarzan Yell" (August 22, 2012).

Introduction

Res humanitatis, A Montage

Objects can make tangible the thoughts, activities, and performances that characterize the lives of everyday people. They also serve as expressive mementos of past events and expectant symbols of desired futures. Poets have said it differently: Only in the world of objects, even the least remarkable ones, do "we have time and space" (T. S. Eliot), so we "can find the entire cosmos" (Wisława Szymborska). Finding these worlds in objects such as potshards has fallen most systematically to archaeologists, but occasionally other investigators have adopted a similar methodology to chart cultures. Archaeologists, anthropologists, and art historians have examined religious relics, ritual regalia, and civic artifacts as well as craft industries, especially ceramics, weaving, and textiles in Latin America. Sam Roberts, in the *New York Times*, pointed to the marks that things – the wheel, the crucifix, the credit card or the computer chip – have made on civilization. Nevertheless, only a few authors have used an object from daily life, one perhaps overlooked and not necessarily handmade, to describe the larger histories it harbors or the episodes that it introduces.[1]

Delight and surprise constitute the goals of this book. Delight comes from an appreciation of the imaginative and resourceful aspects of everyday lives that individuals develop in their homes and communities. Surprise comes from their efforts to make lives well lived despite daunting obstacles and haunting legacies of conquest, colonialism, nationalism, and inequalities of resources and authority.

Things, that is, objects, provide lessons that make evident both these sentiments. These objects have obvious material properties, but serve as more significant cultural phenomena and point to episodes of everyday life. The different objects examined here each contain several general expressions. Only two of the objects as the subject of chapters deal specifically with visual media, but all of them in some way have been featured in movies, documentaries, television or all three. This, it seems to me, confirms their popular appeal to the general public. Moreover, all the objects are associated with music, another factor that accounts for their ubiquitous popularity. Popular or local religion can be identified as well; it appears obviously in three of the chapters, and more subtly in the others, but it occurs in each, providing a constant thread in Latin American culture and life.

For Latin America, the best example of studies based on objects must be Fernando Ortíz's now classic investigation *Contrapunteo cubano del tabaco y el azúcar* (*Cuban Counterpoint: Tobacco and Sugar*), published in 1940, that examines the unique experience of Cubans, and captures their history and culture. In his study of tobacco and sugar, Ortíz explained how processes of "transculturation" shaped the meaning of those products through the impact of slavery during Cuba's transition from colonialism to independence.

Beyond Ortíz, a few writers have taken objects as the organizing theme for their intriguing narratives to understand Latin American history after the arrival of the Spaniards and the Portuguese. Nearly as iconic as Ortíz is Sidney Mintz's *Sweetness and Power: The Place of Sugar in Modern History*. Other books include Frederick Smith's *Caribbean Rum*, Gregory Cushman's *Guano and the Opening of the Pacific World*, and volumes on commodities such as bananas, cocaine, and coffee, and others concerned with clothing, cuisine, and identity. These publications for the most part provide an economic rather than a cultural analysis. An exception comes from Salman Rushdie's *The Jaguar Smile: A Nicaraguan Journey*, with a chapter on "Sandino's Hat."[2]

Outside Latin America, other publications have centered on objects to explore historical events. These include Neil MacGregor's

A History of the World in 100 Objects (2011), based on the British Broadcasting Corporation and the British Museum collaboration in a successful radio series called "A History of the World in 100 Objects." The book has been reprinted in 10 languages, and, even more striking, its companion 15-minute podcasts quickly topped 35 million hits and have continued to grow in number. These successes encouraged London's Victoria and Albert Museum's exhibit displaying 99 "disobedient objects" representing movements for social change over the past 30 years, including a "Silence = Death" poster created in response to the AIDS epidemic. Latin American objects in the exhibition included an *arpillera* (a collage made of scrap cloth) during the Chilean dictatorship demanding to know the fate of "disappeared" relatives and cloth dolls dressed with ski masks to represent the Zapatista Liberation Army (EZLN) insurgents in Chiapas, Mexico.[3]

Beyond museum exhibits, a handful of authors have written thought-provoking books on objects. Harold Holzer's *The Civil War in 50 Objects* (2014) has been successful, as have books on individual items such as Henry Petroski's *The Pencil: A History of Design and Circumstance* (2011), Mark Pendergrast's *Uncommon Grounds: The History of Coffee and How it Transformed Our World* (1999), Mark Kurlansky's *Salt: A World History* (2003), and others on cod (1998), oysters (2007), and other foods, Giles Milton, *Nathaniel's Nutmeg: Or, the True and Incredible Adventures of the Spice Trader Who Changed the Course of History* (2000), and Sarah Bowen, *Divided Spirits: Tequila, Mezcal, and the Politics of Production* (2015). Another approach focuses on how certain objects define places such as the book by Sam Roberts, the *New York Times* urban affairs correspondent, entitled *A History of New York in 101 Objects* (2014).

Two other books take the study of United States material culture to the general reader by highlighting iconic objects – a fragment of Plymouth Rock, a presidential button, a soldier's footlocker – and using them to brief readers on an historical event. *Souvenir Nation* by William L. Bird, Jr. and *The Civil War in 50 Objects* by Harold Holzer both offer fine essays and color illustrations meant for the armchair historian in all of us. It comes as no surprise that reading each of these books is like taking a stroll through a great museum – Holzer's book focuses on the collection of the New-York Historical Society, while Bird's book examines the relics in the Smithsonian's National Museum of American History.

The objects in this book explore in numerous ways what critic Gilbert Seldes called the Lively Arts,[4] and their emergence in hemispheric terms (or their transculturation) have shaped the cultures of Latin America in the modern era, that is the years after the end of Brazilian empire (1889) and the defeat of Spanish control of Cuba and Puerto Rico (1898). The objects and episodes make an effort to appeal to all the senses, touch, taste, sight, sound, and smell. They have resulted from serendipitous discovery of unusual and interesting items or they have come from the suggestions of friends. Some initial objects had to be put aside because of an effort to provide coverage of Latin America, and, in the end, this led to surprising (to me) choices that compelled new chapters. Ultimately, I chose the things that resulted in the following 10 chapters: each begins with an object acting as a synecdoche or metonym that provides an introduction. A stimulating and significant example of how metonymic narrative works is *Cinderella in Spain*[5] with its examination of the story's motives. The metonyms in this volume I have, as Sam Roberts says, "inflated" in order to consider as a cultural topic or to introduce a cultural episode with international dimensions.

In many instances, the object named in chapter titles only provides a keynote to related but different episodes. In these cases, it is not the object that comes into focus, but the episode that it introduces. Oddly, this connects this undertaking with archaeology, I suppose, where reassembling potshards into an object is not the goal, but one step toward recreating a social practice or lost society. Rather than an emphasis on cause and effect beginning with the object, the narration proceeds to an episode through the concatenation, sometimes improbable, of events. This approach poses questions: Is this historical stream of consciousness or perhaps only the correlation of individuals after sociology or statistics, or does it represent the joining together of the subtexts, weaving together information read between the lines, or listening to the silences surrounding objects and their meaning? Are they the traces that Carlo Ginzburg referred to as an indexical paradigm? These interpretative and methodological theories deserve discussion. Just not here, where the emphasis is not on interpretation but explanation of objects and episodes. These comprise in the same sense as Carlo Ginzburg's narratives a montage.

Finishing the manuscript led to some suggestions of other topics and surprises. My editor had five anonymous readers vet the original proposal, and each of the five offered comments that proved helpful. Many made suggestions for additional objects and episodes for this book. These possibilities exist for additional investigation for books, articles, graduate theses or term papers. Of these, the most difficult to forego was the recommendation of the moustache as an iconic male style throughout Latin America and its metonymic symbolism for masculinity and issues of gender in the region. Other intriguing objects proposed included the Bolivian-made knock-off women's undergarments marketed on street corners in Buenos Aires as French lingerie. No doubt this involves as well La Salada, South America's largest marketplace for fraudulently labeled clothing.[6] There are also the department store mannequins with physical proportions and the department store mannequins with physical proportions copied from Venezuelan winners of the Miss Universe contest that serve as guides for women from the circum-Caribbean region seeking plastic surgery. A fascinating introduction to a transcultural topic came from Peter Steiner, a graduate student at the University of Wyoming, who wrote about the collaboration of Vans Shoe Company in the U.S. with Huichol artisans in Jalisco and Nayarit, Mexico, known for both yarn painting and beaded objects, including a totally covered VW bug (called a vichol). The company and the Huichol, in a 10-month hand-done process, produced two shoe styles incorporating both bead decoration and yarn painting in limited editions of 360 pairs each. Released September 20, 2014, the shoes celebrated one tradition of the Huichol.[7]

Courtesy of Jaramara Mendoza Sandoval.

Latin America provides the book's general location, even with discussion of global associations and transcultural appropriations. Nevertheless, in Latin America, Italians and Italian culture have a remarkable, unexpected presence. This includes, for example, the Peru–Argentine soap opera "Nino." Why this Italian presence happened remains unexplained, beyond piecemeal investigations.

Notes

1 A good example is David M. Guss, *To Weave and Sing: Art, Symbol, and Narrative in the South American Rainforest* (Berkeley: University of California Press, 1990). The American Historical Association published a roundtable on material culture in *American Historical Review* (December 2009); see also Sam Roberts, "Object Lessons in History," *New York Times* (September 27, 2014).

2 Sidney Mintz, *Sweetness and Power: The Place of Sugar in Modern History* (New York: Penguin Books, 1985). See also Frederick H. Smith, *Caribbean Rum: A Social and Economic History* (Gainesville: University Press of Florida, 2008); Gregory Cushman, *Guano and the Opening of the Pacific*

World: A Global Ecological History (New York: Cambridge University Press, 2013); Salman Rushdie, *The Jaguar Smile: A Nicaraguan Journey* (New York: Random House, 1987).

3 "¿Qué son los Objectos Desobedientes?" (August 9, 2014), http://www.bbc.co.uk/mundo/noticias/2014/08/140801_finde_cultura_objetos_desobedientes_ch.

4 Gilbert Seldes, *The 7 Lively Arts: The Classic Appraisal of the Popular Arts: Comic Strips, Movies, Musical Comedy, Vaudeville, Radio, Popular Music, Dance* (Mineola, NY: Dover Publications, 2001; originally published in 1924).

5 Maia Fernández-Lamarqu and Foreword by John Stephens, *Variations of the Story as a Socio-Ethical Text* (Jefferson, NC: McFarland & Company, 2019). This investigation came as a wonderful suggestion from one of the reviewers.

6 Matías Dewey, *Making it at Any Cost: Aspirations and Politics in a Counterfeit Clothing Marketplace* (Austin: University of Texas Press, 2020).

7 Peter Steiner, "A Suit Fit for A King: Narratives from a Cultural Empire" (Seminar paper, University of Wyoming, 2014); https://vimeo.com/channels/596143/103385088.

Acknowledgments

This book has taken a long time but has been a pleasure to complete. It owes its existence, in the first instance, to several persons who have given assistance or made suggestions at critical times. Series editor Jürgen Buchenau patiently allowed me to tinker with the project until it reached this form. Editor Peter Coveney suggested ways to make a half-baked idea a full-blown proposal and then insisted on a narrative that matched the subject; he did, surprisingly, have an absolute aversion to titles using Latin phrases. Since Peter's retirement, Jennifer Manias has continued his careful and professional guidance to authors. Carmen Nava, the unofficial cronista of Mexico, the city she loves, answered obscure questions, made smart suggestions, and laughed at foolish mistakes. William E. French, a fellow traveler throughout Mexico to puppet museums, impromptu accordion concerts, and regular mezcal tastings, converses with the past and always reconceptualizes the context of individuals and events. Our discussions always prompt me to rethink the narrative. There are no better friends.

Two other people serve as accessories to this project as they have for others. David Yetman and Dan Duncan make Emmy-winning programs for television, especially PBS's "The Desert Speaks," and now "In the Americas with David Yetman." The opportunity to travel with them as a guest for some episodes resulted in the discovery of some of the objects included in this book. Dave and Dan always provided challenging and amusing conversations over dinner and drinks, wherever we were in a half dozen Latin American locations.

Finally, this book is dedicated to Nic Beezley and his brother Matt and cousins Virginia and William, to Rosy, with whom I walk each morning around 4 a.m. While she sniffs the trails of rabbits or squirrels, I ponder the morning's writing project. Of course, it is also dedicated to Blue.

1

Bowler Hats

Hugh Threlfall/Alamy Stock Photo.

Bowlers, often called derbies, for the women of La Paz, Bolivia have become the expression of their identity, community, and locality. Not surprisingly, a recent television program of professional wrestling featured La Paz women, reputedly housewives, wearing their iconic derby. The origin of these hats has been tangled up in a thicket of Aymara romance, town memory, and urban folklore.

Latin American Cultural Objects and Episodes, First Edition. William H. Beezley.

Largely ignored has been the essential role of merchants from the Italian Piedmont.

Other hats beside bowlers top off the typical clothing of indigenous women in the Andes. Hats appear in Peru, Ecuador, northwestern Argentina, northeastern Chile, and, especially, Bolivia, where they make a statement as an emblem of identity. Especially for women from La Paz, consumption of derbies also allows urban Aymara ladies the conspicuous display of their social status. In one of South America's poorest nations, the derby predominates in some communities but there exists a wealth of more than 100 hat styles for both women and men in a population of 6.4 million. Some women, preferring another style, have adopted a Stetson known locally as a "J. R. Dallas," because it resembles what J. R. Ewing wore on the once popular television series (1978–1991). Gunnar Mendoza, director of Bolivia's National Archives in Sucre, once declared, "I don't know of another region in the world that has such a variety of hats." Nevertheless, the derby, called in Spanish a bombín or sombrero hongo (a mushroom hat), predominates as the stereotypical female headgear especially in La Paz. Aymara women, who have dominated market trade, wear black, brown or gray bombines while selling fruits, vegetables, and today, home computers and compact discs. With their hats, they have become a picturesque part of the Bolivian city best known to visitors. Other women wear them throughout the Andes. As a result, hat-making thrives as a business, from home shops and, until recently, the industry-leading but now closed Charcas Glorieta factory in Sucre. Although typical today, the bowlers and similar hats preserve neither preconquest vestige headgear nor uniquely Aymara objects.

Shortly after arriving in the Andes, the Spanish brought guild workers who produced felt to make hats.[1] The fabrication involved the use of arsenic, and ingesting the chemical resulted in madness among the workers. In a strange episode, an entire guild of hat makers went crazy at the same time in Potosí, Bolivia – the richest and largest city in the Americas at the time – and they rioted through the streets. Despite the spectacle of mad hatters, production continued for Spaniards; for the indigenous new felt hat styles came only later.

Indigenous peoples did not immediately adopt Spanish hats because they had long used traditional head coverings, as demonstrated today by archaeological evidence. The monoliths and ceramics of the ancient Tiahuanaco culture centered near Lake Titicaca feature headgear of a flat, rectangular style. Later the ancient Aymara, confirmed in burial remains, adopted a conical hat without a brim. The Inca ruler did not use a hat at all, rather a head band that signaled his authority, although the men and women of this empire wore various caps.

The derbies, now traditional women's wear especially in La Paz, had been typical for barely a century and a half when their adoption completed the evolving women's clothing adaptations in the Andes. Following the Túpac Amaru Rebellion that racked the region from 1780 to 1782, the Spanish crown sent a Royal Inspector with extraordinary authority to evaluate its causes and make proscriptive changes. Inspector José Arreche concluded the rebellion, as a kind of cargo cult, had resulted from identification with traditional Inca society, so in order to destroy the collective memory of the indigenous greatness of the pre-Spanish empire, he ordered prohibitions against speaking Quechua, celebrating Inca holidays, practicing cultural mores, and wearing of ethnic clothing.[2] One royal decree directed Spanish colonial landowners to require that indigenous peoples on their properties adopt the clothing typical of the Spanish provinces of the owner.[3] Villagers were forced to wear Spanish garments that already had become the clothing of Andean mestizos especially in Peru in an adaptation of the clothing worn by Spanish commoners (in Madrid called the Maja). For women it included a skirt with several petticoats, embroidered wrap,[4] a jacket-like blouse, and often a large hat. Andean peoples resented being forced to wear Spanish clothes, and they tended to make changes, creating community distinctions in color, embroidery, and hat styles.

Villagers covered their heads with hats made of feathers, alpaca, tin, plaster, felt, straw, and *tortora* reeds, a type of bulrush that grows from Lake Titicaca, across Peru, to Easter Island. Perhaps the typical *lluchu*, a woven cap with ear flaps, comes from this era and was modeled loosely on the Catalan beret with flaps from Madrid. An alternative explanation posits that the cap, also called the Ch'ullus in much of highland Peru, dates about 600 CE from the pre-Inca Mocha culture. Female residents of Tarija, near the Argentine border, adopted hats patterned after eighteenth-century women from Andalusia.[5] Men and women from Jatamayu, in the highlands near Sucre, preferred helmet-like headgear, roughly patterned on the helmets worn by sixteenth-century Spanish conquerors, called *monteras*. Here women for weddings and fiestas use a flat hat, with a black cloth brim, two raised points on top, embroidery of green, red, and black threads and an assortment of silver beads and shingles. Various other versions of the montera exist with associated legends that it is a "secret map hat" indicating where Inca treasure had been hidden or that its decoration uses pre-Spanish amulets to preserve indigenous religion. The sheep wool hat called an ovejón became typical in the rural communities of six Bolivian provinces: La Paz, Oruro, Potosí, Tarija, Chuquisaca, and Cochabamba. In the three lower provinces with tropical climates, women use palm hats. The ovejones were made with molds that enabled the shaping of a variety of hats that were worked until they became rigid. In many communities, men, women, and children wore these. For example, women's hats of Ursia have a high crown shaped, according to one writer, like a warhead with a black strip around them at the base. In Potolo and Ravelo, they adopted low crowns decorated in many colors.

Some communities, especially remote ones, had hats that are not of the ovejón type. The members of the Yura community adopted woven hats of dark blue with low crowns that during fiestas were festooned with stars and moons in the shape of the owner's initials. The Tarabuco community in Chuquisaca province had two styles, the shining montera, like the conquistador's helmet with details representing the community, and the Pasha montera, worn only by women, with an elliptical shape reminiscent of Napoleonic-era hats. These were decorated with embroidery, beadwork, and glass. As a base, the Pasha has white fabric that in case of mourning is exchanged for black. Unmarried females choose woolen hats. Boys in this community wear black wool caps covered with embroidery called a jokollo, or tadpole, in part because of the tail of the cap and also referring to their adolescence.[6]

Styles in the provincial capitals varied. Striking women's black hats in Potosí resembled those of medieval European witches. Those of Tarifa, at a lower altitude with warmer weather, were made of lighter cloth with low crowns and were worn on the back of the head. The resulting halo reflected the style of the Andalusian settlers who had come to the region. In Cochabamba, they wore the tarro cochabambino (the Cochabamba jar), an all-white hat with a tall crown and wide brim, that featured a black ribbon. According to legend, a Roman Catholic priest ordered an unmarried Quechua woman living with her lover whom she intended to marry (a practice common among community's engaged couples), as penance for adultery, to wear a black ribbon on her hat. At the next mass, all the Cochabamba women wore black ribbons as a comeuppance to the priest and the style persisted.[7] The women also still perform a dance called La Diablada (dance of the devil) wearing these hats. In La Paz, the women adopted this hat shape in black, brown, ivory, or white color without the ribbon.

Cholitas (indigenous females) in La Paz and cholos (both women and men) in the Potosí and Oruro mining districts changed their hat style early in the twentieth century. Italian merchants selling goods in Bolivia received merchandise, including hats, brought from Genoa by a wholesale enterprise based in Tacna, Peru, Laneri, Solari, & Company. Perhaps Tacna's earliest Italian retail company was Canepa Hmos y Cia, founded in 1862. Several other Italian companies developed after the British, French, and Spanish abandoned the region in 1879 when the outbreak of the War of the Pacific sparked the Chilean invasion of Bolivian and Peruvian coastal towns. Italians, who had been mostly involved in small trades,[8] stayed during the Chilean occupation and came to dominate commerce, including merchandise going to La Paz, Potosí, and Oruro. Tacna offered the shortest distance with its well-established trade route that had existed since the mid-sixteenth century when silver from the mines arrived there for shipment from the nearby port of Arica to Europe and trade goods imported from Europe passed through on the way to Potosí and other mines. Italians, chiefly from Lombardy, Piedmont, and Liguria (especially the capital Genoa), were the largest number of immigrants in Peru from the 1870s until World War II. Tacna's Italians soon became an integral part of the community, recognized in the Plaza de Armas with a portly statue of their national hero, Christopher Columbus. Each October 12, the town firemen cleaned it with their hoses as part of the Día de la Raza, the Columbus Day celebration. The Italian government named one of the resident Italians as honorary consul.[9] The community had an Italian Club (the Círculo Italiano) led by tycoon Dante Abelli, who had tin mines in Bolivia, and Andrés D. Laneri, who managed the wholesale import business from Genoa.[10]

From Tacna, Laneri, Solari & Company shipped to Chile, Peru, and Bolivia various items including luxury clothing and other goods such as Ferrarelle, the famous bottled mineral water from near Naples.[11] The company provided retailers with a multitude of mining tools, preserved foods, and ready-made clothing, including the rather expensive Italian Borsalino and Valera & Ricca hats. The merchandise until early in the twentieth century arrived from the coast after several days' travel by mule when it reached Huanuni near Oruro, and Uncía near Potosí.[12] In Oruro, a group of 40 Italians (in 1889) competed for the commercial trade. In nearby Huanuni, Ludovico Antonio Galoppo, who had left his native Piedmont town of Vallemosse for Chile, lived for some years in coastal mining towns, and then moved to the Bolivian mining zone. He soon created a construction partnership with fellow Italian Marcelo Aglietti di Cossato. Aglietti & Galoppo worked for Simon Patiño's mining company. In 1914, Galoppo turned to retail merchandise with Aldo Ormezzano establishing la Sociedad Galoppo & Ormezzano to import Italian goods to Huanuni. The company successfully sold imported fabrics, draperies, hosiery, hats, stockings, handkerchiefs, shoes, loose wool, and cotton fabrics – all bought from Italy at half price. Galoppo sold his goods in the small general store, where his hats were either tossed in with canned sardines, condensed milk, hard cheeses, other foods, hammers, nails, and dynamite, or they were dangled from the ceiling between slices of smoked lard and Oxford pig feet. Workers selected hats and other items and the mining company deducted the cost from their pay.

Galoppo's business acumen and market intuition after some years resulted in two decisions on March 17, 1914. His success in developing interest in hats led him to drop the sale of general merchandise and focus only on hats in the hope of obtaining an exclusive contract with the Italian company Borsalino. He wrote to Borsalino's wholesaler that the obstacle to major hat sales, especially to women, was the cost. Women costumers liked the style but only wanted or could afford to spend about 2 lire, so he proposed that Borsalino produce for them a hat made of less expensive materials than the usual quality felt or wool. He wanted bowler-style hats described in the 1912 catalog, but made as "qualitá superiore," with the lowest price materials. He proposed these hats, to appeal to the women, be called the Cappello da Ciola – the Chola hat.[13] It became the iconic derby of women in the Bolivian and Peruvian Andes.

Galoppo's plan worked. The Borsalino Cappello da Ciola had a good reception and other derbies became popular with men in Huanuni in 1915. For the following year, Galoppo ordered 28 dozen cloth hats for men and 18 dozen Cholas for indigenous women and an additional two dozen elegant samples, with brims of at least 5½ or 6 centimeters (about 2 to 2½ inches), stating, "there is nothing worse than a hat without a brim." He also ordered four dozen tongos (caps). Galoppo did not want Borsalino to supply the women's hats to other retailers in Bolivia and suggested such business with other companies might prejudice his dealings with Borsalino.[14]

Galoppo's comments reflected the local competition for hat sales. The Portillo company of Uyuni had begun selling Borsalinos in Huanuni, and in Oruro, Filippo Nannetti had been selling general goods for years. The Marin company had opened a shop in the same community to sell Borsalinos. The hats represented only part of the Italian goods sold by both companies. The Laneri wholesale company did not want to jeopardize successful general sales to these companies in Huanuni, Uncia, and other nearby places. The company opposed the idea of the Borsalino company giving Galoppo exclusive rights and noted that Portillo and Marin were two of its best customers with business valued at thousands of pounds sterling each year. Marin & Co. of Oruro, for example, had developed a strong relationship with Laneri, who provided an endless variety of assorted merchandise, and the company's warehouses stored products, it was said, "from all climates" with an assortment as complete as the trade fairs of Leipzig and Nizhny Novgorod. Galoppo soon opened Sombrerería Nacional, which eventually earned a reputation for its hats throughout Bolivia.

Even more intense competition existed in La Paz. As early as 1884, the Italian consul in La Paz, Roberto Magliano, reported 300 Italians in the country, with the majority in the capital. They included merchants and pharmacy, clothing, and general store owners, along with 150 Franciscan brothers and 36 Santa Clara nuns.[15] The capital Italians felt numerous and successful enough in 1910 to found the "Sociedad Italiana de Beneficencia Roma." By 1919, G. De Nota was selling Borsalinos in La Paz. His offerings for men included the old style with loose, silk lining. He bought a minimum of 100 dozen per year. The male consumers here, according to reports, wanted a hat that featured both aesthetics and durability. Beyond Laneri's retail clients in the city, another source of hats resulted from his sales to a dealer in the Peruvian town of Yunguyo on Lake Titicaca bordering Copacabana, Bolivia, a short distance from La Paz. The Yunguyo retailer, beyond limited local sales, filled resale orders from nearby La Paz, apparently largely delivered by smugglers. The contrabandistas, who were perhaps women,[16] soon specialized in Ciola or Cholita hats.

The hat vendors in La Paz included a second-generation Italian immigrant couple, Domingo Soligno and his wife, from Buenos Aires, perhaps by way of Salta. They arrived in La Paz confident they could succeed in the haberdashery business with a shop popularizing imported men's hats. Perhaps the Solignos were familiar with their countrymen's enterprise in Bolivia through the trade from Salta to La Paz that had been disrupted by, if not completely replaced with, goods shipped from Antofagasta to Oruro when a railroad opened in 1892.

Soligno ordered a supply of derbies, the style called bowlers by the Irish railroad construction workers who wore them as they built a railroad in Bolivia. The hats that arrived were too small for most workmen and they were brown, and the workmen wore black. Neither the workers nor Bolivian men wanted them. At that point Soligno developed a marketing strategy, perhaps even giving some away as samples, to sell the hats to the Cholitas.[17] He promoted them as more fashionable than the ones with provincial Cochabamba origins they were wearing, indicated the crowns had space for their braids that would hold the hats without pins, and, as an added appeal, claimed that the crown's height signaled the marital status of the woman to potential suitors. Another popular tale claimed Soligno's Borsalinos increased the fertility of women.[18] These Borsalino hats, the bombín, became widely adopted and because of their higher price became the ultimate expression of conspicuous consumption for Cholitas who wanted to demonstrate their economic success.[19] Within a few years, the bowlers became standard. Successful Cholitas displayed their status with lavish jewelry, especially large, dangling earrings, nylon stockings, vicuña shawls, and several Borsalino hats in different colors.[20]

The success of these Italian hat vendors and other merchants who were members of the Italian Club resulted in 1926 in the presentation to La Paz of a statue of Genoese navigator Cristóbal Colón in honor of the centennial of independence. The statue stands in the center of July 16 Avenue in the center of La Paz.

Soligno, José Escobar (who would become a well-known hat maker) and others soon imported the derbies, probably through the Lineri company. Several of the Italian merchants decided to join together to create a factory for clothes items, but they could not agree, and only Soligno continued with the plan. Eventually, he established the Lanificio Boliviano Domingo Soligno (The Domingo Soligno Bolivian Wool Clothing Factory), likely inspired by Lanificio F.LLI Cerruiti,[21] founded in 1881 and based on an earlier company in Biella, Piedmont, his family's Italian homeland. The hats he made and sold, along with those sold by other merchants, connected the Cholitas to

Italy's most fashionable milliner, and the Solari company remained the most important wholesale business for years, at least until sometime between 1929 and 1936, when European events disrupted Italian businesses and American trade.[22]

Since the mid-nineteenth century, Borsalino had been a name synonymous with Italian hat-making. Its founder, Alessandro Giuseppe Borsalino, was born in 1834 in Alessandria, a small town in northwest Italy. By the age of 14, he was working in a hat factory. After visiting other factories across Italy and France to learn more about the trade, in 1850, the aspiring entrepreneur went to Paris, the center of fashion including hats, as an apprentice in the Berteil company. Seven years later, in 1857, he and his brother Lazzaro opened the Borsalino workshop and Giuseppe introduced new handmade, elaborate processes that took many weeks to produce the felt hats. This Italian business pioneer soon became a global captain of industry as the company began the export of hats that became popular after 1914 in Andean South America.

The company made different styles, but two models in particular became associated with Borsalino: the Panama, made from paja toquilla fiber (*Carludovica palmata*), found particularly in Montecristi, Ecuador, processed with a technique called "the fuma" to produce its unique ivory color, and the derby, which was and still is made of felt and a mixture of different furs including rabbit, treated until it produces a soft fabric. The latter became extremely popular and was exported worldwide under the patented name "Borsalino." Its unmistakable shape has reached iconic status over the years. The hats made the company a success. From the beginning, Giuseppe had respect for his workers and their needs, so he developed for them both health insurance and a pension fund. At his death in 1900, the company had nearly a thousand workers, boasted an annual production of one million hats, and exported 60 percent of its production overseas. Teresio Borsalino succeeded his father, headed the company for 39 years, and added to its success. By 1913, it employed more than 2,500 workers with an annual production of more than two million hats sold throughout the world. Teresio Borsalino's nephew, Teresio Usuelli, the last heir of the Borsalino family, took over as chairman and served until 1979, when he left the company in the hands of Vittorio Vaccarino. In 1986 the company moved from its factory originally located in the center of Alessandria to a new, more efficient and modern site in the town's suburbs. Initially, the old factory housed a hat museum until a few years ago, when the museum moved and the site became Eastern Piedmont University.[23] Roberto Gallo now holds the title of CEO and president of the company and has expanded it to include Asia and the U.S. (with Borsalino America). There are now more than 15 flagship stores in Italy, France, and China. The Borsalino name has continued to figure prominently in fashion history. Today Borsalino's hats extend beyond the classic felt derby and the famous straw "Panama-Montecristi" to new styles targeting the young hat wearer. All the world's fashionable stores, such as Harrods in London and Saks on Fifth Avenue in New York, stock Borsalino's famous hats. The company now has men's, women's, and children's ready-to-wear collections as well as accessories from perfumes to eyewear. With an annual turnover of almost 30 million Euros, Borsalino remains the leader in Italian hat manufacturing. Over the years the Borsalino family has not only made an impact on the history of fashion with their famous hats, but also they have influenced the history of their town. They are renowned for the charitable work they have done since the company started. They have financed public works, from the aqueduct to the orphanage to the old sanatorium, for the city of Alessandria.[24]

Adopting these derbies, the Cholitas joined other famous groups and individuals wearing the iconic Borsalino hat. The Pope had one, as did other church prelates, and they were worn by the Royal Canadian Mounted police, Sephardic Jews, and New Yorker Emma Stebbins, who sculpted the Angel of the Waters at the Bethesda Fountain in Central Park.[25] In the 1920s movie stars adopted the hat. In Hollywood, Charlie Chaplin's Tramp character, Greta Garbo, and Lou Costello, along with Stan Laurel and Oliver Hardy, were well known for their bowler hats, which they used as accessories, twisting the rim, doffing them, and adjusting the angle on their heads to denote mood. A mainstay expression of anger or frustration, especially in silent films, had an actor punch out the crown of his derby; part of the joke was that the actor could not break the hardened shellac hat unless it previously had been weakened. Later Humphrey Bogart wore a Borsalino, notably in *Casablanca* (1942), as did the famous World War II correspondent Ernie Pyle.

The derby connected the Cholitas to wider styles than the Borsalino. The hats had prominence in England, where they had originated and are called bowlers. Milliners Thomas and William Bowler created the first one in 1849. The Bowlers made the hat to fulfill an order for the firm of hatters Lock & Co. of St James's. Lock & Co. had been commissioned by Edward Coke, the younger brother of the 2nd Earl of Leicester, who had designed a close-fitting, low-crowned hat to protect his gamekeepers' heads while on horseback from low-hanging branches. The keepers had previously worn top hats, which were easily knocked off and damaged. Lock & Co. then commissioned the Bowler brothers to produce the design. They responded with a distinctive hat with a hard shellac resin-treated crown. When Coke arrived in London in December 1849 to collect his hat, he reportedly placed it on the floor and stamped hard on it twice to test its strength; the hat withstood this test and Coke paid 12 shillings for it. In accordance with Lock & Co.'s usual practice, the hat was called the "Coke" hat (pronounced "cook") after the customer who had ordered it. This is most likely why the hat became known as the "Billy Coke" or "Billycock" hat in Norfolk.

This hard hat proved suitable for a number of occupations – street traders, cab drivers, fishmongers, shipyard stevedores, and construction workers. Others such as salesmen, insurance hacks, civil servants, and bank managers quickly adopted it to replace the upper-class top hat and the lower-class cloth cap. The bowler went on to be associated with businessmen in the City of London as part of their dress code. Beyond London, the bowler had several other lives.

It has been largely forgotten, but the bowler, rather than a Stetson or sombrero, was the most popular hat worn in the western United States. Perhaps Frederick Remington's cowboy paintings and

Hollywood western movies popularized the historical inaccuracy. Cowboys, miners, lumberjacks, and railroad workers preferred the bowler, and so did lawmen and outlaws, including Bat Masterson, Butch Cassidy, Black Bart, Billy the Kid, and the Wild West Show's outlaw Marion Hedgepeth, commonly called "the Derby Kid." They all wore the hat with its shellacked crown because it worked as head protection and did not blow off easily when horseback riding or sticking one's head out the window of a speeding train or in any strong wind.[26]

Another region that took up an appreciation of the bowler hat is the Niger Delta of Nigeria. Men of this region use the hat along with a walking stick. Introduced by British colonials in the 1900s, these fashion accessories have become a staple part of the regional costume to indicate social status. Recently a "Bowler Hat Bash" has become part of Nigerian Independence Day celebrations.[27]

In Northern Ireland, the bowler became common in shipyards. Along with a pair of white gloves and a sash, the bowler hat represented the traditional clothing worn by Loyalist fraternities, such as the Independent Loyal Orange Institution, the Royal Black Preceptory, and the Apprentice Boys, when they marched.

Except in these Irish parades, the wearing of the bowler in Great Britain in the 1960s began declining. Central heating was being installed in new homes and in workplaces and hats became less necessary for warmth. Moreover, the rapid growth in private car ownership often made wearing a hat difficult. Coincidently, mass media influences, particularly in music, film, and television, worked against hats. Celebrities and star performers stopped wearing them. Traditional hats fell out of fashion and were replaced by baseball caps, beanie hats, skull caps, hoodies, and cheap umbrellas. Even at weddings, high society horse races, and church, hats for both men and women gave way. They largely died out during the 1970s. One factor that perhaps contributed most to the hat's demise was its association with Captain Mainwaring, in the BBC television series *Dad's Army*, in which as a banker wearing a bowler and as captain of the home guards he represented an outdated, conservative, and pompous comic character. Another likely cause was the TV comedy show *Monty Python*, in which John Cleese used the bowler in sketches such as his Ministry of Silly Walks. This did nothing for the bowler's social image.[28]

In Bolivia, the importation of Borsalinos ended when World War II prevented commerce with Europe. Moreover, Italian wartime demands for shellac used in the production of both airplanes and small boats greatly reduced the material available for hats. In Bolivia, the local Borsalino-style hat factory, Charcas & Glorieta in Sucre, continued to produce the hats, and a similar, knock-off version was being made in La Paz in various colors, crown heights, and material quality in local workshops.[29] Imports resumed after the war, and beginning in the 1950s, the Broadway House sold these Borsalinos, at a rate of three or four a day, at a price equivalent to $75 each, for over 30 years.

The Borsalino factory closed some time later, but much of the demand was met by Charcas & Glorieta in Sucre. This factory had been founded by Princess Clotilde Urioste de Argandona, a Bolivian philanthropist who received her title from Pope Leo XIII in the late nineteenth century, when her husband served as ambassador to the Vatican. In Sucre, she built a castle surrounded by Venetian-style canals, gardens, and a small zoo. She started the hat factory in 1929 to provide jobs for the people of the town. At some point, around 1950, management of the factory was handed to Italian immigrant Mario Nosiglia from Sagliano-Micca in Biela, where the town's nine hat factories had been reduced to one because of the decline of men wearing hats. He directed the 80 employees who used Bolivian, Uruguayan, and Argentine wool to make 35 different hat forms, some based on U.S. and European designs, and, of course, the Borsalino. Under his direction, the workers began producing 7,000 hats each month. The factory's production continued to expand until 1986 when it reached 500,000 hats or unfinished felt hat casings. This production equaled about half of the Bolivian market and it supplied at least 2,000 hat makers in Bolivia, Brazil, Peru, and Chile, who bought casings and molded them into finished bombines that sold for $10 to $20 apiece.

It was well known that during his presidency Victor Paz Estenssoro frequently commissioned Nosiglia to provide his hats.

Charcas & Glorieta in the 1980s relied on the same steam-powered machines installed during construction of the factory. Spare parts and molds had to be made by hand because the factory that built the machinery no longer existed. Perhaps the old machinery explained the company's inability to keep up with demand in Bolivia. In an effort to obtain new or replacement machinery, an executive went to Italy, but unfortunately died just before negotiating for the equipment. So, the company attempted to purchase the Italian hat company Panizza's factory with a $2 million credit, $600,000 of it from the U.S. Agency for International Development. Manager Nosiglia expected the expansion and new machinery to double the factory's output to one million felt hats per year while enabling it to make 60,000 rabbit-fur hats. He said 20,000 felt hats would be exported to Italy for Panizza's former clients. He also claimed the enlarged factory would benefit farmers, who would supply the fur of at least 50,000 rabbits a year and wool from 10,000 sheep, according to company plans. "The economic impact will be extraordinary," Nosiglia declared. Charcas & Glorieta already made beside the derbies thousands of "J. R. Dallas" hats that sold for $15 apiece as well as traditional hats for nearly every region of Bolivia.

Representatives for Sucre's Charcas & Glorieta in the late 1980s negotiated the purchase of the Panizza factory plant and machinery (primarily the front shop, which undertook the first phase of the production of felt). The Bolivian entrepreneurs Alfredo Gimenez and his son Miguel made a partial payment for the restoration of the machinery. Nevertheless, even though the senior Gimenez seems to have been appointed Governor of the Central Bank of Bolivia in 1989, he was not able to provide the necessary amount of foreign currency to pay for the machinery. Consequently, the machinery was never shipped. An Italian intermediary a few years later bought the equipment and probably sold it to one of the former Soviet republics.[30]

When the Nosiglia and Gimenez plans did not work out, the former decided to retire as the Forno family, who owned the majority of the shares in the company, at first wanted to sell the plant, but instead closed it. Nosiglia, rather than lead an idle life, was involved in opening two new hat factories in Sucre, "La Sucre" and "Chuquisaca." These closed after a few years, and a new factory with different owners opened in 1997, Sombreros Sucre Museo y Fábrica. The factory with about 100 workers produced some 2,000 hats a day and the company won international awards for their hats in 1999, 2000, and 2001. The factory included a one-room museum displaying hat styles from around the country. This factory has now closed.[31]

Nevertheless, the derby remains essential headgear in La Paz for Cholas. Worldwide, the Borsalino's unmistakable shape had retained its iconic status. In 1970, the Borsalino gave its name to a box-office hit, *Borsalino*, that starred Jean-Paul Belmondo and Alain Delon as two French gangsters. A sequel followed in 1974, *Borsalino and Co.* The two films relaunched the Borsalino after what had been a fallow period for hat wearing, on the international fashion scene and in films. John Belushi wore one in *The Blues Brothers* and pop star Michael Jackson often wore a fedora matched with a trench coat just like Bogart.

The relationship between Borsalino and the cinema is so strong that it regularly is featured in exhibitions and shows. One example was the recent exhibition *Cinema Wears a Hat*, held in the Triennale di Milano. This trip through the history of cinema and fashion highlighted how the Italian hat is deeply connected with international films. Memorably, the evil henchman Oddjob in the James Bond film *Goldfinger* wielded a bowler as a lethal weapon. Batman's best-known villain, the Riddler, and the evil lead character Alex DeLarge in Stanley Kubrick's film *A Clockwork Orange* wore signature bowlers. Other Borsalino wearers ranged from Indiana Jones to the great western stars, from Johnny Depp to Audrey Hepburn. Current-day popular music performer and producer Pharrel Williams wears one today.

Borsalino even has its own museum. The Borsalino Hat Museum has over 2,000 exhibits and is located in the old Palazzo Borsalino in Alessandria. It was set up at the beginning of the twentieth century by Arnaldo Gardella. Now it hosts shows, exhibitions, and cultural initiatives as well as having a section dedicated to showing how the Borsalino hat is made, still following the same traditional manufacturing process.[32]

Hats remain essential clothing in the Andes. One explanation is that the high altitude, where the sun's rays are more intense and few shade trees grow, make hats a necessity. This accounts for the popular saying, "Use a hat, or your brain will melt."[33] Ecuadorian women still wear hats. They initially wore hats of Spanish origin, but then learned how to make them using sheep wool and felting. Different communities or ethnic groups often have their own variations in the style of hat they wear. The hats became part of the traditional outfit in the countryside. Various highland communities today maintain distinctive hats, ponchos, and embroidered blouses for normal daily wear. Women wear full pleated skirts in bright colors, often with embroidery around the hem. A woolen shawl doubles as a means of carrying shopping or babies on the women's backs. Even in Quito, most of the women and the men dressed in traditional clothing wear felt hats.[34]

The hat, especially in Bolivia, is much more than protection from the sun, according to Haroldo de Faria Castro, a Bolivian author on hats. "It is the most important piece of an outfit" worn by the indigenous, he says. There is no shame in walking barefoot, but one must always wear a hat.[35] In La Paz, it is the ultimate symbol of status. As a result, hat-making remains a thriving business in home industry in Jatamayu and other towns to the current factory in Sucre. The cholas still represent the picturesque in La Paz; as one tourist declared, "the style that immediately caught my eye when arriving was the long silky skirts with layers of puffy petticoats, hand-made shawls, alpaca leg warmers, waist length braids, and tilted bowler hats."[36] Hats also have a significant role in Bolivian fiestas. For El Día de los Fieles Difuntos, the hats are usually covered with red or black paper flowers. For weddings, the hats of the betrothed couple are often decorated with pieces of different-colored paper. In religious fiestas, the pasante (the local name for the person who pays the costs of the celebration) receives guests by placing wreaths of large popcorn on their hats. The guests in turn pin 20 or 50 peso bills on the pasante's hat. Each traditional fiesta has its own clothing with special touches. The Chuncho dancers from Tarija, for example, who dance for San Roque, wear colored feathers on their heads. The Morenada parades feature embroidered and decorated hats as part of this representation of Afro-Bolivian slaves making a satire of Spanish slave-owners. The Tinku ritual combatants wear heavy monteras of hard leather.[37] These are a sampling of fiesta hats. In daily life, hats especially for working men such as miners and construction workers have declined with the adoption of more durable hard hats.

Indigenous women in Puno and in much of Andean Peru also choose to wear the derby-style hat. Coincidentally these indigenous women who wear them are known as Cholas, like those in La Paz, and the hat was styled for them as the Chola hat.

For a sense of identity, status within the community, and definition of style or beauty, many communities continue to wear a representative hat, although the practice probably dates only from the colonial period. The cholitas of La Paz, nevertheless, continue to wear as their status symbol, not much more than a century old, the derby hat.

Notes

This chapter has benefited from the suggestions about research in Italian sources from Lucia Carminati of Texas Tech University, in Bolivian materials from Gabrielle Kuenzli of the University of South Carolina, in fashion essays from Regina Root of the College of William and Mary, and on Italians in La Paz from R. Matthew Gildner, Washington & Lee University.

1 Beverley Chico, "South American Headwear," in Margot Blum Shevill, ed., *Berg Encyclopedia of World Dress and Fashion: Latin America and the Caribbean*. Berg Fashion Library, pp. 456–464. eBook.

2 M. Lissette Canavesi de Sahonero, *El Traje de la Chola Paceña* (La Paz, Bolivia: Editorial Los Amigos del Libro, 1987), pp. 17, 19–21; "Las cholitas luchadores," Mundo Hispano Los Cervantinos, http://mundohispanoloscervantinos.blogspot.com/2013/11/las-cholitas-luchadoras.html. The most thorough account of the rebellion is Charles F. Walker, *The Tupac Amaru Rebellion* (Cambridge, MA: Harvard University Press, 2014).

3 Haroldo and Flávia de Faria Castro, "Bolívia dos Mil e Um Chapéus," *Revista Geográfica Universal*, no. 44 (May-June, 1978), p. 105, http://unboliviable.tumblr.com/post/11006496682/sombreros-bolivianos.

4 Called the mantón de Manila. https://en.wikipedia.org/wiki/Manila_shawl.

5 Canavesi de Sahonero, pp. 25–42; with pictures of Spanish styles, pp. 27–29; p. 28 has a picture of women from Andalusia.

6 Haroldo and Flávia de Faria Castro, "Los Mil y Un Sombreros de la Cultura Boliviana," *Geomunco*, 8, no. 6 (1984), pp. 566–571.

7 "Hats Off to Bolivians - From Derbies to Helmets, They're Tops," *Los Angeles Times* (January 25, 1987).

8 An Italian term baccicia, which translated into the common language as bachiche, used to refer to Italians of modest social status. This term in Peruvian society was used to classify a certain type of business such as pulpero, winemaker, blacksmith, etc. The majority made their way with a small shop, the old pulpería, attended by a man almost always dicharachero, talkative, friendly, a connoisseur of all the neighborhood and sometimes called gringo.

9 Mauricio Belmonte Pijuán, *Polenta: Familias italianas en Bolivia* (Editorial Gente Común: Ambasciata d'Italia in La Paz, 2009), p. 25. See Gabriella De Ferrari's delightful memoir of growing up in her Italian family in Tacna. Her father, Armando, was the honorary consul, and after the monarchy was abolished in 1946, he hosted a party for town elites each June 2, the Day of the Republic. *Gringa Latina: A Woman of Two Worlds* (Boston: Houghton Mifflin Company, 1995).

10 Joaquín Blaya Alende, *El Progreso Italiano en Chile* (Santiago: Imprenta La Ilustración, 1921), pp. 441, 445, with photographs. Selections are included in the online essay at http://www.italianosenchile.cl/documentos/documentos-tacna.html.

11 Alfonso Díaz Aguad and Elías Pizarro Pizarro, "Algunos antecedentes de la presencia italiana en la ciudad de Tacna: 1885–1929," August 29, 2014. http://www.italianosenchile.cl/documentos/documentos-tacna.html.

12 Archivio Storico Borsalino Indice, municipal library, Alexandria, Italy, Mazz 144, 6, 1915–1919.

13 The word "ciola" (without the "h") does not translate into the English language as it is the proper name of the hat in question, which in Peru is named "Chullo." Dario Pavan, archivist, Alessandria Community Library, Italy, to the author, March 28, 2019.

14 "Esclusiva Borsalino. L. A. Galoppo & Galoppo e Ormezzano," Alexandria, Italy, Mazz 144, 6, 1915–1919.

15 Belmonte, "Los sombreros Borsalino de Ludovico Galoppo," pp. 179–182, 60.

16 This seems possible because of the development of smuggling after the plebiscite in 1921 that divided the towns of Tacna and Arica, carried on daily by the women of Tacna, who might well have had knowledge of the practice between Peru and Bolivia. They might even have worn the hats they were smuggling. De Ferrari, pp. 71–72.

17 One travel guide account claims the first shipment of hats was given away to the women. Claudia Looi, "Bowler Hats and the Cholas of Bolivia," http://travelwritingpro.com/bowler-hats-cholas-bolivia/.

18 http://www.bloganavazquez.com/2010/02/07/el-sombrero-bombin-borsalinoy-las-mujeres-de-bolivia/.

19 See the blog entitled "El Mundo Cervantinos," the Hispanic World seen through the eyes of some Italians, "Las cholitas luchadoras" (November 15, 2013). The origin story of the railroad workers is repeated on this website. http://mundohispanoloscervantinos.blogspot.com/2013/11/las-cholitas-luchadoras.html.

20 Lesley Gill, *Precarious Dependencies: Gender, Class, and Domestic Service in Bolivia* (New York: Columbia University Press, 1994), p. 106.

21 Belmonte, p. 89.

22 Archivio Storico Borsalino Indice Mazz 969 Fascicol 13, Rappresentanti cessati dal 1929 al 1936-c/provv:

23 http://www.hathistory.org/borsalino/.

24 http://www.made-in-italy.com/italian-fashion/designers-and-brands/borsalino.

25 https://www.nytimes.com/2019/05/29/obituaries/emma-stebbins-overlooked.html. Liza Bakewell provided this reference.

26 Lucius Beebe, "The Hat that Won the West," *Deseret News*, Salt Lake City, Utah (October 27, 1957), https://news.google.com/newspapers?nid=336&dat=19571026&id=xQQpAAAAIBAJ&sjid=PkgDAAAAIBAJ&pg=7036,5636283&hl=en. Beebe said that he examined thousands and thousands of photographs of westerners for a book and that resulted in his conclusion.

27 *The Guardian* (October 8, 2016).

28 Don Anderson, "Bowled Over by a Hat Beloved by Orangemen," *Belfast Telegraph* (March 3, 2015), https://www.belfasttelegraph.co.uk/opinion/

columnists/bowled-over-by-the-history-of-a-hat-beloved-by-orangemen-30380950.html.

29 http://www.bloganavazquez.com/2010/02/07/el-sombrero-bombin-borsalinoy-las-mujeres-de-bolivia/.

30 Gian Paolo Gamba, Panizza company, email to the author, March 22, 2015.

31 "Las remembranzas de Mario Nosiglia," Belmonte, pp. 223–224. There are some slight differences in this essay with Michael Powell and Jürgen Horn, "A Tour of Sucre's Hat Factory," http://bolivia.for91days.com/2011/06/12/a-tour-of-sucres-hat-factory/.

32 http://www.made-in-italy.com/italian-fashion/designers-and-brands/borsalino.

33 Haroldo and Flávia de Faria Castro, "Los Mil y Un Sombreros de la Cultura Boliviana," *Geomunco*, 8, no. 6 (1984), p. 566.

34 http://movingtoecuador.blogspot.com/2009/10/ecuadorian-hats.html; http://www.ecuadortravelsite.org/traditional_costume.html.

35 "Hats Off to Bolivians - From Derbies to Helmets, They're Tops," *Los Angeles Times* (January 25, 1987).

36 Brittany Robinson, Stars on the Ceiling Travel and Adventure, http://sotcblog.com.

37 Haroldo and Flávia de Faria Castro, "Los Mil y Un Sombreros de la Cultura Boliviana," *Geomunco*, 8, no. 6 (1984), pp. 573–576.

Additional Resources

Readings

E. Gabrielle Kuenzli, *Acting Inca: National Belonging in Early Twentieth-Century Bolivia* (Pittsburgh: University of Pittsburgh Press, 2013).

Zoila S. Mendoza, *Creating Our Own: Folklore, Performance, and Identity in Cuzco, Peru* (Durham, NC: Duke University Press, 2008).

Regina Root, ed., *Latin American Fashion Reader* (Oxford: Berg, 2005).

2

Magic Beans

Ozgur Coskun/Alamy Stock Photo.

A boatload of beans, hoped to be magic enough to solve an athletic and financial crisis, defined Brazilian Olympic participation. In 1932, the ship with the Guaraní name *Itaquicê* left Rio de Janeiro carrying 55,000 bags (an estimated 25 tons) of coffee beans, a delegation of 82 athletes, including a heart-broken rower and the first South American female competitor, a group of 273 officials and family members, and the 50-member National Marine Band destined for

Latin American Cultural Objects and Episodes, First Edition. William H. Beezley.

Los Angeles, California and the Olympic Games. The Great Depression had resulted in the collapse of the international coffee market from 25 to 7 cents a pound and drove many disheartened coffee growers to burn their crop rather than sell at a loss. Moreover, the country remained in turmoil from the 1930 rebellion that ended the First Republic (1889 to 1930) and brought Getúlio Vargas to power. Brazilian Olympic organizers, who had not been able to send participants to the 1928 Games, could not finance the participation of the nation's athletes, nor could President Vargas pay for them. A patchwork solution emerged. Vargas learned the Navy had impressed coastal vessels during the rebellion and fitted them out as transports armed with cannons. He assigned one of them to take the Olympians to Los Angeles with the athletes serving as part of the crew.[1] Growers donated coffee for the leaders of the delegation to sell in port cities along the way to finance the other costs of the trip.

As the journey got underway, efforts to sell the coffee in Brazil's ports north of Rio failed miserably. The delegation leaders, R. de Rio Branco, Arnaldo Guinle, and Dr. Ferreira Santos, had hopes to sell large amounts once the ship arrived in Port of Spain. Unfortunately, Trinidadians, with their oil industry crippled and singing their desperation in Depression-inspired calypsos such as "Send Your Children to the Orphan Home" and "I Don't Know How the Young Men Living," did not, or perhaps could not, buy a single pound of coffee.

This sent the ship and the Olympians to their first major crisis at the Panama Canal. Transit tolls through the Canal charged to commercial vessels were waived for ships of war. The *Itaquicê*'s captain, without sufficient money, and on the technicality the ship was part of the Navy, ordered the band members in uniform topside, more or less in battle stations around the two small cannons mounted on the deck, and presented the *Itaquicê* as a Brazilian ship of the line. Canal officials, laughing at the exaggerated status of the transport, demanded the ship's passenger list and information on its destination. While discussions ensued, the Brazilian water polo team played a pick-up squad from the Canal Zone. The Brazilians won easily and hoped their victory was a preview of Los Angeles. The captain, with his ruse exposed, radioed a distress signal to the Banco do Brasil, which managed to scrape together some money, and dispatched a messenger who arrived with sufficient cash for the tolls a few days later.

The ship steamed through the Canal to the Pacific and the Olympic Games. It stopped at several ports in Central America and Mexico, but the captain had meager success, selling perhaps 300 pounds of the coffee, and he had on hand only $24 on July 22 as the *Itaquicê* docked at San Pedro, the Port of Los Angeles. The Brazilians immediately encountered a new crisis: The ship's captain and team members learned that the Immigration Service charged a one-dollar tax on each person entering the U.S. The coffee money could only pay for 24 athletes to go ashore. Officials chose the contestants they felt had a chance to win medals and whose events were scheduled early in the program. They also paid for swimmer Maria Lenk, the first South American woman to compete in the Olympics. Once ashore, the Olympians each needed to pay a two-dollar entry fee at the Games. Fans and crew pooled their money to pay this fee.

On July 30, 24 Brazilians marched among the 1,500 athletes into Olympic Stadium (today the University of Southern California football stadium), where U.S. Vice President Charles Curtis (President Herbert Hoover chose to campaign for reelection rather than attend) proclaimed the Games open before the athletes and 100,000 spectators. This Parade of Nations marked a success for the Los Angeles committee because so many nations faced financial problems. Travel distances coupled with the worldwide Depression made the cost of sending a team formidable. Entries plummeted. Only 1,500 athletes competed compared with 3,015 at the 1928 Amsterdam Games. Nonetheless, 37 countries managed to send Olympians. Some coped with the financial exigencies by drastically reducing the size of their teams: China, Haiti, Uruguay, and Egypt sent one-person teams and Colombia sent two representatives.[2]

The other 45 Brazilian athletes who remained on board ship hoped for a miracle to pay their disembarkation tax. The head of the delegation sent another desperate radiogram, this time calling on the Brazilian consul in San Francisco to help the team. The consul quickly responded the best he could and sent a courier with a check in Brazilian currency equivalent to 45 dollars. When the messenger departed the exchange was three milreis to the dollar; by the time he arrived in Los Angeles the currency's value had plummeted to 17 dollars and, worse yet, it was refused for insufficient funds.[3]

Selling the coffee initially proved impossible because of the 1930 Smoot–Hawley Tariff, the highest in U.S. history, and authorities demanded an import payment from ship authorities to unload the coffee. Without money or buyers, the captain argued that the coffee did not belong to the Olympic delegation but was part of a private negotiation. This ruse failed; and the captain decided the ship should depart L.A.

The *Itaquicê* sailed with the rest of the athletes and other delegates to San Francisco with the goal of resolving legal issues and in the hope of selling coffee. The delegation negotiated the sale of some coffee, in spite of tariff regulations. For those on the ship, more complications followed with the outbreak of a revolution against Vargas, centered in São Paulo. Harbor officials placed attachments on the ship for immediate payment of the tariff and other harbor fees because payment of promissory notes seemed unlikely with the rebellion.

In the midst of the legal controversy, 10,000-meter runner Adalberto Cardoso feared the *Itaquicê* would not return to Los Angeles in time for his event. Determined to compete, he jumped ship in San Francisco, sold a little coffee in town, and hitchhiked to the Los Angeles Coliseum. He managed to arrive only minutes before his event. He ran and finished last. Nevertheless, he was loudly cheered by the audience who learned of his tenacious efforts to participate. Later fans in Los Angeles contributed money to present him a special medal for his effort.

Eventually, promissory notes were accepted to resolve the legal technicalities and the ship returned to Los Angeles.[4] The trip north had managed sales that financed the debarkation of the water polo, rowing, and pole vault competitors. These athletes did not fare as well as Cardoso or receive as much popular acclaim. Despite their match in Panama, the water polo players did not know the international rules and suffered defeats to the U.S. and German teams. After losing 3–7 in the match against Germany, the Brazilians assaulted the Hungarian referee, Bela Komjadi, one of the founders of the sport, and caused a riot at the pool. The Brazilian team was disqualified and the ruling committee then indefinitely banned Brazil from international competition. Only the rowing team, pole vaulters, and Lenk did well in the Games. The rowers claimed a fourth and fifth place; pole vaulter Lucio Almeida Prado de Castro finished sixth and a teammate claimed eighth place – out of the medals, but excellent nevertheless. Lenk, who used something like a butterfly form, was disqualified for illegal turns, but experienced international competition, styles, and coaching for the first time that she brought back to Brazil. Fifteen athletes had to remain on the ship because of paltry coffee sales and did not have the chance to participate in the Games.

The trip home, which began August 19, was no easier for the athletes. While they were on their journey, the São Paulo State revolt continued against the Vargas government and when the athletes arrived in Rio the 32 Paulistas in the delegation learned the federal army had blocked the road and rail routes to their home. They were marooned once again. They were invited to remain in a safe retreat in Rio, but voted to decline the offer. Instead, they found a friendly captain of a freighter leaving for São Sebastião Island, who gave them free passage to Ilhabela, where they got small boats to use in the São Sebastião canal, then some, including young Maria Lenk, proceeded on foot through the rugged mountains of the Serra do Mar. They hiked for eight hours, foraged for food, and spent the night in a deserted hillside shack. The next morning they marched higher up the mountainside until they found a compassionate truck driver, who gave them a ride to Cacapava, where they caught a train to São Paulo. Although they did not return victorious, the Brazilians had reason to be proud. They held to the statement of the Roman poet Propertius that said, "In mighty enterprises, it is enough to have had the determination."

Maria Lenk stands out. Her family had emigrated from Germany to São Paulo, where she was born. She trained in Amparo, a nearby rural town. Brazilian parents resolutely refused to allow their daughters to wear swimming costumes and they were supported by church prelates. Lenk, who was determined to swim in the Olympics, ignored the restrictions and was excommunicated by the local bishop. The 1932 Olympic team represented one of the last vestiges of *café com leite* culture, in which the non-white population and popular classes had only tacit social and political incorporation.[5]

Vargas had adopted a form of populism with a program to appeal to the greater racial dimensions of Brazilian national identity. Certainly, the Afro-Brazilian influence was recognized and applauded in music, dance, and other cultural practices, including sport. Political publicity exaggerated the emergence of a racial democracy, but major steps were taken to create a society that included more of the racial components of the population than it ever had before.

The *Itaquicê* continued through the 1930s as a coastal steamer, leaving Rio to make a five-day trip, stopping at Vitoria, Bahia, and Maceió to Recife. It stopped in Bahia, so passengers had time for a shore excursion as part of these vacation excursions.[6]

The coffee episode left a bitter taste of disappointment for Mario Cunha, one of the rowers. Mario belonged to the prominent Rio de Janeiro society. His father helped found the Flamengo rowing club in Rio in 1895, although Mario rowed for Vasco da Gama. These boating clubs soon expanded their activities and formed major soccer teams that popularized the sport in the 1930s. Mario had driven a float – his car, actually – during the 1932 Carnival parade in Rio, carrying his girlfriend, an aspiring singer, who had just recorded her first hit song. Even though her brother was the lead rower in Mario's two-man boat, the singer had opposed Mario's trip to Los Angeles. She told him to choose between her and the Olympics. When he took ship, he carried with him her popular hit on a Brunswick record, "Prá Você Gostar de Mim" ("To Make You Love Me"), a traditional *marcha* tune by composer Joubert de Carvalho, to play during the voyage. The marine band no doubt learned it as well. Once the *Itaquicê* arrived in California, meager coffee sales in both L.A. and San Francisco meant insufficient money for all team members to participate. Cunha was one of the fifteen athletes who stayed on board the ship. When he returned, he learned his singer had achieved a popularity that took her to Broadway in 1939 and then Hollywood in 1940. She took the U.S. music and movie world by storm. According to the stories, Mario's onetime girlfriend became the international star Carmen Miranda.[7]

The coffee beans did not prove to be as magical as hoped, but they did inspire the Brazilian committee, athletics, and fans to participate in the Olympics. Questions remain: What did athletes who had to remain on shipboard do to pass the time? Were the ship and its passengers visited by curious individuals in Los Angeles and San Francisco? Did the ship captain sell or give away the rest of the coffee, dump it overboard, or return home with some of it? Perhaps some obscure reference will provide answers. The coffee episode provides a microcosm of the early years of the Vargas government and connected to other cultural events of the time in Brazil, especially the evolution of Carnival, the popularization of samba, and the promotion of soccer.

Carnival today in Brazil climaxes with the sensational three-day celebration in Rio de Janeiro, but the dance and music groups called samba schools, which also had parades and the crowning of royalty, did not have the same overwhelming popular character, neither in Brazil nor in global terms, in the 1930s. Carnival rather had regional dimensions; for example, in the Northeast the celebrations of Salvador de Bahia and Recife differed from those in Rio and included resistance to Rio's prevalent samba music. Rio's organizers made clear their national intentions in 1936 when they required the schools to use songs and floats with a nationalistic theme. In Salvador and other places in the Northeastern zone, Carnival committees would have none of it. Although some sambas appeared in this region in this decade, more significant were the *afoxés*, a tradition of music and dance that drew on the Candomblé of the Afro-Brazilian majority of the community. In Recife, local elites tried to give Carnival an official character beginning in the mid-1930s. Although the rules for participants connected to ideas of nationalism, the regional character prevailed with the encouragement of costumes, heroes, and agricultural products typical of Pernambuco – the province including the community. This resulted in suggestions that women participate dressed as "tomatoes, pineapples, mangoes, cotton, even lobster or processed sugar."[8] The local officials described samba, the chief expression of the Rio Carnival, as a dance that was slow and monotonous, especially when compared to the more raucous local frevo. In this community, clubs devoted to frevo music and dancing (called passo) had been organized as early as 1889 and several remained in existence in the 1930s. Frevo and passo were both described as activities that combined hints of the indigenous peoples, the music of Afro-Brazilians, and the dance of the white population. As such, they perfectly represented the region beyond anything brought from Rio could do. Nevertheless, samba nationalism pushed forward in the region, despite resistance, and by the 1950s it had prevailed. Then it declined with the growth of the re-Africanization of Northeastern culture, in part inspired by renewed pride in the earlier black performances, and the Civil Rights and Black Power campaigns in the United States. Today, Carnival in Salvador, Recife, and the region generally is different from what tourists and television audiences see performed by samba schools in Rio.

The Carnival issue most at stake was whether or not samba represented Brazilian nationalism or whether it was simply an imposition of the national authorities in Rio de Janeiro, the capital at that time. Samba, so it was claimed, came to express the racial democracy of the nation. The 1930 revolution led by Getúlio Vargas focused on Brazilian nationalism above race, class, and regional identities, and in theory and somewhat in practice succeeded in these efforts. In particular, Afro-Brazilian culture was brought through radio and recordings into the cultural mainstream, although it was done through white social filters. Early composing, playing, and dancing of what would become sambas as well as some rituals of Candomblé occurred in the houses of *Tias Baianas* (Bahian aunts) who migrated to Rio in the beginning of the twentieth century. The first recognized samba, "*Pelo Telefone*" ("By Telephone"), was recorded in 1917. Created by musicians who met regularly at the house of Aunt Ciata, it was recorded by Donga (Ernesto dos Santos) and Mauro Almeida. "*Pelo Telefone*" achieved some success and contributed to the popularization of samba. At the end of the 1920s, composers from carnival "blocks" (groups) in central and hillside neighborhoods gave samba a more urban expression. It began to be played on radio stations, although affluent residents of Rio at first rejected it because of its Afro-Brazilian roots. Eventually, its joyful rhythms and satirical lyrics won over the white middle class. Ismael Silva added to samba's popularity when he established the first escolar de samba or samba school, named Deixa Falar (Let it Speak), and transformed the samba beat to make it fit the carnival celebrations and street parades with fast-paced drum orchestras.[9] As it spread across the country, initially associated with Carnival, samba soon developed its own place in the music market.

The clearest example of samba's increasing popularity came with the performances in Afro-Brazilian and working-class popular music, dance, and humor given by Carmen Miranda – known as the Queen of Samba – at the same time as the popularization of Carnival was occurring through the samba schools. Samba lyrics and music, often imbued with satire, sarcasm, and parody, achieved popularity in clubs, on the radio, and through recordings. The words brought a streak of humor to national culture. Carmen Miranda quickly became the symbol of samba, and she did it by serving as a bridge between the people and music of the favelas – poor neighborhoods – and middle- and upper-class society through performances and recordings. Now classics, her samba recordings provided a foundational text for national music. Eventually, Carmen fixed as her stage persona the Bahiana, the icon Afro-Brazilian woman from Bahia, whose costume included a colorful dress and a basket for a hat filled with fruit.

Vargas wanted to promote national culture, both across the country and beyond – one reason he had supported the Olympic team, difficult as it was, to go to Los Angeles. He gave samba official recognition as the "official music" of Brazil. It resulted in its status recognized in intellectual and artistic circles. Classical composer Heitor Villa-Lobos arranged a recording session that involved the participation of the maestro Leopold Stokosk and samba singers Cartola, Donga, João da Baiana, Pixinguinha, and Zé da Zilda in 1940.

Iconic recordings of samba have been made by outstanding Brazilian artists. These musicians include Zé Kéti, born José Flores de Jesus, who began his career in the 1940s in Portela samba school. His classic song is "A Voz do Morro" (1955). Aloysio de Oliveira is famous for singing "Aquarela do Brasil" in the Disney films in the 1940s that popularized the song. He and his ensemble, "Bando da Lua," were involved with the career of Carmen Miranda in the U.S., and he made dozens of popular sambas. Angenor de Oliveira, known as Cartola, has the reputation of being the best samba musician, as a singer, songwriter, musician, and poet. Perhaps his most popular song is "As Rosa Não Falam." Founded in the 1940s in São Paulo, the group called Demônios da Garoa have sold millions of records and their emblematic song remains "Trem das Once." Elza Soares was declared "Brazilian Singer of the Millennium" in 1999 by BBC Radio in Brazil. She brings to performances her incredible musical repertoire, outgoing personality, and edgy style. Among her many samba hits, "Malandro" is one of the most well known. Dona Ivone Lara is another successful samba star, whose popular song "Sorriso Negro" – "Black Smile," a reference to skin color, is one of the most famous sambas in the country and is regularly performed during Rio de Janeiro's Carnival. Recordings and some videos of these samba stars are widely available on the internet.[10]

Outside Brazil, samba's popularity came with the international success of "Aquarela do Brazil" composed by Ary Barroso. It did not make the finals of the Carnival Song of the year in 1939 and even after it was recorded by popular singer Francisco "Chico" Alves, it still did not gain great success. That changed when Aloísio de Oliveira sang it on the soundtrack for a Walt Disney animated film in 1942. This occurred as a result of a trip made by Disney employees, who called themselves El Grupo. Their journey came in response to a U.S. government appeal through the Office of the Coordinator of Inter-American Affairs (CIAA) that was created to produce films in an attempt to counter Nazi propaganda in Latin America. "El Grupo," under the Disney contract, was supposed to make 12 shorts for the U.S. government, and produced two feature films. The first film had Donald Duck and Goofy traveling in South America.

Disney's connection with the CIAA demonstrated this agency's commitment to use movies to carry out its propaganda mission in Latin America. Created in 1940 with Nelson Rockefeller as its director, the CIAA had two immediate and major goals: to initiate economic programs to meet Latin American financial, agricultural, educational, and public health needs, and to manage what was called "psychological warfare," that is, propaganda against Nazi German activities in Latin America. The Museum of Modern Art, with Rockefeller family ties, became the center of CIAA production of documentaries and dubbing for Latin American distribution. Disney was recruited in this effort, not just because he served as a movie mogul but also because of his reputation as an artist throughout Latin America. As early as 1933, Argentina's Escuela de los Artes Decorativas de la Nación had honored him for animation and other honors followed from Brazil and other South American nations. On the trip, the Disney group looked for new material, possible collaborators, and considered the possibility of opening a South American studio. Group members had carried out several months of research before departing on the tour. They generally downplayed the group's ties to the CIAA and official government sponsorship. The first stop on the tour was Brazil, and by the second day, Walt had changed the musical focus from Brazilian classical music to the samba, and soon signed an agreement for the movie rights to "Aquarela do Brasil" by Ary Barroso, a song so internationally popular it was described as the unofficial national anthem of the nation. The successful visit was extended from 10 days to three weeks, as Walt had meetings, spoke in Portuguese as Mickey Mouse on the radio, and the group made drawings, listened to music, and took photographs and shot film footage. Besides the samba, the group also designed a parrot, soon called Joe Carioca, as the logical choice for stories about Brazil (Dan MacManus, one of the illustrators of Joe Carioca, was Mexican, and soon emerged as the leader of the Disney educational films for Latin America). The research and filming in Brazil became the basis for the animated film *Saludos Amigos* that premiered in Rio de Janeiro and then Buenos Aires. It was a huge success throughout Latin America and the United

States, then in England, and was quickly translated into Swedish, French, Russian, and even Italian and German.[11]

The samba "Aquarela do Brasil" was included again two years later in Disney's *The Three Caballeros*. After the film, the song became known not only in Brazil, but worldwide, with recordings in the U.S. by Xavier Cugat and Django Reinhardt. The huge popular interest encouraged Bob Russell to create an English-language version copyrighted in the U.S. as "Brazil." Jimmy Dorsey first recorded the song with the English lyrics sung by Bob Eberly and Helen O'Connell in 1942. Other recordings followed and it became the first Brazilian song to be played over a million times on U.S. radio. The recording industry in 2009 added the Dorsey recording to the Grammy Hall of Fame.

Once World War II began, in 1941 the Office of the Coordinator of Inter-American Affairs sent Orson Welles on a government tour to counter the Nazis. The Welles tour was supposed to result in a film, which he named *It's All True*, but Welles never finished it. In a 1993 documentary, the surviving Welles footage was assembled, including a nearly full-length version of his Brazilian fishermen saga, "Four Men and a Raft," from the initial tour. It was only when he realized that samba was the Brazilian counterpart to jazz (a passion of his) and that both were expressions of the African diaspora in the New World that Welles opted for the story of Carnival and the samba. Most pertinent here, the Welles footage showed Rio's Carnival in all its dimensions. Welles later said U.S. movie producers rejected this rough cut of a documentary on Carnival because it featured almost exclusively Afro-Brazilians. Welles added the executives never bothered to listen to the music, but just rejected the footage because of the individuals on the screen.[12] Orson Welles never finished *It's All True*, but the legendary movie fragment was partially restored and edited as *It's All True: Based on an Unfinished Film by Orson Welles* in 1993.[13] The RKO management wanted a film that would have the popular appeal of the performances, recordings, and films of Carmen Miranda.

Samba did become internationally popular, both in its Carnival, festive form and in a slower version danced by couples in clubs and ballrooms. This latter version transformed into the global phenomenon in both popular and jazz performances in the 1950s called Bossa Nova, played by Stan Getz in the U.S. and, especially, the song "The Girl from Ipanema."

Carnival and samba gave Brazil a presence and drew tourists, music fans, dance clubs, and moviemakers after World War II. Reinforcing these cultural practices beginning in the 1930s as part of the Vargas cultural nationalism was the rise of futbol, called soccer in the United States. Organized soccer began in 1888 in the São Paulo Athletics Club, but Brazilian fans regard its actual founding in 1930 when a national team was assembled to play in the first World Cup tournament. The team eventually achieved a world reputation for its fluid, imaginative play, achieving beauty on the field not known in the European matches. This was confirmed when Brazil won the World Cup in 1958, 1962, and 1970 and followed with two more championships in 1994 and 2002. It has international followers who continue to make the team a favorite whenever or wherever it plays. Beginning in the Vargas era, Brazil quickly became known as "The Country of Soccer."

The most popular and best-known club teams come from Rio de Janeiro and from São Paulo. They maintain an intense rivalry. Rio has Fluminense, Flamengo, Vasco, and Botafuga. The annual match between Fluminense and Flamengo, called the Fla-Flu Derby, captures national attention among soccer fans. It was first contested in 1911 when 10 disenchanted players from Fluminense abandoned the team and went to Flamengo to create a squad. This remains the most intense club match. In São Paulo, the most popular and most successful clubs are Corinthians (adopting the name of a visiting English side), São Paulo, Palmeires, and Santos. The latter has a place in memory held by every fan because it was the home club of the legendary Pelé, the greatest player in Brazilian and probably world soccer history.

Vargas had a major impact on Brazilian soccer in the 1930s when he saw it as a way to promote popular nationalism. Football had the potential for unifying the people of Brazil as a single nationality. Crucial for this to happen, the national team had to use the best players regardless of racial or class backgrounds to compete in international games. Afro-Brazilian and working-class players achieved celebrity status from their performances. This contributed to the Vargas promotion of what was being called "racial democracy." Nevertheless, below the national selection, the teams remained tied to aristocratic, white social clubs managed by privileged white administrators as amateur squads during the 1930s and 1940s.

The first World Cup for the international soccer federation's championship occurred in 1930, with 13 teams in Montevideo, Uruguay. Many European teams could not afford the travel costs and did not participate. The Brazilian team, all players from Rio clubs, except one from São Paulo, played in a group with Yugoslavia and Bolivia, and lost to the former 2–1, and defeated the latter 4–0, but did not advance to the next round. Uruguay defeated Argentina in the final. The success of its two South American rivals encouraged changes in Brazil's approach to international competition.

The 1934 World Cup held in Italy gave Benito Mussolini the opportunity to use sport to promote his fascist regime. Italy defeated Czechoslovakia 2–1 in the final. In the knockout arrangement, Brazil lost its first match to Spain 3–1 and was eliminated. The entire tournament provided another example to Vargas of the potential to use sport for political goals.

Inspired by Vargas's concerns, the Brazilian team showed the significance of the changes in the next World Cup in 1938, held in France. The best players were selected regardless of club managers trying to pressure for certain individuals and the team also held a month-long training camp in Caxambu, famous for its medicinal waters, in Minas Gerais State. One method for physical preparation had the players carry around pieces of logs to build strength. The squad also played with the nation's first Afro-Brazilian star, Leônidas da Silva, called the "Diamante Negro" or the Black Diamond. The team defeated Poland, in extra time, and drew with Czechoslovakia before facing Italy in the semifinal. A widely repeated story regarding da Silva concerned his absence in the semifinal match because of a reported injury. Stories circulated that Mussolini sent agents to persuade the Brazilian coach to leave da Silva out of the game. Italy won 2–1, with a disputed penalty kick awarded against the Brazilians. Da Silva returned a couple days later for the third place match, in which Brazil defeated Sweden 4–2 for the third place medal.[14] Da Silva earned his reputation by inventing the bicycle kick, scoring seven goals during the tournament – the highest scorer and, according to folk stories, scoring his last goal barefooted, using black mud to hide his lack of shoes from the referee. This was the beginning of Brazil's ascension to the top of world soccer that would take place following World War II and the rise of fervent passion among Brazilians for their team.[15]

Samba is frequently associated with soccer and Carnival. Samba achieved an international audience, and Brazilian soccer established the standard for other teams worldwide. Carnival has been recognized as the celebration, fiesta, and party without rival, surpassing even Mardi Gras in New Orleans, and other variants throughout Latin America and Europe. The rise of samba, Carnival, and sport, especially soccer, created a new national popular culture in Brazil. It also created a new dimension to national populist politics. The activities inspired celebrities popularized in the media of newspapers, radio, movies, and newsreels. Vargas recognized the political value of all three and built a populist regime using them.

Beyond politics, new cultural activities added commercial activities as well. After the national soccer team returned from Europe with its third-place victory, a group of entrepreneurs launched a chocolate bar called "Diamante Negro" to profit from da Silva's achievements. Even today, it remains among the most sold candies in Brazil, although many, perhaps most, people do not know its connection to the nation's first soccer star.[16] Samba, with its popularity, inspired the music industry, certainly dependent on foreign companies from the U.S. and Europe. As visible as records were, sheet music remained the lucrative side of the business. Records and movie appearances did not have the profit margin of the compositions. This resulted in a good deal of international exploitation of Brazilian musicians whose music and lyrics were copyrighted elsewhere and used to make records abroad. Musical movies had popular followings and gave some performers such as Carmen Miranda international followings, sales, and popularity. Samba schools at Carnival, soccer teams at the World Cup, and samba recordings and sheet music created an image of Brazil that attracted travelers, imitation, and admiration in the Americas and beyond.

These cultural developments had appeared, if only as implications, during the voyage of the *Itaquicê* and the disappointments that came at the 1932 Olympics. Nevertheless, as the decade progressed, these cultural activities became more popular. In the last decades of the twentieth century, Brazilians achieved world stature in both men's and women's soccer, with recent stars Neymar (Neymar da Silva Santos Júnior) and Marta (Marta Vieira Da Silva) ranked among the world's best players. Additional athletic success has come in Olympic basketball, track and field, and volleyball. Coffee remains a major product and an everyday addiction. Perhaps the beans did prove magical for Vargas and Brazil after all.

Notes

1 *Brooklyn Daily Eagle* (November 11, 1930), p. 4.
2 Jerry D. Lewis, "Brazilian Athletes Perked Up The 1932 Games With Their Coffee Caper," *Sports Illustrated* (August 11, 1980), pp. 11–12.
3 Mark Palmer, "InterMat Rewind: 1932 Olympics" (August 11, 2008), http://intermatwrestle.com/articles/3962/Rev-Rewind-1932-Olympics.
4 *New York Times* (August 4, 1932), p. 23; *Los Angeles Times* (August 19, 1932), Shipping News, p. 7.
5 José Sergio Leite Lopes, "Class and Ethnicity, and Color in the Making of Brazilian Football," *Daedalus* 129, no. 2 (Spring 2000), pp. 239–270.
6 Walter Stafford Swetnam, *Kith and Kin*, https://archive.org/details/KithAndKin_808.
7 Ruy Castro, *Uma biografia de Carmen Miranda* (São Paulo: Companhia das Letreas, 2005), pp. 26–28.
8 Jerry D. Metz, Jr., "Carnival as Brazil's 'Tropical Opera,'" in William H. Beezley, ed., *Cultural Nationalism and Ethnic Music in Latin America* (Albuquerque: University of New Mexico Press, 2018), p. 185.
9 "History of Samba Music," https://www.brazilcultureandtravel.com/history-of-samba-music.html.

10 For example, Sarah Brown, "The Top 15 Brazilian Samba Songs to Add to Your Playlist Right Now" (October 3, 2017), https://theculturetrip.com/south-america/brazil/articles/the-top-15-brazilian-samba-songs-to-add-to-your-playlist-right-now/. The songs are available on YouTube or on recordings.
11 J. B. Kaufman, *South of the Border with Disney: Walt Disney and the Good Neighbor Program, 1941–1948* (Burbank, CA: Disney Press, 2009).
12 Darién J. Davis, "Racial Parity and National Humor: Exploring Brazilian Samba from Noel Rosa to Carmen Miranda, 1930–1939," in William H. Beezley and Linda A. Curcio-Nagy, eds., *Latin American Popular Culture: An Introduction* (Wilmington, DE: SR Books, 2003), pp. 183–200.
13 Catherine L. Benamou, *It's All True: Orson Welles's Pan-American Odyssey* (Berkeley: University of California Press, 2007).
14 "Brazil in the World Cup 1938 – France," http://www.v-brazil.com/world-cup/history/1938-France.php.
15 Janet Lever, *Soccer Madness: Brazil's Passion for the World's Most Popular Sport* (Long Grove, IL: Waveland Press, 1983).
16 "Brazil in the World Cup 1938 – France," http://www.v-brazil.com/world-cup/history/1938-France.php.

Additional Resources

Readings

Luciano Aronne de Abreu, Luis Carlos dos Passos Martins, and Geandra Denardi Munareto, *Embracing the Past, Designing the Future: Authoritarianism and Economic Development in Brazil Under Getúlio Vargas* (Brighton: Sussex Academic Press, 2020).

Mauricio A. Font, *Coffee and Transformation in São Paulo, Brazil* (Lanham, MD: Lexington Books, 2010).

Alma Guillermoprieto, *Samba* (New York: Vintage Books, 1991).

Video

Carmen Miranda: Bananas is My Business. Documentary filmed and directed by Helena Solberg (1995).

3

Red Flags

Westend61 GmbH/Alamy Stock Photo.

Small red pennants on bamboo (tacuara) poles along the shoulders of Argentine roads mark handmade shrines dedicated to the popular saint Gauchito Gil or Curuzú – the Guaraní word for cross – Gil. Although not recognized by the Catholic Church, Antonio Mamerto

Latin American Cultural Objects and Episodes, First Edition. William H. Beezley.

Gil Nuñez from Corrientes province was executed, although innocent of wrongdoing, and became a folk saint. As a martyred innocent, it is believed, he has access to the divine to work miracles and protect travelers. A huge following of Argentines offers him devotion and seeks his assistance in their daily lives, especially if traveling. The red banners serve as a material metonym of the Gauchito.

Sometime during one of the incessant civil wars between the Liberals (or Celestes) and the Autonomists (or Colorados) between 1840 and 1848, perhaps even 1890, Gauchito Gil in Mercedes, Corrientes, was accused of desertion from the army and arrested by a Colonel Zalazar. Many people considered him a traitorous criminal guilty of many unpunished crimes, but others knew him as a "Robin Hood," who robbed those who took advantage of the poor. Doing what others dared not do, he was, they said, the avenging gaucho who righted injustice. The colonel ordered a sergeant and three men to escort him to the town of Goya for trial. Gil's friends knew prisoners seldom arrived at the court because on the journey they were shot to death, it was said, attempting to escape. Friends gave evidence of Gil's innocence to Colonel Zalazar, who issued a belated pardon on January 8, but Gil and the escort had already left for Goya.

Along the way, eight kilometers from Mercedes at the crossroads of modern routes 123 and 119, the escort stopped. The gauchito grasped the situation and told the soldiers he knew a pardon was on its way. The sergeant only laughed and ordered the soldiers to execute Gil at a tree off the road. Gil cautioned the sergeant that when he returned to Mercedes he would learn that his son was dying, but the sergeant ignored him. Gil then told the sergeant to pray to him because he would die an innocent who could intercede with God for the life of the son. Contradictory stories describe what happened next. Several accounts say the soldiers formed a firing squad, but their bullets could not harm Gil because he was wearing the amulet of Santa la Muerte; finally one bullet entered his heart to kill him. Other stories say all the bullets failed, so the soldiers hanged him by his feet until he was dead on the solitary tree. And, in a third version, they hanged Gil head down from the locust tree and then beheaded the body because they knew that he had the ability to hypnotize individuals by looking at them in the eyes. After the execution, the escort returned to Mercedes and learned about the pardon.

Back at his home, the sergeant discovered his son was ill to the point of dying and he immediately prayed to the Gauchito, asking for a miracle. The son recovered overnight and the sergeant then made a wooden cross of *ñandubay*, a flowering tree (*Prosopis affinis*) that figures in local Guaraní lore. He took the cross to the crossroads and into the field where the execution had taken place. The location quickly became an oratory, a site where pilgrims burned votive candles to accompany their prayers for help.

Miraculous stories quickly circulated about Gauchito Gil and the site of his death. On January 8, thousands of pilgrims would come to the location, off the road, in the field of a large landowner (called an estanciero). As the number of pilgrims increased, the estanciero feared their candles would cause a fire in his fields. He decided to have the oratory moved to a local cemetery. Immediately he and his family began to suffer. The family fortune declined as the fields dried up, one of the landholder's sons died of a strange disease, and the owner himself developed an illness that doctors could not diagnose. Finally, he called a curandera, a faith healer, who told him that he would recover only when he returned the Gauchito's oratory to its proper location. The landowner immediately ordered the construction of a mausoleum that contained a cross of beautiful wood at the site of the Gauchito's execution and donated additional land for the pilgrims who visited. Even though the body remained buried in the cemetery, the fortune and health of the landholder and his family returned.

Another legend recounts provincial government plans to pave the highway. The engineers decided at the same time to straighten the road to shorten the distance between towns. The newly planned route went directly through the Gauchito's oratory, and therefore it would be necessary to move it. Opposition developed to the road because it crossed a place sacred to the people of Corrientes province. Once construction approached the site, workmen, equipment drivers, and even crew chiefs refused to continue work. The engineers, after discussions, decided to respect the desires of the workers and honor the Gaucho's oratory by maintaining the curve around it.

The sanctuary remains at the crossroads near Mercedes. Pilgrims recognize the site from a distance as hundreds of bamboo poles with red pennants become visible. On arrival, they visit the mausoleum with its plaques giving thanks to the Gauchito and an enormous number of offerings that include wedding dresses, children's toys, miniature houses, little cars, and prayer cards of the saint with handwritten requests for assistance or expressions of gratitude.

January 8, regarded as the anniversary of his death, witnesses a major celebration. In the days before the fiesta, vendors and musicians arrive at the sanctuary and set up a tent town. They create temporary businesses, dance halls (called bailantas in the Lumfardo slang of Buenos Aires) for chamamé, and booths that sell drinks, chipá (the traditional Guaraní cheese bread), and souvenirs. On the land donated by the landowner was constructed a platform for offerings and candles, bathrooms, bars, and other amenities for those who came to pray. The documentary "Antonio Gil" by Lía Dansker shows the celebration and tells the legends of his martyrdom, miracles, and his popularity.[1]

Lía Dansker made the documentary over a decade, filming the processions at the annual celebrations from 2001 until 2010 and captured the voices of pilgrims that she said formed a composite of the belief in el Gaucho. The director argued that disparate legends about the Gauchito result from the needs of the popular classes in each community to resist repression and protect themselves. As an example, she said that it is no coincidence that, in the slum neighborhoods of Buenos Aires, the Gauchito "is the saint of the 'chorros' (thieves)," a dimension different from that of his myth in rural regions.[2] The documentary about the festival shows how the responses of both the local government and the Catholic Church have gone from dismissal of the event to an attempt at appropriation of the saint. But the Gauchito remains part of the popular community. "I don't know if I need another god," says one of the interviewees.

Today Gauchito Gil's popularity as a saint of the people can be seen everywhere along all the stretches of the nation's highways with their ubiquitous red pennants on tacuara (bamboo) poles that indicate a shrine. Red is Gauchito Gil's emblem, used for candles and ribbons with written requests or thanks. The requests to the Gauchito typically concern health, money, work, love or the courage to face difficult situations. Above all else, travelers ask for his protection during their journey. Drivers often stop briefly at the shrine. Pilgrims tie a ribbon to those already at the shrine. They take another one giving thanks for a blessing received and tie it on their wrist or the rearview mirror or put it in the house some place to protect the home. In the northeastern province of Formosa, the common practice is for drivers to honk their car horns as they pass a shrine. This insures the Gauchito's protection during the trip. Not honking risks some misfortune during the journey.[3]

Legends about Gauchito Gil and the methods of devotion to him demonstrate the vitality of locality in popular culture, vernacular language, collective memory, and local folklore. Locality places a community and gives expressions of its uniqueness. Gil's hometown of Mercedes (formerly Pay-Ubre), in Corrientes province in the region of Entre Ríos, Argentina's Mesopotamia between the Paraguay and Paraná rivers, has distinctive customs, all of which form a part of the traditions of El Gaucho Gil. He is regarded as the most famous person born in the province. This distinctive ecological region, with native bamboo, was inhabited by Guaraní people when the Spanish explorers arrived. It has a distinctive cultural heritage expressed in the language combining Spanish, Buenos Aires Lumfardo, and indigenous words. It has a unique music called chamamé.

The environment appears in specific plant types in the legends of the Gauchito, including the wood of the cross dedicated to him, the local bamboo used for the poles of his pennants, native red flowers, and references to other local plants. The legend of the landowner required the intervention of a native healer, or curandera, to provide a solution to his and his family's bad fortune. The annual celebration demonstrates the merging of Spanish and Guaraní with Lumfardo, slang from lower-class Buenos Aires (the slang of the early Tango), in the naming of dance halls and bars.[4]

The unique music can be traced to the arrival in Corrientes of the Jesuit priest Antonio Sepp from Tyrol in modern Italy in April 1691. Although he stayed only until the end of 1693, he nevertheless introduced European music, opened a large workshop in Yapeyu that made musical instruments of all kinds, including organs, organized the first polyphonic choir, and created a music school for indigenous peoples. Sepp taught the local Guaraní to dance the classic Viennese waltz, and, according to traditional stories, the dancers called for a faster and faster rhythm. To please the dancers, Sepp composed a waltz that became known as chamamé and the musical style has come to express the wild and free character of Corrientes and the Northeast. A modern composer, Roberto Galarza, has written several chamamés, including one dedicated to the Gauchito called "Unjustly Condemned."

The Gauchito has been celebrated in poems as well. For example, there are those by the well-known poet Florencio Godoy Cruz. Sometimes printed on cards with images of the Gauchito, the poems are taken as offerings to the sanctuaries of other popular saints such as the Difunta Correa (the dead mother). The Gauchito and other popular or folk saints capture the essence of daily religion. Their prevalence in everyday life resulted in the Difunta Correa becoming the protagonist in Vicente Blasco Ibáñez's celebrated novel, *El préstamo de la difunta* (1921; translated into English as *The Mad Virgins and Other Stories*, 1926).

The Gauchito is one of innumerable saints not recognized by the official Roman Catholic Church, but revered, worshipped, and above all trusted for help, comfort, and assistance with the trials of daily life. Individuals bring symbolic items to the shrine as a thank you for the Gaucho bringing success, happiness, joy, and surprise to life.

The devotion to El Gauchito demonstrates a pattern typical of practices in Catholic parishes and dedication to popular saints from the colonial era not only in Latin America but also in Portugal (e.g., Dr. José Tomás de Sousa Martins)[5] and Spain and perhaps other Catholic regions as well. Journeys away from family and community have been recognized as dangerous, with successful departure and return dependent on divine assistance in the face of natural and human risks. Visits to the local church before and after the journey became regular practices and this continued with local, unofficial saints, such as El Gauchito, becoming a protector during journeys. This evolved into making offerings of images and objects or requests for help, and, if successful, making offerings of other placards or items, first to the parish church, but later to popular saints.[6]

Late in the nineteenth century, with better media communications and increased travel by foreign writers, popular saints became better known outside of their own communities. El Gauchito Gil is an example. Elsewhere, Santa Teresa in the Sierra Madre of Chihuahua and Sonora, Mexico had a huge following with her miracles and inspired the inhabitants of the village of Tomochic to refuse to accept government authority over their community. The federal government sent Santa Teresa into exile in the southwestern United States, but the entire community of Tomochic continued its struggle against federal troops. Eventually, after suffering several humiliating defeats, an army of over a thousand men placed the village under siege. In its final days, the village as it burned witnessed an image of Santa Teresa rising from the smoke to the heavens.[7] In Venezuela, José Gregorio Hernández from a mountainous state brought together local folk practices and schooled medicine in Caracas until his death in a bizarre streetcar accident. He soon was transmogrified into San Gregorio, a folk saint. Stories reported holy water seeping from his tomb and that his spirit performed miraculous cures, including surgeries. He had followers throughout Venezuela, Colombia, and Ecuador, while his statue and prayer cards could be found in Peru and even in the southwestern U.S.

A typical popular saint, known as Sarita, appeared in the community of Callao, Peru, in the early twentieth century. Stevedores working in this port went to the common grave in the Baquijano cemetery as the burial place of locally known saintly individuals, believed to be able to perform miracles. Soon marginal individuals, prostitutes, peddlers, and others desperate for aid began to meet there to ask for help.

Some community saints were known as "the Little Unknown Soldier," Sister María, Isabelita, and Brother Ceferino. All these cults were subsumed in 1970 in a new popular devotion.

Sarita Colonia Zambrando had been born in 1914 in the poorest neighborhood in the Andean town of Huaraz. Her father, a carpenter, after a few years took the family to Lima in search of improved opportunities. The move allowed Sara to attend Santa Teresita Elementary School, where she mastered reading, writing, and sketching. After three years, she had to leave school and return to Huaraz to help with her ailing mother. Following her mother's death, the family returned to Lima, moving from one poor neighborhood to another, and finally settled in Callao. Sara's extended family was extremely religious, and her aunts were so committed to the church they were regarded as nuns. Holy images, especially of San Martín de Porras whom Sara regarded as her patron and the saint of the humble, filled the family's home. She worked as a domestic, sold vegetables in the market, and cared for her younger family members. She managed to spend time in prayer and found ways to share what the family had with people in need. In 1940, aged 26, she died of malaria and was buried in the common grave.

A cult developed around her. At first only her family came to the site, but then a woman known as Señora Zoila began promoting the devotion to Sarita as the most significant of the holy persons in the cemetery. Soon the desperate began to visit and ask for her assistance. These included, according to observers, longshoremen, prostitutes, petty criminals, homosexuals, abandoned mothers, housewives, unemployed workers, small merchants, and bus and taxi drivers. Those who came contributed what they could, a few coins, or materials, or labor to build a small chapel – in the style of rough hovels of the neighborhood. Once completed, the chapel's exterior walls were covered with votive candles and flowers, and the interior walls held small signs or notes giving thanks for the miracles performed by Sarita. Outside the chapel, vendors sold amulets and prayer cards of the popular saint. A sampling of the requests and the expressions of gratitude revealed that men most often sought assistance with business, work, and health issues. Women needed aid with work and health issues that usually involved their children, parents, or other loved ones.

Ignored by religious officials, Sarita was recognized for being humble, pure, charitable, and willing to share with the most needy neighbors. These virtues, it was said, gave her the ability to support requests for miracles. Moreover, the desperate could approach her because, as one said, "She too was poor and Peruvian."[8]

Another popular saint, as baffling for his sanctity as Gauchito Gil, appeared in Tijuana, Mexico, across the border from San Diego, California. He, too, became popular with the ordinary population. Juan Soldado, idiomatically translated as GI Joe, Juan Castillo Morales, raped and killed 8-year-old Olga Camacho. He was killed trying to escape after being convicted of murder in 1938. Stories casting doubt on whether the crime occurred followed stories of blood oozing from his grave. Other stories quickly circulated that the poor enlisted soldier and murderer in life, after death, had healed the sick and comforted the wretched. His grave soon became a pilgrimage site and followers constructed a chapel above it. The church continues to ignore him, but many come with health problems, migration hopes, love conflicts, and other everyday issues to seek his assistance.[9]

Other well-known Mexican popular saints are Jesús Malverde and La Santa Muerte. Malverde has become known as the patron of drug dealers and others in the Northwest region of the nation. His legend builds on the life of Jesús Juárez Mazo, who was born in 1870 near the Sinaloa capital of Culiacán. He lived an exemplary life until the death of his parents, when he turned to banditry and gave money to the poor. The authorities captured him only after his betrayal by a follower. Soon celebrated as a folk saint, he received the name el ángel de los pobres – the Angel of the Poor – and his miracles and aid remained typical of other folk saints. In the 1980s and 1990s, leaders of drug cartels in the region adopted him as their patron and began to promote a deliberate public relations strategy. Their efforts resulted in increased popularity of Malverde. This campaign included paying regional bands to write and sing songs, now known as *narcocorridos*, and the funding of three movies. They appropriated his Robin

Hood-like support for local communities as part of their criminal enterprise. Malverde has been featured in three films, *Jesús Malverde*, *Jesús Malverde II: La Mafia de Sinaloa*, and *Jesús Malverde III: Infierno en Los Ángeles*. These feature tales of drug trafficking with musical interludes by Norteño bands playing and singing *narcocorridos*.[10] Perhaps the best example of the widespread yet selective support for Malverde, despite his popularity in the Northwest and his increasing association with the illegal drug industry, came in 2013 in a parade for "Justice and Dignity" in which a marching police officer wore a baseball cap depicting Malverde in the southern village of Aytla de los Libres, Guerrero. Malverde's cult includes many followers who manage to ignore the connections to the cartels.

Some have raised suspicions that La Santa Muerte, Sacred Death, like Malverde, has developed her popularity through connections with illegal drug dealers and other criminals. Considered by some as Mexico's most popular religious figure, second only to the Virgin of Guadalupe,[11] the unofficial saint Santa Muerte and her cult have been condemned as blasphemous. Pope Francis, when he visited Mexico in 2016, repudiated Santa Muerte on his arrival as a dangerous symbol of drug cartels and their culture. Neither the Pope's rejection of the popular saint nor the alleged association with drug-related practices have reduced the growing number of her followers, perhaps 20 million in Mexico, the United States, and parts of Central America.[12] This is attributed to her assistance with the desperation of many in society, especially those ignored by both the government and the church. She performs, according to her followers, miracles of healing and protection, and assists with safe delivery to the afterlife.

Male counterparts of "Sacred Death" exist in other parts of Latin America, such as the folk saints who appear as skeletons, San La Muerte in Paraguay and Rey Pascual in Guatemala. Many draw connections to both Aztec and Maya gods and the celebration of the Day of the Dead, but specific references to the veneration of Santa Muerte have been documented in the 1940s in Mexico City's working-class neighborhoods such as Tepito, where the Romero family became connected to the cult. In 1962, Enriqueta Romero took over her aunt's shrine and became its chaplain. Other sources show its origins around 1965 in the state of Hidalgo.

Public worship of the saint increased after one believer, David Romo, founded Mexico City's first Santa Muerte church at the end of the twentieth century. The church had a statue of La Santa Muerte alongside the main altar. In 2007, Romo replaced the statue with a dressed mannequin, the Angel de La Santa Muerte, with the hope of preventing its association with criminal acts. At present Santa Muerte can be found throughout Mexico and also in parts of the United States and Central America. There are videos, websites, and music composed in honor of this folk saint.

Originally a male figure, Santa Muerte generally appears as a skeletal female figure, clad in a long robe and holding one or more objects, usually a scythe and a globe. Her robe can be of any color, as more specific images of the figure vary widely from devotee to devotee and according to the rite being performed or the petition being made.[13]

As the worship of Santa Muerte was clandestine until the twentieth century, most prayers and other rites have been traditionally performed privately at home. Since the beginning of the twenty-first century, worship has become more public and shrines to this image have been mushrooming. Chapels and shrines have proliferated and at times have provoked hostile, even violent reactions. Some shrines have been defiled or destroyed, and in March 2009, the Mexican army demolished 40 roadside shrines near the U.S. border.[14] The shrine on Dr. Vertiz Street in Colonia Doctores is unique in Mexico City because it features images of both Jesús Malverde and Santa Muerte.

All the popular chapels and shrines have space for gifts to the saint. These objects often are luxuries in the lives of ordinary individuals, small pleasures that assuage the daily demands of work, illness, and family needs: a few cigarettes, an alcoholic drink, a coin or two, fresh flowers, copal or some other incense, votive candles, sweets, especially chocolate, and personal items such as pictures, locks of hair or replicas of body parts (called milagros) that represent the offering. Often individuals tell the story of their saint and a miracle through an ex voto.

Essential with each of these popular saints is the personal relationship between the individual and the saint. Individuals might have a similar personal connection to one of the church's saints as a patron, but rarely does this become too personal, even irreverent. Perhaps the exception was San Antonio, with whom individuals felt a close enough connection to stand his image on its head or place it in a closet until he had helped find a missing object.

More generally, one expression of gratitude might be displayed in the parish church or popular shrine by ex votos (from the abbreviated Latin term *ex voto suscepto*, "from the vow made"). These votives fulfilled a vow or were made in gratitude or devotion. They were hung on a wall of the church or at a shrine to remain on display as a public offering of thanks as well as a reminder to others that prayers were indeed answered.

The painted ex voto originated in Italy in the fifteenth century. Wealthy patrons commissioned artists to make a visual representation of miracles they had been granted or ones that they hoped for. According to a patron's social standing, the painting would then be hung in a church, private chapel, or at home. When ordinary individuals adopted the practice, it fell out of fashion with the upper classes. Commoners made some significant transformations, especially the reduction in size (from full-size paintings to little paintings), the use of inexpensive materials (wood, occasionally metal laminates and glass in Italy; wood and zinc in Mexico), and the detailed visual and verbal narrative of the miracle it represented. The "commissioning" of the painting, which originally marked status and wealth, remained a part of painted ex votos well into the twentieth century, although usually the commission went to unlettered anonymous artists. Soon the tradition spread to Europe and the custom of offering gifts to the Divine in thanksgiving for a miracle flourished from the arrival of the Spanish in the Americas. In rural areas, the gifts were individually made or commissioned from a neighbor or local painter, and were generally small, done in oil paint on tin or wood. The ex voto provided a material representation of the miracle and remained "as public affirmations of God's constant powerful presence in the lives of the faithful – poor or otherwise – and…to acknowledge it, to communicate it to others, to celebrate it."[15]

Each ex voto depicted the event as well as the saint who assisted or performed the miracle. The untrained artists often used bright colors along with Roman Catholic iconic symbols that identified the holy figures, and these attributes of color and symbol were given to popular saints as well. The spatial arrangement, adopted from the Italian painted ex votos, had two distinct and uneven parts: the smaller part, usually but not always in the left upper corner, pictured the heavenly figure, who might stand on clouds or against the heavens. The saint's gaze or hand was stretched out to the supplicant, shortening the distance between them. The larger, remaining space was given to the visual representation of the miraculous event. At the bottom, each ex voto carried an inscription, the name of the supplicant, the date of the event, occasionally, but rarely the name of the painter, and brief accounts of the specific miracle. Italian examples used votive acronyms: *P.G.R.*, Per Grazia Ricevuta; *E.V.*, Ex Voto; *V.F.G.R.*, Voto Fatto Grazia Ricevuta. The description accounting for the miracle was usually misspelled and grammatically incorrect and sometimes seemed cryptic on account of the dialect. During the late 1800s and early 1900s many small paintings lined the walls of Mexican churches as gestures of thanksgiving. They pictured the intimate dramas of everyday life, bull fights, lightning strikes, work accidents, ill health, and false imprisonments. Divine intervention was believed to have made possible survival and reprieve. Diego Rivera and Frida Kahlo popularized these images when they began collecting them, and individuals and museums soon followed.

Also called retablos, *laminas*, or "miracle boards," ex votos picture direct and personal relationships with the saint that bypass the ecclesiastical rituals and pastoral mediation of the Catholic Church. Although they hang on the walls of churches and shrines, they are not ecclesiastically sanctioned professions of faith. This may explain the church's ambivalence toward them, selling or discarding them to make room to display more. As genuine acts of faith, ex votos belong to "vernacular Catholicism."[16] Unlike the static statues of saints, the ex voto narrates a saint in action, intervening in a disaster, accident, or illness that befalls ordinary human beings or animals. Each one commemorates the saint's miraculous intervention and expresses the gratitude of the survivors or loving families.

The tales of life or death told in pictures with written testimonials are bound up with real-life dangers and near fatal events. Perils include being hit by carts, streetcars or cars; accidents with boiling water, hot tallow and electricity; threats from animals – bulls, wild cats, snakes, rats, and wolves – and natural disasters – fires, falls, and floods, earthquakes, storms, and disease. All these happened with alarming frequency. Manmade catastrophes occurred as well – soldiers, bandits, police, and drunken husbands constituted reasons for alarm that were full of risk and fear. Expressions of fatalism resound throughout these tales. Every scene of daily life – no matter what or where the drama is – "painted as if lifted from a book of magical realism showing two levels of time past. There is the pluperfect – *what happened* – theft, collision, illness of the flock – and then the more recent past – *what happened next* – the attentive mercies of the chosen saint, whether floating, ethereal, or descending close as a confidant to reassure the family of the stricken one." The ex voto shows "a grim, even catastrophic event, involving the world of mortals, followed by the divine intervention by the saint. Even though time passes between the event and intervention, 'a miracle,' wrote Anita Brenner, 'is a thing without chronology. A picture is therefore closer to its nature than the story. Even the written information about it on the margin below the painting is not a sequence.'" Ex votos provide the essence of personal despair helped with divine assistance.[17]

The risks of travel have become magnified for those who cross into the United States. For many, the first step is a visit to San Juan de Los Lagos in Jalisco, where they offer prayers for a safe journey. If it goes well, the individual will often return to the church and leave an ex voto in thanks. On the other hand, the increased availability and visibility they grant them might well generate and nurture a rekindled interest in their religious and cultural function.

John Mitchell/Alamy Stock Photo.

Since the rise of interest by collectors in this popular art form, numerous fakes have also appeared in public markets, antique stores, and online sales. Photography has made possible assemblages of prayer cards, photos, and written notes. Unlike Italian ex votos, Mexicans have adopted several "popular" ways of keeping alive, reappropriating, and transforming the ex voto tradition: ex votos are tourist souvenirs, or items sold on the streets, embroidered by women living in small village communities, mainly in central Mexico, who sell them to support their families;[18] they have become decorative pieces for homes, offices, public places; they have been painted on room dividers, fireplace screens, refrigerator magnets.[19] From a religious point of view, these transformations desacralize ex votos.

In some examples of ex voto, artists take this popular form to produce everyday art. Like those who have produced fanciful lotería games, these painters do ex votos that comment on aspects of everyday life. For example, one subtitle thanks the Virgin of Guadalupe for helping learn about Viagra so that he can pursue a woman who has attracted him. Others regard rescue from aliens and the opportunity for a woman to live with her friend, that they no longer have to hide their relationship. In another that makes a commentary on Mexican society, Carlos thanks San Sebastian for helping him after many years to look like he feels, a woman. The saint also got his family to accept him for what he is.

Vernacular, that is, everyday religion has a rich variety of popular saints, holy patrons, ex voto traditions, and objects as diverse as tattoos and gearshift knobs. Ex votos are now increasingly being made by the supplicants themselves. The practices extend well beyond church-sanctioned practices and icons and may appear to some as superstitions, even heresies, but for those who see them as essential to making life good and understandable, they provide the comfort of the divine in personal terms.

Notes

1 "Antonio Gil," documentary by Lía Dansker, premiered at BAFICI (Buenos Aires International Festival of Independent Cinema), 2013, Competencia Argentina; CDROM - Almas Milagrosas, https://www.equiponaya.com.ar/forms/suscripcion_almas.htm.

2 "El Gauchito Gil, el santo popular que conquistó la Argentina," https://www.elmundo.es/america/2013/04/17/argentina/1366226839.html.

3 "Culto al Gauchito Gil," Diccionario de Mitos y Leyendas, https://www.cuco.com.ar/gauchito_gil.htm.

4 "Culto al Gauchito Gil," Diccionario de Mitos y Leyendas, https://www.cuco.com.ar/gauchito_gil.htm.

5 Buenos Aires high school teacher Adrienne Talamas to author, October 30, 2015.

6 Adrienne Talamas to author, October 30, 2015.

7 Paul Vanderwood, *The Power of God Against the Guns of Government: Religious Upheaval in Mexico at the Turn of the Nineteenth Century* (Stanford: Stanford University Press, 1998).

8 "Profile: Sarita – The People's Saint," in William H. Beezley and Colin M. MacLachlan, *Latin America: The Peoples and their History* (Ft. Worth, TX: Harcourt Brace College Publishers, 2000), pp. 250–251.

9 Paul J. Vanderwood, *Juan Soldado: Rapist, Murderer, Martyr, Saint* (Durham, NC: Duke University Press, 2006).

10 R. Andrew Chesnut, "Jesus Malverde: Not Just a Narcosaint," HuffPost (January 9, 2014, updated March 11, 2014), https://www.huffpost.com.

11 R. Andrew Chesnut, *Devoted to Death: Santa Muerte, the Skeleton Saint*, 2nd edition (New York: Oxford University Press, 2018).

12 Ibid.

13 See https://en.wikipedia.org/wiki/Santa_Muerte.

14 Chesnut, *Devoted to Death*.

15 Mariolina Rizzi Salvatori, "Understanding Ex Votos," http://www.mariolinasalvatori.com/understanding-ex-votos/; and "Porque no puedo decir mi cuento: Mexican Ex-Votos' Iconographic Literacy," in John Trimbur, ed., *Popular Literacy: Studies in Cultural Practices and Poetics* (Pittsburgh: University of Pittsburgh Press, 2001).

16 "Ex Votos – Mexican Folk, Peruvian Milagros," https://marciaweberartobjects.com/artists/ex-votos-mexican-folk-art/.

17 Rosamond Purcell, "The Stories of Strangers: Mexican *Ex-Voto* Paintings," *VQR*, 84, no. 2 (2008), https://www.vqronline.org/vqr-gallery/stories-strangers-mexican-ex-voto-paintings.

18 Salvatori, "Mexican Ex-Votos' Iconographic Literacy," pp. 38–42.

19 Tony Cohan, Melba Levick, and Masako Takahashi, *Mexicolor: The Spirit of Mexican Design* (San Francisco: Chronicle Books, 1998).

Additional Resources

Readings

R. Andrew Chesnut, *Devoted to Death: Santa Muerte, the Skeleton Saint*, 2nd edition (New York: Oxford University Press, 2018).

Frank Graziano, *Cultures of Devotion: Folk Saints of Spanish America* (New York: Oxford University Press, 2007).

June Macklin, "Two Faces of Sainthood: The Pious and the Popular," *Journal of Latin American Lore*, 14, no. 1 (Summer 1988). The entire issue is devoted to folk saints.

Sam Quinones, *True Tales from Another Mexico: The Lynch Mob, the Popsicle Kings, Chalino and the Bronx* (Albuquerque: University of New Mexico Press, 2001).

Alfredo Vilchis Roque, photography by Pierre Schwartz, foreword by Victoire and Hervé Di Rosa, *Infinitas Gracias: Contemporary Mexican Votive Painting* (San Francisco: Seuil Chronicle, 2004).

Videos

"Antonio Gil," documentary by Lía Dansker, premiered at BAFICI (Buenos Aires International Festival of Independent Cinema), 2013, Competencia Argentina; CDROM - Almas Milagrosas, https://www.equiponaya.com.ar/forms/suscripcion_almas.htm.

La Santa Muerte (Saint Death), full-length documentary, Spanish, with English subtitles, http://evaaridjis.com/lasantamuerte.html.

4

Roasted Chicken

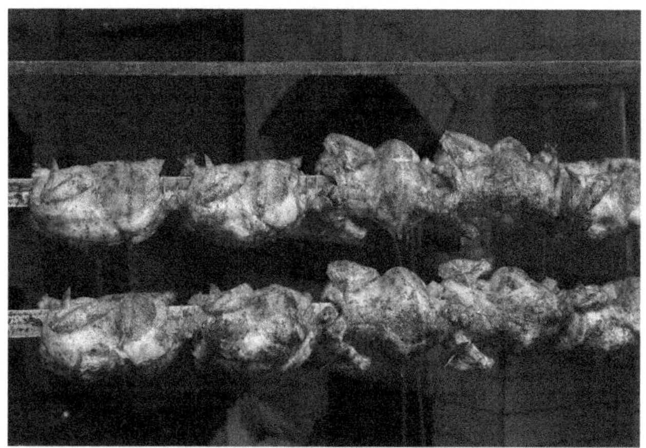

David Wall/Alamy Stock Photo.

Lima, Peru has become a destination for food tourists as its cuisine is now rated among the top three or four in the world by culinary magazines and travel lists. Along with the specialties of ceviche and anticuchos (beef kabobs) appears rotisserie or roasted chicken – el pollo a la brasa, which has become a favorite of gourmets as well as nearly all Peruvians. As chicken in green sauce, it has developed

Latin American Cultural Objects and Episodes, First Edition. William H. Beezley.

popularity in the United States. The emergence of roasted chicken has been a recent development, even though it appears that the domesticated birds arrived by canoe with travelers from the Polynesian islands as early as about 1400, one hundred years before Europeans appeared in the region.[1]

The rise to popularity of chicken meals did not occur until the 1950s, when, according to Carlos Magdalena, the national government developed a strategy of building hundreds of large chicken farms. The widely popular account says that just before this government program, a Swiss resident in Peru, Roger Schuler, took an interest in chickens. In 1946, he started a farm that he called "La Granja Azul" in the Santa Clara zone of greater Lima. At first, he sold eggs and chickens in wealthy neighborhoods such as Miraflores. After about four years, his business was losing money and he had to find something different to do with his chickens. He saw his cook working outside in the shade of false pepper trees, called *molles*, at his hacienda Santa Clara in the Chaclacayo neighborhood. She fixed a chicken dish according to local accounts seasoned only with salt, served with French fries, and eaten by hand, although others say it was prepared with local products, rosemary, huacatay (called by various names, including Peruvian black mint and Mexican marigold), ají panca (the chile powder or paste widely used in Peruvian cooking), and pepper. The cook skewered young birds end to end and roasted them over a wood fire. Schuler enjoyed the dish and saw an opportunity if he could make the dish efficiently. He began by tinkering with the recipe until he perfected the taste he wanted by marinating the chicken in panca, soy sauce, huacatay, salt, and pepper. He asked his compatriot, Franz Ulrich, to develop a metal cooker with an iron rod that would hold about eight chickens. Ulrich soon developed a mechanized rotisserie to cook several chickens at once that he called the "rotombo," made from a large metal barrel with a skewer for the chickens. The process was called the planetary (planetario) cooking system. Just as critical as the chickens, the recipe, and the oven was algarrobo charcoal – often described as the product of the Peruvian carob tree, noting its similarity to the Mediterranean carob. But, in fact, the charcoal came from a kind of mesquite called the huarango (the *Prosopis pallida*) tree found throughout Peru, Colombia, and Ecuador. With everything in place, Schuler decided that he, his cook, and his friend Franz should open a restaurant that he named La Granja Azul featuring the chicken plate. He advertised the restaurant with a sign on the road saying, "Eat All the Roasted Chicken You Want for 5 soles" (1 dollar U.S. in 1950).

The cheap price soon brought in customers. Lima's aristocrats crowded the suburban restaurant as a place where they could go for lunch, use their hands, and eat all they wanted. One guest described the scene: "Seeing a woman with a wide sombrero with an air of Mona Lisa and eating with her hands created a Dantesque painting." Students from the medical school at the San Marcos University came when they learned the meal was free for anyone beating the record for eating the most chicken in one lunch. The record holder had his name and picture placed in the dining room. In 1979, a group of students graduating in sociology from Garcilaso de la Vega, the Inca University, celebrated with dinner at La Granja Azul. The restaurant soon became the preferred location for graduation dinner dances for university students. The pollo a la brasa was the featured meal served with French fries, salad, and a variety of sauces, especially huacatay aji and yellow aji, and the students hired popular music groups, especially the well-known cumbia band Orquesta de Los Hermanos Silva.[2] Among many of the stories about the popularity of La Granja Azul were repeated rumors that Gina Lollobrigida, when the glare of public attention became too great in Europe, fled to Peru and hid out in the restaurant.

Other restaurants soon followed. In 1957, another Swiss resident named Steinmann, using the planetary system, opened El Rancho in Miraflores. Within five years, to meet the growing demand, there were 10 Lima restaurants serving the chicken.[3] Other famous locations appeared. In 1966 La Caravana in Pueblo Libre, and in the 1970s others in the center of Lima, El Kikiriji and El Sótano. Together they made the dish one of the most popular among all classes in the city and it quickly spread across the country. The chicken, rotisserie, and charcoal remained the same, but the marinade varied according to the cook, who might use dark beer or pisco, rosemary, huacatay, salt and pepper, cumin, soy sauce, and panca. The plate always came with French fries and a lettuce salad, except in the Amazonian region where fried yuca or banana accompanied the chicken.

In the early 1970s, another boost to eating chicken came from some marine biologists concerned with El Niño. This phenomenon occurs when reduced upwelling of cold oceanic water brings warmer water with fewer nutrients, and fish and seabirds vanish. From 1971 to 1972, the fish harvest collapsed from 10.3 million metric tons to 4.6 million metric tons, so there were limited supplies of fish, affecting both food and fishmeal, nor was there guano for fertilizer. Some marine biologists, uncertain about the recovery of the fishing industry, encouraged a shift to chicken.

The popularity of pollo a la brasa continued to grow. A study in 2007 reported that across Peru, individuals bought more than 373 million plates of pollo a la brasa each year. The Peruvian Institute of Culture in 2013 found in a survey that 95 percent of Peruvians named pollo a la brasa as their favorite meal, 9 out of 10 ate it every week or so, with 45 percent going to a restaurant to have it every week. This explains a report by the National Institute of Statistics and Informatics in 2014 showing that nationwide every month restaurants served 12 million pollo a la brasas and each family consumed 24.4 kilos of pollo a la brasa. In 2017, Peruvians ate 48 million broilers a month, not all of them as roasted chicken, of course.

To keep up with the demand, the raising of chickens greatly expanded, with a predicted growth rate from 2012 to 2020 of 23.5 percent, that is from 1.08 million metric tons in the base year to 1.31 million metric tons. Agronomists estimate that over 68 percent of domestically produced yellow corn goes to feed the chickens in the country's 1,000 plus poultry farms and other individually owned, unreported chicken enterprises. And that was not enough chicken. Peru became and remains a net importer of poultry meat. In 2012, poultry imports totaled 27,000 tons. The major supply sources, in 2017, were Brazil (31%), U.S. (27%), Chile (25%), Argentina (11%), and Bolivia (6%).[4]

Roasted chicken spread everywhere Peruvians migrated, so it is available now in Brazil, Chile, Venezuela, Ecuador, Argentina, Bolivia, Colombia, Mexico, Spain, Japan, and China. In the United States, 441 restaurants in 20 states and all major cities offer pollo a la brasa. The popularity of the dish reached the Food Channel's television program *The Kitchen*, where an episode on May 5, 2018 offered instructions to prepare a version of it called "Peruvian spatchcock chicken" in the oven.[5] The incredible success of pollo a la brasa persuaded the Ministry of Agriculture in 2010 to declare the third Sunday in July as "Roasted Chicken Day" (el Día del Pollo a la Brasa).[6]

The tasty chicken dish with its phenomenal success came at a price. The Spanish horticulturalist Carlos Magdalena explained, "When I first arrived in Peru, I was taken with this delicious chicken dish." But the delicacy required an essential, particular charcoal, whose production endangered the huarango tree – the price, as Magdalena and others learned, for pollo a la brasa. Insect plagues have limited the supply of charcoal at a time of extraordinary demand. Two outbreaks in 2003 began to defoliate the already threatened forests across the region. By 2004, the demand for charcoal to fuel restaurant grills (and, incidentally, for use in alcohol distilling industries) and insect pestilence meant most of the old-growth huarango forest, "even the most ancient specimens, known in Spanish as *huarango milenario*, the 'millennial trees,'"[7] as Magdalena discovered, had been destroyed, placing the tree on the verge of extinction.

The loss of the huarango would mean more than changing the chicken preparation; it is an indispensable part of the coastal ecosystem. It has the deepest root system of any tree species in the world, going down more than 75 meters in search of water. It is also the world's second hardest wood. It condenses water from fog on its leaves and stems at night that trickles down to its roots, and equally as important, it captures nitrogen from the air through its leaves, using a special bacterium.

Traditionally the huarango has been seen as the tree of life, woven into mythology since pre-Columbian times. As the keystone species in the southern coastal region surrounding the town of Ica, it served as a resource that provided food, forage, and fuel for local people for at least 7,000 years. Its forests formed the backbone of the Nazca people, famous for the giant line drawings in the desert and sophisticated agriculture between 500 BCE and 500 CE, but they deforested much of the region by cutting the huarango. The tree with its long roots had served to palliate the flooding caused by El Niño. Once they had receded, the floods caused erosion and washing away of many other plants, leading to a desert environment that contributed to the collapse of the Nazca culture. Today, although basins in the lower Ica Valley are almost completely abandoned, they contain extensive archaeological evidence of previous human habitation, ancient irrigation, and agricultural systems. The surviving huarango still underpin biodiversity and make invaluable contributions to the desert ecosystem including soil fertility, water desalination, climate improvement, and some refuge for animals including the slender-billed finch (*Xenospinus concolor*) that has declined along with plants and other rare birds. *Prosopis pallida* is remarkable for the desert environment, providing islands of fertility, moisture, and, for cattle and locals, shade.

As the huarango became endangered, the national government classified it as a threatened species and the regional government made all huarango cutting that resulted in deforestation illegal (Ordenanza Regional 0009, 2007 GORE, Ica). Despite these legal measures, enforcement has remained weak. Some local communities started attempting to publicize the issue and to protect mature trees. Joining those working to protect the tree, scientists from Kew Gardens, London, arrived in 2005. With individuals from Ica, they tried to combine experiential knowledge and interdisciplinary science to create an ecosystem approach. Individuals from the town and the botanical garden planned an extensive conservation program that began when locals identified productive plague-resistant tree varieties and collected seeds from a number of locations in Ica. Next, they established a nursery to produce seedlings for a free planting program along streets and in other areas. Moreover, they organized a Huarango Festival to publicize the significance of the tree. The project received support from the Darwin Initiative (a non-profit foundation in the

United Kingdom) and other non-government organizations for the efforts to build sustainable agriculture and ecosystem survival.[8]

One botanical horticulturalist from Kew Gardens, Carlos Magdalena, took an active role in efforts to restore the plant. Workers from Kew and local groups such as the Asociación para la Niñez y su Ambiente (Association for Children and their Environment) planted over 100,000 seedlings, but only one in ten survived because of the harsh desert ecosystem and the numerous animals that graze on them.[9]

The Huarango Project resulted in school programs and the annual festival, both helping with the emergence of a generation with a greater appreciation for the environment and for the huarango. For over a decade, these individuals and many new migrants into the region have experimented with sustainable economic opportunities, offered especially by the pods of the tree. Similar to the huarango (*Prosopis limensis*), pods from the algarrobo tree (*Prosopis juliflora* and *Prosopis pallida*) of the dry forests of northern Peru are used to make a number of products. Encouraged by an enthusiastic women's group in Ica, project members visited pod processing communities and cottage industries in the Piura and Tambogrande region.

Around Ica, the trees each year produce a large crop in April and a smaller one in October of sweet yellow pods (called huaranga). One tree, 20–70 years old, can produce 110 to 220 pounds of pods each year. They constitute a "complete" food because their nutrients contain high levels of carbohydrate and protein, vitamins A, C, E, B1, B2, folic acid, and minerals (calcium, magnesium, potassium, and iron). Humans have eaten them for at least 7,000 years, and it has been estimated that in pre-Columbian times, they sometimes provided an estimated 50 percent of the local diet.

Another significant local product associated with the tree is honey. Many species of *Prosopis* yield excellent pollen, considered by some experts to be of the highest quality. Nevertheless, the surviving forests of Ica are generally species-poor and honey production from a single nectar-producing plant is difficult, as bee hives must be moved to provide nectar throughout the year. Nevertheless, in one of the reforestation areas (Samaca), organic farming practices have preserved wide borders of native species around the fields, especially chilco (*Fuchsia magellanica*), and shrubby species like toñuz and lucraco. Together with huarango and espino, these provide nectar and pollen for profitable year-round beekeeping without moving hives.

The project members studied honey production from native stingless bees (meliponines). An Ica beekeeper received training in management from a capacity-building course in Piura, northern Peru. Stingless bees offer both advantages and disadvantages: the bees are comparatively easy to manage, but they have relatively low productivity. The honey has a high market value because of its medicinal and nutritional properties. Most disappointing, these bees are in decline due to insecticide use and lack of investment.

The project in 2006 supported the establishment of a small huarango products company called Miskyhuaranga associated with a network of family pod producers. The goal was for the pod suppliers to form a cooperative, investing in the company with labor or pods. Most producers needed cash for their pod crop that could otherwise readily be sold for forage. Miskyhuaranga purchased the crop, paying extra for the cleanest pods, and providing training and advice to producers. The company experimented with production of pod syrup, sweet flour, and a coffee substitute, and opted to produce flour made from the finest sieved portion of milled pods, as well as a coffee substitute made from the toasted coarser-sieved quantity (30% of original weight). The pod flour has the advantage over the syrup of requiring lower energy demands for processing.

The project teamed up with a small but efficient local milling plant. The high sugar content of the pods caused the flour to solidify and required developing several drying stages to permit milling. The seeds were also milled with the flour as they are exceptionally high in protein and nutritionally rich. The resulting pod flour was then sieved into three varieties: fine and sweet, coarse "bran," and tough "bran" of seed packet.

Before issuing a permit, authorities required a detailed description of the product as it was the first time it had come to market. It was sent for analysis before allowing its sale on the open market and was found to have microbial contamination above regulatory limits. The source was thought to be due to producers collecting pods where domestic animals ranged. Another production step was added, washing the pods in disinfected water and rinsing while harvesting them. Analysis showed this reduced contamination. Washing required further drying, done with a solar dryer to save costs. The reduced microbial levels met regulations and the permit was issued for the sale of the flour.

Miskyhuaranga sold the flour in Lima and it was available in Ica's local shops, during promotional events, and at the Huarango Festival. The best sales came from cakes made from the flour sold in corner shops and at tree planting events. Packets of the coffee substitute were made by pan-toasting the coarser-sieved variety.

The Miskyhuaranga coop did not recover its costs the first year. The group has been contacted by ice-cream manufacturers and investors as it seeks to expand the company with several products. The group continues to train teachers and children in local schools in the processing of pods and several schools are now producing their own products. Miskyhuaranga found that capacity building is essential, especially for insect plague management, harvest, storage, and hygiene, to enable pod producers to achieve quality of production. Marketing can be the highest single cost, but local radio helps in an effective way to publicize these products.[10]

The pods, the huarango trees, and the roasted chicken have come to represent a treasure for the Peruvian people, especially in the southern coastal regions. Together they provide an unexpected discovery in the search for Inca wealth that has persisted since the arrival of the Spanish and formed the basis of much popular culture in Peru. Environmental wealth, nevertheless, has less glitter than precious metals, especially gold and silver, and its protection proves much more difficult against both natives and foreigners who want easy access to it. Environmental wealth notwithstanding, the search for precious minerals persists. Tales of pre-Columbian treasure of silver and gold, rather than environmental wealth, have continued.

When Columbus arrived in the Americas, he caused a gold rush, first in the Caribbean and then on the mainland of the Americas. Spaniards followed by other European adventurers sought the treasure of indigenous peoples, especially the great Inca and Aztec cultures. These bedazzled treasure hunters relied on legends, folktales, rough-drawn maps, and counterfeit travelers' stories that reported extravagant accounts of emerald buildings, silver streets, and golden cities that resulted in the race of conquistadors who pursued glory, God, and gold. Their letters and the names they gave to new provinces and cities reflect the conquistadors' lust especially for gold, silver, and emeralds. The theme persisted into the twentieth century, when histories, novels, radio soap operas, and especially movies repeated the tales of the covetous search for treasure and the indigenous efforts to protect it. These accounts from Peru, Mexico, and the rest of Latin America inspired domestic and foreign filmmakers from Hollywood, New York, and even Italy. Persistent accounts concerned hidden treasures of indigenous cultures and formed a cultural substratum in much of Latin America.

The treasure motif in Hollywood resulted in various movies, especially the 1954 classic *Secret of the Incas* that starred Charlton Heston and featured the famous Peruvian singer Yma Sumac. The film illustrated three interlocking cultural themes: representations of the great indigenous culture of the past to show their achievements and nobility, the authentic fashions and beliefs of the indigenous peoples, and stories about the search and theft of indigenous treasures that serve as celluloid homilies. *Secret of the Incas* managed to relate the indigenous treasure tale with Cold War conflict. The plot centered in Cuzco, Peru, where a legend claimed that the Inca Empire had been destroyed by the gods following the theft of a gold and jeweled starburst from the Temple of the Sun centuries ago. The legend told that the return of the treasure would restore the Inca civilization. Based on new information, adventurer Harry Steele (Charlton Heston) searches for the artifact, as does his nemesis Edward "Ed" Morgan (Thomas Mitchell) and Romanian Elena Antonescu (Nicole Maurey), an Iron Curtain refugee. Paramount Pictures became the first major

Hollywood Studio to film on location in Peru at the archaeological sites in Machu Picchu and Cuzco. Five hundred local indigenous residents appeared as extras in the film. Curiously, some of the cast did not go to Peru but were filmed in Hollywood. One who remained in California was Peruvian singer Yma Sumac. She played the role of an Inca princess, who sang what was supposed to be a traditional song, "Virgin of the Sun God," to the extras. The song was actually written by her husband, Moisés Vivanco, and was arranged and conducted by well-known band leader Les Baxter. Sumac and her song became popular in the U.S.

Born in highland Peru, Sumac worked to develop her career during the late 1930s and 1940s. She had changed her given name, Zoila Augusta Chávarri del Castillo, to Yma Sumac to give her an identity in the 1930s as an Inca princess. Well-known folklore musician Moisés Vivanco de Allende became her manager and promoter. They married in 1942. Vivanco romanticized her story, claiming that he had discovered her in her native Cajamarca. He spun a fantasy that the government had decided to take her to perform in Lima and the decision nearly "caused an uprising among some thirty thousand Indians over the loss of their revered ritual singer." Such exaggerations caused some highland audiences to resent the star and her manager-husband.

Sumac first appeared on radio in 1942 and recorded at least 18 tracks of Peruvian folk songs for the Odeon label in Buenos Aires in 1943. As she and her husband tried to build her career, they had the international success of Carmen Miranda as a model and the cautionary tale of Chilean Rosita Serrano. Sumac and her husband eventually followed Carmen to the United States and avoided Germany, where Rosita (María Martha Esther Aldunate del Campo) had had great success singing Chilean folksongs on radio and recording for Telefunken. Rosita's voice and whistling resulted in the nickname *Chilenische Nachtigall* (Chilean Nightingale), but her popularity had collapsed in 1943 in Sweden. Nazi German officials accused her of being a spy after she had donated a benefit performance to Jewish refugees. She fled to Chile to avoid arrest and her songs were banned in Nazi Germany. After the war, Serrano attempted a tour in the United States in 1950, but even a television appearance created little interest in her music. In 1951, she went to West Germany for a role as a Cuban singer in the film *Schwarze Augen* (Dark Eyes), and the next year she sang in the film *Saison in Salzburg*. Nevertheless, her attempts to restart her career ended poorly and she returned to Chile. The public never forgave her for performing in Nazi Germany and she died in poverty.[11] Nevertheless, she stands as the third of the great singers from Latin America who at the time had an international reputation.

Sumac decided to follow Carmen Miranda and arrived in the U.S. in 1946, with plans to popularize her extraordinary voice – said by some to range through four octaves, and by others, including the singer, that it reached five. She also wanted to avoid the folkloric status that Miranda had achieved, especially with her tutti-frutti hats. She moved away from traditional Andean singing toward a quasi-operatic style by wearing gowns and adorning herself with Peruvian jewelry. Although she never achieved the popularity of Carmen Miranda, certainly she had a successful performing and movie career in Hollywood. Her popularity as a Peruvian singer resulted in 1953 in her joining the cast of *Secret of the Incas* and shortly afterward, in 1957, she appeared in *Omar Khayyam*. Her career would experience several ups and downs in the U.S., and when her popularity declined in the 1960s, she had sold out audiences in the Soviet Union, and toured Europe, Asia, and Latin America for four years. Her popularity would continue to have twists and turns, including being featured in a German-made documentary, "Hollywood's Inca Princess" (1992). Her following in the U.S. had another upsurge during the decade before her death in 2008. Showing the imagination of popular culture, an anecdote circulated at the time she was not an Inca at all but in reality a bored housewife, some said from Brooklyn, named Amy Camus, who spelled her name backwards to appear as a Peruvian priestess.[12]

The *Secret of the Incas* narrative follows the efforts to find a missing piece of a stone treasure map, the theft of a plane, attempted murders, and the appearance of major characters Pachacutec, the leader of indigenous peoples at Machu Picchu, and his sister Kori-Tika

(Sumac), and U.S. archaeologist Dr. Stanley Moorehead, who is leading the search for the tomb of the Inca leaders. The group find and open the tomb and discover the sunburst. A battle ensues in which the villain Ed wounds Pachacutec and flees with the relic. Harry Steele catches him and they fight on a mountain ledge; Ed falls to his death, but Harry saves the sunburst and briefly celebrates the fact that he has it. Then he returns it to Pachacutec, the rightful owner, and proposes marriage to Elena Antonescu, the Romanian runaway – a thrilling, dramatic romance of a film. In December 1954, Charlton Heston and Nicole Maurey, Harry and Elena, reprised their roles in a *Lux Radio Theatre* version of the story for radio broadcast.

The film had an enduring influence through its male star, Charlton Heston, the Peruvian singer Yma Sumac, and the ruins of Machu Picchu. Its popularity resulted in increased tourism in Peru, especially to the Inca capital, throughout the 1950s. Charlton Heston's character, the intelligent, sensitive anthropologist adventurer Harry Steele, influenced many who saw the film, notably young George Lucas, who later created the character Dr. Henry Walton "Indiana" Jones, Jr. in homage to this and other movie heroes of the 1930s. Moreover, Lucas placed Indiana Jones in the same hat and leather jacket worn by Harry Steele.[13]

Another film focused on Inca treasure resulted from an Italian and German collaboration. Italian moviemakers Arpad DeRiso and Piero Pierotti wrote the script for *Sansone e il Tesoro degli Incas*, made in 1964. A western with bandits and good guys, it also involves the search for Inca treasure.[14]

Another version of lost Inca treasure circulated stories about Atahualpa's ransom. Somewhere deep inside the Llanganates mountain range of central Ecuador between the Andes and the Amazon, stories have claimed there exists the fabulous Inca hoard hidden from Spanish conquistadors. The legend began in the sixteenth century, when Atahualpa, an Inca king, after warring with his half-brother Huáscar for control of the empire, was captured at his palace in Cajamarca in modern-day Peru by Francisco Pizarro. The Spanish commander agreed to release Atahualpa in return for a roomful of gold, but changed his mind and had the Inca king put to death before the last and largest part of the ransom had been delivered. So the Incas, the story goes, buried the gold in a secret mountain cave. For those who have tried to find it, the essential source is Valverde, a Spaniard who some 50 years after Atahualpa's death was said to have become rich after being led to the gold by his Inca bride's family. When he died, he left written directions to its location, the so-called *Derrotero de Valverde.*

English botanist Richard Spruce, working for the Royal Botanical Gardens at Kew, traveled to Brazil, Ecuador, and Peru from 1849 to 1864 collecting plants, including the seeds of the cinchona tree, whose bark and seeds were used to produce the antimalarial drug quinine. Once he finally returned to Great Britain, he reported that he had uncovered Valverde's guide and a related map, made by someone named Atanasio Guzman.

Treasure seeker Barth Blake followed up Spruce's discovery in 1886. If his writings are to be believed, Blake was the last person to find the gold. He described it in a letter: "There are thousands of gold and silver pieces of Inca and pre-Inca handicraft, the most beautiful goldsmith works you are not able to imagine." He found as well life-size human figurines, birds, and other animals, flowers, and corn-stalks, as well as "the most incredible jewelry" and "golden vases full of emeralds." He concluded, "I could not remove it alone, nor could thousands of men." Taking only what he could carry, Blake left. While traveling to New York, where he planned to raise funds for an expedition to recover the prize, he disappeared overboard. Some claim he was pushed to protect the treasure.

Many who have since attempted to retrace Blake's steps into the Llanganates have also died in their efforts. Mark Honigsbaum wrote *Valverde's Gold* (2004) about his efforts to find the treasure. He and two adventurers made the attempt to find the lake Valverde described. "The legend essentially is that the Inca took the gold out of the Llanganates and then returned it," Honigsbaum said. He never found the site and suggested it probably had been lost as a result of the earthquakes that regularly rock the region.

Archaeologist Johan Reinhard, an explorer-in-residence at the National Geographic Society, has an explanation for why numerous expeditions in search of the gold mine and artificial lake mentioned by Valverde have failed. "Most have followed Guzman's map that does indeed lead to some mines located on the northern end of the Llanganate range, but not to the area as can be ascertained from Valverde's description," Reinhard explained, but he says the directions do make sense against modern maps of the region. While Reinhard doesn't believe Atahualpa's gold will ever be found, he says there's still a good chance of discovering Inca sites such as those referred to in the *Derrotero*. "Thus," he said, "a serious archaeological expedition would likely add significantly to our knowledge of the Inca presence in the region."[15]

Treasure of precious minerals over the environment shaped films in Mexico with the stories of Aztec wealth. Mexicans developed the treasure-horror genre starting with *La Momia Azteca* (The Aztec Mummy) in 1957. Its success resulted in succeeding films that featured the living mummy Popoca, destined to guard an ancient Aztec treasure for all eternity. The plot used the stereotype of an heir to indigenous nobility with secret knowledge of treasure, caught between evil profit seekers and trustworthy scientists. In this case, a doctor (Ramon Gay) learns his fiancée is the reincarnation of an Aztec princess who was killed in a ceremony involving Popoca. With information he has gained using hypnosis, he attempts to gain entrance to the tomb for scientific reasons. They soon learn a master criminal, the Bat, is following them in order to steal the treasure. The scientist himself snatches the treasure and the mummy rises to seek revenge. The Bat turns out to be a friend of the doctor and the mummy is finally laid to rest again.

Other accounts of the Aztec Emperor Montezuma's treasure hidden from the Spaniards have resulted in equally implausible but persistent stories and elaborate treasure hunts. The whereabouts of Montezuma's hidden treasure, according to one report, is in a mysterious pond in Utah.[16] For over 100 years, residents of Kanab, Utah have insisted that Montezuma's treasure lies at the end of a tunnel below Three Lakes Pond. In February 2014, landowner Lon Child and producer Mike Wiest along with a crew from Jubal Productions decided to tell the story of Three Lakes, Montezuma, and the treasure hunters whose attempts to recover the gold have failed.

The pond, located near U.S. 89, according to local legend holds the lost treasure worth perhaps more than $3 billion. Although details vary, locals believe Aztecs fled from central Mexico in 1521 and eventually reached Utah, where they dug the Three Lakes Pond to cover the treasure's cavernous hiding place in a water trap on the pond's west side. Once dug, they diverted a river to the pond, filled it, and walked away from the ordinary-looking pond with a valuable secret. This far-fetched tale has circulated throughout southern Utah since 1914, when someone named Freddy Crystal showed up with a map that he claimed showed the treasure's location. In the 1920s, he found a series of sealed tunnels in nearby Johnson's Canyon and people began believing his story. Some joined his unsuccessful hunt for the gold.

In 1989, Brandt Child, a Kanab resident, bought the pond and the surrounding property. He claimed that the clues in Johnson Canyon were only decoys, and that the treasure rested in a water trap 36 feet below the pond's waterline, indicated by a symbol on the cliff above the cave. Repeated efforts to dive into the caves ended after divers said they became disoriented and saw the ghosts of Aztec guardians. Nevertheless they claimed they could see metal at the end of the tunnel.

Child prepared to drain the pond, but this plan faltered because the U.S. Fish and Wildlife Service put the amber snail on the endangered species list in 1992. The small, rare creature has as its only known habitat Three Lakes Pond. One killed can incur a $50,000 fine. "I can't do anything to my own property that might disturb those snails," Child told the *Deseret News*. "It doesn't look like anyone will get the gold."

Mike Wiest, producer, has been interested in the property since he was 12 years old and his father mentioned the pond was haunted. He only learned more a few years ago when friends told him about Three Lakes' history. He has said, "We think more importantly than finding if there's in fact treasure there, it's knowing why it's there, who put it there, who it was being hidden from and who was it intended for?" His most recent plan calls for submarines carrying lights and cameras into the cave. The remotely operated underwater vehicles (ROVs) are well suited to high water pressure and immune to human fears of the supernatural that have impaired scuba divers in the past. The crew, Wiest said, believes there is something down there, and something is protecting it, whether it's supernatural or explained away by science. He is not ready yet to discredit the supernatural as an explanation for the strange occurrences surrounding the cave. He said he wants to go into the filming with an open mind and is even ready to send in a scuba diving exorcist, if necessary. "Nothing is too farfetched at this point only because, at this point, we can't afford to discredit anything."

If the submarines do find anything, Wiest said, they likely wouldn't remove it from the cave. Lon Child, one of Brandt Child's 10 children, has expressed that it belongs down there. "I'm most excited to actually get a camera and film something that's never been filmed ever in the history of mankind, that's never been seen and recorded," Wiest said. "I'm thrilled to get some footage, as poor as the footage may be. I'm just thrilled to get something. At the end of the day, we're just storytellers. Hopefully this will be a good story."

Should this work out in the end, it will be a story in which environmental interests dominate wealthy dreams. The ROVs would also be better able to avoid smashing any of the small snails, who protect Montezuma's treasure, if it is there. Meanwhile, across Latin America, the need exists to recognize the riches offered by the environment, the animal and plant varieties of the region that express its wealth.

Notes

1 John Noble Wilford, "First Chickens in Americas Were Brought From Polynesia," *New York Times* (June 5, 2007), https://www.nytimes.com/2007/06/05/science/05chic.html.

2 Jorge Yeshayahu Gonzales-Lara, "La historia del pollo a las brasas peruano Patrimonio cultural e identidad gastronómica," Monografias.com, https://www.monografias.com/trabajos82/historia-pollo-brasa-peruano/historia-pollo-brasa-peruano.shtml.

3 "Pollo a la brasa... divine pleasure!!!!!" Gringo Peru, https://gringoperu.blogspot.com/2016/05/pollo-la-brasa-divine-pleasure.html.

4 "USDA International Egg and Poultry: Peru Poultry Production to Increase," https://www.themeatsite.com/reports/?id=3751.

5 Guillermo Torrejon Nava, "Pollo a la brasa," Sabores de mi Tierra (October 28,2013),http://amoperusaboresdemitierra.blogspot.com/2013/10/pollo-la-brasa.html. This blog includes a recipe to try at home.

6 "Día del Pollo a la Brasa: entérate cómo empezó la historia," Peru.com (July 16, 2017), https://peru.com/estilo-de-vida/gastronomia/dia-pollo-brasa-enterate-como-empezo-historia-noticia-523670. The cooking program can be viewed on demand.

7 Carlos Magdalena, *The Plant Messiah: Adventures in Search of the World's Rarest Species* (New York: Doubleday, 2017), p. 192.

8 Kew Royal Botanical Gardens, "Conservation, Restoration and Sustainable Management of Dry Forest in Southern Peru: *The Huarango Project*," https://www.kew.org/science/tropamerica/peru/index.htm.

9 Magdalena, pp. 192–193.

10 Kew Royal Botanical Gardens, "Working alongside Community: The Huarango Festival," https://www.kew.org/science/tropamerica/peru/activities.html.

11 https://en.wikipedia.org/wiki/Rosita_Serrano.

12 Zoila Mendoza, "From Folklore to Exotica: Yma Sumac and the Performance of Inca Identity," *The Appendix*, http://theappendix.net/issues/2013/7/from-folklore-to-exotica-yma-sumac-and-inca-identity; Nicholas E. Limansky, *Yma Sumac: The Art Behind the Legend* (New York: YBK Publishers, 2009); "Sumac, Yma," Encyclopedia.com, https://www.encyclopedia.com/education/news-wires-white-papers-and-books/sumac-yma.

13 "*Secret of the Incas* (1954)," Turner Classic Movies, https://www.tcm.com/tcmdb/title/89450/Secret-of-the-Incas/notes.html.

14 https://www.comprar-peliculas.com/pelicula/sanson-y-el-tesoro-de-los-incas.aspx#sthash.EF97iCI7.dpuf.

15 James Owen, "Lost Inca Gold," National Geographic, https://www.nationalgeographic.com/history/archaeology/lost-inca-gold/.

16 "Filmmakers search for Montezuma's treasure in Three Lakes Pond," https://whatliesbeyond.boards.net/thread/1160/filmmakers-search-montezumas-treasure-haunted.

Additional Resources

Reading

Rafael Climent-Espino and Ana M. Gomez-Bravo, eds., *Food, Texts, and Cultures in Latin America and Spain* (Nashville: Vanderbilt University Press, 2020).

Shawn William Miller, *An Environmental History of Latin America* (New York: Cambridge University Press, 2007).

Sarah Pruitt, "6 Famous Missing Treasures: From the Ark of the Covenant to the Aztec gold of Montezuma, these six historic treasures continue to elude us," https://www.history.com/news/6-famous-missing-treasures.

Video

See notes or search "pollo a la brasa" on YouTube or any similar site.

5

Eye Patches and Telenovelas

Medios y Media/Getty Images.

Latin American Cultural Objects and Episodes, First Edition. William H. Beezley.

The eye patch became the signature of Catalina Creel, the rich, fashionable, and evil matriarch of a powerful Mexican dynasty whose devotion to haute couture resulted in designer dresses with matching shoes, purse, and eye patch, covering a healthy eye she claimed to have lost. Like those used by pirates, the eye patch provided a constant reminder of Catalina's wickedness because she swore she had lost her right eye in an accident involving a toy top caused by her stepson Juan Carlos, whom she wanted to disinherit in favor of her son for ownership of the family's pharmaceutical company.

Catalina Creel, eye patch and all, as played by actress Maria Rubio, fascinated viewers of the soap opera *Cuna de lobos* ("Den of Wolves"), through 85 one-hour episodes in 1986–1987. The chronicles of her deceit and murder quickly drew huge national and international audiences, and the series finale made Mexico City a ghost town as residents stayed off the streets to see the conclusion. The Mexican magazine *TVyNovelas* named the series the best program in 1986 and, in 2011, the greatest telenovela of all time. Catalina, with her covered eye, became the metonym for evil and has been called the greatest television villain of all time. Her character has served as the role model for evil on other television programs and in Latin American culture generally.

Cuna de lobos is just one of the mass media melodramas that have entranced both Latin American and international audiences. Other radio and television melodramas have drawn on the tradition of nineteenth-century newspaper serials offered in installments (called folletines) and later U.S. soap operas, both of which provided a model for them. Lux soap sponsorship gave the genre its name in English. Chicago radio station WGN broadcast the first soap opera, "Painted Dreams," on October 20, 1930. This and other early serials had daytime broadcast times, usually five days a week, when most of the listeners were housewives; thus, the shows were written with themes that writers believed would interest the predominantly female audience. Evening broadcasts occurred, such as the first nationally broadcast soap opera *Clara, Lu, and Em* aired on the NBC Blue Network at 10:30 p.m. Eastern Time on January 27,

1931. Colgate-Palmolive and Lever Brothers soap companies also sponsored similar programs.

Shortly after the development of the genre using the new radio technology in the United States, radionovelas quickly appeared in Cuba, Mexico, and the rest of Latin America. Cuban writers and broadcasters in the 1930s initiated programs based on newspaper patterns and U.S. models. Cubans had the same soap sponsorship as in the U.S. These radio romances began with *Los precios fijos* (Fixed Prices) that perhaps had a double meaning for the drama and the prices of sponsor's products. Luis Aragón Dulzaides inaugurated the show on CMQ Radio in 1938 and it continued into 1939. The program was later broadcast on the national radio chain, RHC Cadena Azul, as predecessor to the emblematic literary series called *La novela del aire* that first adapted literature to radio and then added original scripts.

The success of *Los precios fijos* encouraged other Cuban and Latin American radio stations to seek similar programming. The Cubans continued to lead the way, and from the 1930s through the 1950s, they exported more radionovelas for daytime and nighttime play than any nation in the Spanish-speaking world. This inspired aspiring writers to produce scripts for romantic melodramas. Among the successful programs in the 1940s were *Ave sin nido* ("Bird without a Nest") by Spaniard Leandro Blanco, who was living in Havana; *El collar de lágrimas* ("Necklace of Tears") by José Sánchez Arcilla, which still holds the Cuban record for episodes with 965 chapters that ended in December 1946; and *Por la ciudad ruega un grito* ("A Cry is a Prayer for the City") by Reinaldo López del Rincón. The best-known actor in these radionovelas was probably Minín Bujones, known as the Lucille Ball of Cuba.[1]

Among these early Cuban writers, author Félix B. Caignet first achieved success by composing children's songs. One of them, "El ratoncito Miguel" (Mickey Mouse), was performed to raise funds in the campaign against President Gerardo Machado (1925–1933). After several performances at the Teatro Rialto in Santiago in 1932, officials banned the song and jailed Caignet. He was released three days later when his fans, including many children, demonstrated outside the

Moncada garrison. He also had success in 1934 writing and narrating a radio detective drama, *Chan Li Po*, based on the U.S. Charlie Chan movies, broadcast on CMKD.

None of his scripts or songs rivaled his sensational novel and radionovela entitled *El derecho de nacer*, first broadcast in 1948. It became popular throughout Latin America. With a plot that featured an overbearing grandfather (Rafael Del Junco), a pregnant unwed granddaughter (Maria Elena), and the hiding of the newborn son by the nanny (Maria Dolores) to save him from death ordered by the grandfather. The child (Alberto Limoneta) grew up, became a doctor, and fell in love with someone who at first was revealed to be a blood relative. The discovery immediately caused his grandfather to suffer a stroke and he could not tell anyone the truth. The revelation that the doctor's beloved was adopted, his real mother was in a nunnery, and she finally revealed everything allowed for a happy and just ending. For more than a year, Monday through Saturday, the 314 episodes, in the words of one critic, "shook all of Cuba." Listeners around the Caribbean, in Latin America and other parts of the world heard it on short-wave broadcasts of CMQ Radio. It was sponsored by Bestov Products, the representative in Cuba of a diverse line of U.S. food and medical products, including Kresto chocolate (still popular in Puerto Rico), that produced its own publicity and advertising at its own transmitter. The program set a record for listeners across Cuba. The short-wave presentation encouraged other scriptwriters outside of Cuba to consider national adaptations.

El derecho de nacer has been voted by television experts as the greatest radio and television melodrama in Latin American history with a huge impact on music and movies as well. This story was reincarnated time and again as a novel, radio and television serial, and a movie whose theme music became well known. Caignet's Cuban novel and radio script inspired radionovelas in Mexico, Peru, Venezuela, and Brazil, movies in Mexico, Venezuela, Argentina, and Spain, and television soap operas in Mexico (twice), Brazil, and Argentina. The song for its Mexican productions included "El derecho de nacer," sung by Lucho Gatica.

Considered the pioneer of Latin American mass media melodrama, it has received a good deal of analysis by academics in scholarly forums and by fans on social media. For example, the Spanish social critic living in Colombia, José Martín-Barbero, said it represented the Latin American search for belonging, identity, and origins (recognition by the father in the most philosophical and social sense), reflecting the identity in process characterized in the story by showing encounters among social groups, races, and parentages that build a community.[2]

Venezuelan writers adapted the Cuban version of *El derecho de nacer* as a radionovela venezolana and broadcast it in 1949 and 1950. Years later, writers reprised it in the form of a miniseries and most recently rebroadcast it in 2010.[3]

Mexican writers revised the story for national radio in 1950 with Dolores del Río as María Elena del Junco, Manolo Fábregas as Albertico Limonta, and Fedora Capdevila as Mamá Dolores. It quickly appeared in other Latin American countries. In Colombia in 1951, the station Nuevo Mundo de Caracol, which generally presented classical music and drama programs, broadcast the radionovela, winning the audience away from Radio Cadena Nacional which was airing a popular sporting event, the national bicycle race. In Peru it became one of the country's earliest and most successful radio programs. The role of the grandfather, Rafael del Junco, was played by Carlos Ego Aguirre, who portrayed his evil behavior so well that one day the actor was assaulted by a group of women listeners who surrounded him on a Lima street. *El derecho de nacer* changed the daily schedules and customs of its audience, who altered work and family habits to listen to the most widely heard program on radio.[4]

The program's immediate success motivated Cubans at radio network CMQ to develop El Servicio Internacional de Grabaciones de Audio, S.A. – SIGA. They recorded electromagnetic tapes as they broadcast the radiodramas and then distributed the tapes to the rest of Latin America. SIGA also sold scripts of radio and later television programs. A sample of 124 scripts for radionovelas of the 1950s in the archive of Caracol radio network in Bogotá showed the largest number came from Cuba.[5] The dramas relied on stories about the typical conflicts between men and women, parents and children, upper and lower classes, and city and countryside, reflecting the daily life and language of couples, families, school, work, and neighborhoods.[6]

Imitation may not be the sincerest form of flattery in the lively arts, but it certainly serves as inspiration for productions in different media such as film, television, and musical recordings. *El derecho de nacer* demonstrated all these crossover production and collaborative marketing possibilities. Its popularity drew movie producers, who repackaged the story as a film, and with the development of television the melodrama was remade as a TV series. The story also included music that proved popular. The Mexican movie production premiered in 1952, directed by Zacarías Gómez Urquiza and starring Jorge Mistral and Gloria Marín, a special performance by Lupe Suárez in the role of "Mamá Dolores," the selfless black woman who took charge as the nanny for Albertico Limonta, and María Montecristo. It immediately broke box-office records. The movie was shown in Central America, for example at the theater El Circuito Margat in Managua, Nicaragua.[7] In 1966, Tito Davison directed Aurora Bautista and Julio Alemán in a new Mexican version of the story.

Television writers in Cuba produced a version of the 1948 radionovela in a 1952 television series starring Salvador Levy, Violeta Jimenez, and Carlos Badia with immediate success. Puerto Rican television produced its own version in 1959 with Helena Montalban and Braulio Castillo. With the advent of television in Ecuador, one of the new broadcast company's first programs was *El derecho de nacer* in 1960. Two years later, Peruvian television added its production of the program. In Brazil, three versions of the story captivated national audiences: *O direito de nascer* on Rede Tupí in 1964, starring Amilton Fernandes and Nathalia Timberg, again in 1978 with Eva Wilma and Carlos Alberto Strazzer, and network SBT remade it in 2001 with Guilhermina Guinle and Jorge Pontual.

The final episodes of the 1964 program, recalled historian Bert Barickman, were shown in Rio's Maracanã stadium that seats just short of 79,000. On the other telenovelas that appeared on Brazilian television he added, "In Brazil, novela mexicana means an overly melodramatic, sappy telenovela, often of poor quality. I am inclined to believe that the expression arose in the late '60s or early '70s when minor networks, lacking the wherewithal to produce novelas, started showing dubbed Mexican telenovelas and also, I imagine, novelas from elsewhere in Spanish-speaking countries."[8] This certainly did not describe the masterful story of *O direito de nascer* broadcast in the stadium so those with televisions could see the finale.

Venezuelan television, broadcast on Radio Caracas Television (RCTV), in 1965 presented the program as the first to have hour-long episodes. The series told the story through 600 hour-long chapters directed by Juan Lamata and starring Raúl Amundaray and Conchita Obach.

It was not until 1966 that Telesistema Mexicano (today Televisa) first brought the story to the small screen starring María Rivas and Enrique Rambal. In 2008, a panel of Mexican television experts chose *El derecho de nacer* as the most influential telenovela in all of Latin America because it defined the genre as it shaped a collective imaginary. The performers who appeared in the series represent a who's who of major actors.[9]

Recording companies found that theme songs and soundtracks sold well to large audiences. Cuban writer Félix B. Caignet who had created *El derecho de nacer* was also a songwriter and performer. He and Raúl Lavista coauthored the soundtrack for the 1952 Mexican film with "Ven" as its theme song. Verónica Castro sang it again as the theme song when she and Salvador Pineda starred in the Mexican television remake of the series in 1981, but Televisa's 2001 version starring Kate del Castillo and Saúl Lisazo featured "Quisiera" by Alejandro Fernández as the theme song.

Although today Mexico and Brazil have reputations as leaders in the production of telenovelas, other countries have attracted international audiences with their television melodramas. These include programs such as Venezuela's most popular soap opera, *La viuda joven* (called the Black Widow in English, 2011), a mystery thriller and love story that attracted such a huge audience that a million followers came online to discuss the identity of the murderer.

In Colombia *El derecho de nacer* established great popularity by all accounts. Because it was broadcast on commercial radio, almost no sound archives were retained and little information exists about it, but it inspired the broadcast of other radionovelas.[10] In 1940, Colombia's national government established an educational radio station. Its programs included radioteatros (radio theater) or dramas radiales (radio dramas) that focused on the era of independence and the heroes who struggled to achieve it. The style and tenor of these radio programs broke with the dithyrambic style of hero creation to make the leaders of independence human beings, with great streaks of heroism and plenty of failings. Professor Mary Roldan has said that "there should be *far* more research done on telenovelas for Colombia that is extremely important and notable – especially beginning in the 1980s – for being focused on social and political issues in ways that distinguish the genre from its Venezuelan, Mexican and Brazilian counterparts."[11]

This resulted in Colombia's first and classic 1994 telenovela, *Café, con aroma de una mujer*, which achieved what the Cuban scriptwriter Félix B. Caignet explained was the goal for listeners and viewers of these stories, who "took on the feelings of one or another character who was suffering and, without being aware of it, associated their own pain with that of the fictitious figure, and cried with him or her."[12] The telenovela demonstrated the pattern of turning popular novels into television series and the production of revised versions in other countries. In this case, Colombian author Fernando Gaitán's novel of the same name provided the story of Gaviota, a young woman who worked in the coffee harvest, and her love affair with Sebastián, the grandson of a powerful coffee producer. The location for filming in Antioquia has become a popular attraction. Two Mexican adaptations were produced when TV Aztec filmed *Cuando seas mía* in 2001 and Televisa created *Destilando amor* in 2007, replacing coffee with tequila.

Caignet's explanation of the allure of telenovelas and radionovelas held true in Sonora, Mexico as well. Anabelle Galindo recalled her mom saying that in Sonora she listened to a couple of radionovelas, *El derecho de nacer* and *Apague la luz y escuche*. She said, "My dad used to remember all the neighborhood kids gathering outside a pharmacy to listen to the scary stories of *Apague la luz*, then no one wanted to walk back home because they were too scared…I guess what made it worse is that they lived in front of the cemetery."[13]

Mexico and Brazil continue to dominate the production and export of telenovelas, followed by Colombia. But television production companies from other nations produced them and sometimes have had success not only nationally but also in the export market. A significant example was the Argentina telenovela *Los Roldán*. In Mexico, it was remade as *Una familia con suerte* and ran from 2011 until 2012 with 265 episodes. A summary of the characters and their relationships to each other demonstrates the complexity and coincidences that shape the narrative. The story follows the López family and the lives of the family members in Mexico City (relocated from Buenos Aires in the original). Pancho, played by Arath de la Torre, is the patriarch. He drives a grocery delivery truck and, despite his tragic backstory involving the death of his wife, he always tells jokes and laughs with customers. Pepe, played by Pablo Lyle, is the eldest son and a mechanic. Lupita, played by Alejandra García, is the second oldest. She is sweet and wants to be a teacher. The second daughter and Pancho's third child is Ana, played by Sherlyn. She is a bit of a tomboy and wants to become a famous singer. The youngest child is Cuautemóc, although everyone calls him "Temo." Ever since Laurita, Pancho's wife, died giving birth to Temo, Chela has raised the children. Chela is Pancho's sister-in-law (Laurita's sister) and is played by Luz Elena González. Pancho's adopted sister, Candy, also lives with the family. She is played by Miss Universe Alicia Machado. The López family lives in poverty, but they have each other and they are happy. One day Pancho saves the life of a wealthy businesswoman (who turns out to be Pancho's birth mother) named Fernanda. She leaves all her money to Pancho. The lives of the family change forever. Throughout the series, the López family deal with funny mishaps. Among them, each member of the family finds love and they all live happily ever after. The Mexican production company replaced the Argentine theme song "Gente Buena" composed by Palito Ortega with "Día de Suerte," sung by Alejandra Guzmán, a well-known Mexican singer.[14]

All these telenovelas achieved their popularity, according to social philosopher Jesús Martín-Barbero, by connecting viewers to the universe of legends and heroes and the stories of mystery and fear that were common in the countryside before television and have been displaced to the city, often with new media. For example, in Brazil, cordel literature has moved to the comic book or fotonovela, a photomagazine; in Mexico, the corrido has become the narcocorrido, singing the stories of the narco leaders; and in Colombia, the vallenato that once sang messages from one village to another has been linked to a new urban music style. The telenovela links with this oral culture, establishing dramatic continuity and achieving its great popularity.[15]

Whether linked to oral traditions or not, the popularity of telenovelas results in periodic panels and magazine articles deciding on lists of the best or most popular or most dramatic of these programs, such as "My Top 27 Favorite Colombian Soap Operas."[16] In the regional magazine *Cosmopolitan for Latinas*, for example, in 2020 Alanna Nunez and Alex Brady published "These Are the Absolute Best Telenovelas of All Time."[17] They chose for their list rather recent programs and none that were based on earlier radionovelas. They selected the following:

1. ***Rebelde.*** Recalling the extremely popular ***Elite***, this telenovela builds on the adventures of students in an elite boarding school as a remake of the Argentine series *Rebelde Way*. The authors call it a knock-off of the *Breakfast Club*, with students dressed for a Britney Spears music video.
2. ***Rubí.*** Another remake of an earlier soap opera (2004) based on a short story from the 1960s, this follows the career of an anti-hero femme fatale who compensates for her impoverished childhood by seduction, adultery, and manipulation. It becomes a melodramatic attempt at murder and amputation. There are cliff-hangers aplenty and opportunities to discuss the gossipy side of relationships on a regular basis.

3. ***Yo Soy Betty La Fea.*** Originally a Colombian telenovela about a homely but brilliant secretary working at a high-pressure fashion company, which ran from 1998–2001. The theme that "intelligence and integrity will triumph over skin-deep beauty" drew about one in five Colombians to watch the program. The program saved the Colombian network RCN, which created it, from financial ruin. Ana Maria Orozco, who played Betty, became a star across Latin America. As the character became successful, she began to undergo a makeover that some fans saw as a copout. When the series wound down after 300 episodes over a year and a half in 2000 and 2001, audiences were obsessed with the finale in Bogotá and in 21 other countries. The program had a fan base of about 80 million viewers across Latin America to Hungary and Israel and was watched on the international Spanish-language network, Telemundo. The story resulted in dozens of remakes, adapted versions, and was introduced to broad-based U.S. viewers when it became the primetime, successful soap opera, *Ugly Betty*.[18] The authors at one time declared it "the most successful (and probably the most popular) *novela* of all time."
4. ***Juegos de Fuego.*** A Chilean production. Nunez confessed she is Chilean, and for that reason as well as an excellent soundtrack, notable for "Mi Historia Entre Tus Dedos," available on YouTube, she chose this telenovela. She added that it was actually quite bad, so bad it was good.
5. ***Marimar.*** A remake of another Mexican telenovela, *La Venganza*, 1977. Starring Helena Rojo, it narrates the tale of forbidden love in which the protagonist Marimar (played by Thalia, considered one of the most successful Mexican artists worldwide) falls in love with Sergio, the son of a wealthy farmer, much to the chagrin of his parents and grandparents. Filmed on location with beautiful beaches, demonstrating the significance of landscape, critics declared it combined elements of Cinderella, Pygmalion, and *The Taming of the Shrew*.
6. ***La Reina del Sur.*** Translated as "The Queen of the South," *La Reina* takes place in Mexico and chronicles the rise of Teresa Mendoza, who works her way up to become the most powerful drug lord in the country. This telenovela in English has become widely available on several streaming services and has a growing audience.
7. ***La Patrona.*** This telenovela from Mexico features the main character Gabriela Súarez (played by Aracely Arambula) as the only female miner in a small town. It is a remake of the 1984 Venezuelan telenovela

La dueña, loosely based on "The Count of Monte Cristo." It tells the story of Gabriela who is framed for the death of her father by starting a mine explosion that killed many miners. She is sent to an insane asylum and has to endure shock therapy and yet she perseveres and manages to exact revenge.

8. ***El Zorro La Espada y La Rosa.*** Based on the 1998 film, the serial, which ran in 2007, has the masked hero constantly in torment because of his feelings for his love and his commitment to achieve justice for the residents in Spanish California. Music fans love the fact that Beyoncé sang the theme song.
9. ***El Clon*** ("The Clone") is a Spanish-language telenovela released in 2010, produced by the U.S.-based television network Telemundo, the Colombian network Caracol Television, and the Brazilian network Globo. It is a remake of *O Clone*, a Brazilian telenovela that originally aired on Globo in 2001 and on Telemundo in 2002. This melodrama, which starred Mauricio Ochmann and Sandra Echeverría, deals with topics such as drug trafficking, Islam, and cloning. The incredibly farfetched story focuses on Jade, a young Arab woman in Morocco, and Lucas, the son of a powerful businessman. The couple cannot be together. Two decades later, a strange turn of luck brings the pair together. Then Jade also meets Lucas's clone, who is twenty years younger. She faces the choice between the man she loved and the memory she cherishes.
10. ***Martin Rivas.*** A Chilean historical television series adapted from the 1862 novel of the same name by Alberto Blest Gana, which aired on TVN and TV Chile for several months in 2010. Relying on a common trope, it features forbidden love between Martin Rivas, the impoverished protagonist, and Leonore Encina, the wealthy daughter of the family Rivas lives with.
11. ***La Usurpadora.*** This classic has an extremely complicated narrative, called a doozy by the reviewers, that aired in 1998. Twin sisters Paulina and Paola are separated at birth, and when they manage to reunite as adults, Paola (the evil twin) blackmails Paulina to switch places so she can leave her husband for a year-long vacation with her lover. Paulina reluctantly agrees, and while living with Paola's husband, she falls in love with him.
12. ***Dos Mujeres, Un Camino.*** This 1993 show featured Johnny, a truck driver who travels between Mexico and the U.S. and juggles a relationship with two women, his wife Ana Maria, and his love

> Tanya. Johnny ends up wrongly blamed for the death of a youngster and Tanya dies, taking a knife intended for Johnny's wife. Johnny's wife finally decides to leave him. This production drew fans across 47 countries.

All of these telenovelas merit viewing and show the dimensions of programs based on novels, earlier television programs, and movies. The twists and turns, the coincidental romances, and revenge for the most part create a good feeling for audiences.

Production did not shift only to television programs, at least, not in one case. The Cuban passion for soap operas that had emerged with *El derecho de nacer* continued through the 1959 revolution. From the 1930s through the 1950s, Cuba produced and exported radio serials. After Fidel Castro's revolutionary victory, many Cubans fled to Miami. Some supported the creation of the U.S. anti-Castro campaign as part of the anti-revolutionary policies of the Cold War. A new production of Cuban soap operas began operations in Florida as Cuban emigres in Miami began making original Spanish-language radionovelas broadcast on more than 200 stations worldwide. The stories heard throughout Latin America revealed a nascent middle class searching for a new way to live. Many of the programs aimed at housewives used the frequent breaks in the action to allow advertisers to pitch household and luxury items.

From 1963 to 1970, America's Productions Incorporated made more than 130 Spanish-language serials. The company had its office and studios in the Freedom Tower in Miami and the company hired displaced Cuban writers, directors, actors, musicians, and engineers. Perhaps the best-known actor in the radionovelas was Minín Bujones.[19] Louis Boeri, an Italian-born American businessman, who was the husband of Bujones, founded America's Productions Incorporated. Boeri remains a mysterious character. Before the early 1960s he was a magazine publisher in Florida. In the final years of the Batista regime, he took a job with the Cuban government to promote U.S. investment and tourism there. But when Fidel Castro achieved power and made Cuba a partner with the Soviet Union, Boeri left his home and fortune in Havana and relocated to Miami.

Boeri's family suspects he worked for a U.S. intelligence agency. Zenia Robertson, his daughter, recalled that he took a lot of flights to Washington, DC. That may account for why Cold War politics seem so evident in these radionovelas. The protagonists openly embrace democratic and capitalist ideals. They do not say exactly who or what they are fighting against. The Tulane Library archivist Ida Schooler explained, "They don't want to say 'Communists,' so the big sub-in is always 'The Existentialists...So in multiple series you'll have like, 'It was the kind of bar where Bohemians and students and Existentialists hang out.' And they'll talk about Sartre and his philosophy."

Some of Boeri's radionovelas were pure propaganda, made to counter the ideals of the Cuban Revolution. But the serials broadcast on commercial radio, so they were not completely dogmatic – they managed to be both ideological and thrilling. The Cuban actors in Miami cultivated a rare skill – the ability to speak "Continental Spanish." "It would be the equivalent to the Trans-Atlantic accent," Schooler says. "So they'd figured out a way to alter their voices so that it was not region specific and it wasn't class specific." Boeri once said that in his radionovelas, "The American way of life shines, but without saying so."[20]

Telenovelas Redux

The popularity of a number of Mexican telenovelas considered classics, timeless programs that captured the attention of millions of people throughout Latin America and beyond in the 1980s and 1990s, now are little known by the current generation of television viewers. This resulted in plans to remake several of these classics and bringing them up to date, with well-known actors, and reimagined for the new generation. Televisa scheduled 12 iconic telenovelas for new productions to form a collection to be called *Fábrica de sueños* (the Dream Factory). They were also to be broadcast on Univision, with the anthology called "The Collection." The producers listed for this project the telenovelas *El maleficio*, *Rubí*, *Colorina*, *Los ricos también lloran*, *Rosa salvaje*, *Corona de lágrimas*, *Quinceañera*, *El privilegio de amar*, and *Corazón salvaje*, and scheduled the first two, *La usurpadora* and *Cuna de lobos*.

The first of these programs, *La usurpadora* ("The Usurper"), is regarded as one of the most popular of all Mexican telenovelas. Cuban writer Inés Rodena's novel served as the basis for her script for the 1998 telenovela, which also had a series of predecessors that drew on Daphne du Maurier's 1957 novel, *The Scapegoat*, and several television programs, two made in Venezuela, one in 1971 and another version called *La intrusa* in 1986. The first Mexican adaptation of Rodena's novel came in 1981 when Valentin Pimstein made *El hogar que yo robé*. A 2012 remake coproduced by Mexico with Colombian and the U.S. assistance was broadcast as ¿Quién eres tú? Claimed as a major difference compared to the 1998 show, the producers insisted on using the modern United States condensed format of 25 episodes that are produced in one block; despite this oddity in terms of Mexican productions, Carmen Armendáriz, the director, said the series maintained its essence as a telenovela.

Updating the story's context, the writers had the President and the First Lady replace the successful businessman and his trophy wife; added an international dimension with locations that included Colombia; and changed the two sons of the original into a stepson and stepdaughter. The crucial element in the plotline remained the same, the story of two identical twins, the First Lady, the character Paola Miranda, who discovers she has a twin sister Paulina. Paola has an unhappy marriage to Carlos, the President, wants to escape, and seeks to switch with her newfound twin Paulina. The plan is for her to stand in as First Lady at an Independence Day celebration and kill her, allowing Paola to run away with her lover Gonzalo.

Paulina lives in Bogotá, running an orphanage and tending to her aging mother, Olga. She mysteriously receives large donations from a Mexican benefactor, travels to Mexico, and is kidnapped by Paola, who blackmails Paulina into assuming her identity for two weeks under the threat of murdering Olga. Paulina becomes the "usurpadora" and moves into the presidential palace. The plan goes awry at the

Independence celebrations. Paulina is shot, but not only does she live, the National Intelligence Agency also begins an investigation into the shooting, thinking that the President was the target. The President also hires a private detective to investigate. Paola has already run away with Gonzalo to Bora Bora; she is not happy, kills her lover, and returns to Mexico City to cover her tracks. Paulina takes to her role as First Lady which allows her to engage in social activism. Paola tries to kill her again, but she survives and returns to Colombia, trusting the President's agent to find out everything, to make sure that her mother is still alive. Paola tries to return to her role. Paulina is not willing to sacrifice her position of social influence and begins her own scheme, acting crazy and using the real story to receive a diagnosis of multiple personality disorder, finally becoming committed to an asylum. Paola tries once more to kill her. The President's agent breaks Paulina out of the hospital and takes her to the countryside; Paola is taken to Colombia after being misidentified as her sister after the attack, with her confusion ruled as post-traumatic stress. The mother recognizes who Paola really is, at the same time that Paulina returns to the presidential home, supposedly cured; Paulina convinces Carlos that she isn't crazy and has him travel to Colombia with her to meet Olga. Paola, Paulina, and Olga come to an agreement whereby the twins will continue swapping lives for a little longer, so that Olga has some time to get to know Paola. Only a few days later, though, she dies, with Paola determinedly returning to Mexico. Despite its abrupt ending, the remade program was highly praised and the story remained, as one critic put it earlier, a doozy.[21]

The second of these classic remakes was *Cuna de lobos*, one of the most iconic dramas of all time, starring Paz Vega with an eye patch as a modern version of the iconic Catalina Creel, whose beauty is only surpassed by her cruelty. The Spanish star Vega has received multiple awards, including the Chopard Trophy at the Cannes Film Festival and the Film Critics Society award. She gave new overtones of evil to Creel. She is known for her film performances in *Rambo V*, *Talk to Her*, *Carmen*, *Lucia y El Sexo*, and *Spanglish*. On television, she has appeared in several successful series, notably *7 Vidas*, *Más que amigos*, and *Compañeros*. Her widespread popularity gave the new version of *Cuna de lobos* a celebrity cast. Giselle González, known for producing *Caer en tentación* and *Yo no creo en los hombres*, took charge of *Cuna de Lobos*. The series features performances by Paulette Hernández, Flavio Medina, Azela Robinson, Gonzalo García Vivanco, Nailea Norvind, and Jose Pablo Minor. The all-star cast and production crew created an instant audience in the Spanish-speaking world.

Ambition and treachery drive the story in this new account of the classic tale about the mother of all telenovela "villains" – Catalina Creel. After causing the death of her wealthy husband Carlos Larios (Leonardo Daniel), Catalina will do anything for the unconditional love she feels for her son Alejandro (Diego Amozurrutia) and will go to any lengths, no matter how despicable, to secure her fortune and her bloodline. Taking advantage of social media, the new production provides viewers a chance to join the conversation by providing twitter information, especially the opportunity to discuss the moment after Catalina's death when the patch is removed and it is discovered it was unnecessary.

The one-eyed villain can likely be tracked back at least to the cyclops of the *Odyssey*, and certainly it has ties to highwaymen and pirates of later centuries. More than ever, in the world of the telenovela, the symbol of evil remains the eye patch.

Notes

1 Mayra Cue Sierra, "Radionovela 'El derecho de nacer' (Tercera Parte y final)," *el arte de hacer radio* blog (April 27, 2008), https://haciendoradio.blogspot.com/2008/04/radionovela-derecho-de-nacer-tercera.html; Gwen Thompkins, "Massive Digitization Effort Is The Latest Plot Twist For Cuban Radio Soap Operas," *Repeating Islands* blog (July 26, 2019), https://repeatingislands.com/2019/07/26/massive-digitization-effort-is-the-latest-plot-twist-for-cuban-radio-soap-operas/.

2 http://es.wikipedia.org/wiki/El_derecho_de_nacer, comments August 8, 2009 (no longer accessible).

3 https://es.wikipedia.org/wiki/El_derecho_de_nacer_(telenovela_de_1965).
4 Nelson Castellanos, "Historia de los medios: *El precio de un pecado*: Oír radionovelas a escondidas," *Signo y Pensamiento*, 48 (January/June 2006), p. 93.
5 Castellanos, p. 93, n. 2.
6 Federico Medino Cano, "La radionovela y el folletín," *Revista Universidad Pontificia Bolivariana*, 47, no. 145 (September 1998), p. 91.
7 *La Prensa* (Managua), June 1, 1955.
8 Barickman in discussion with the author, April 22, 2012.
9 https://es.wikipedia.org/wiki/El_derecho_de_nacer_(telenovela_de_2001).
10 Email to the author from Mary Roldan, Professor of Latin American History, Hunter College, CUNY/Graduate Center, August 11, 2013.
11 Ibid. Professor Roldan could not identify any serious studies of this issue.
12 Félix B. Caignet, interview with Orlando Castellanos on Radio Havana, Cuba, August 30, 1972, https://en.wikipedia.org/wiki/F%C3%A9lix_B._Caignet.
13 Interview with Anabelle Galindo, Tucson, AZ, March 22, 2011.
14 Information on *Una familia con suerte* provided by University of Arizona student Elizabeth Garcia.
15 Jesús Martín-Barbero and Sonia Muñoz, *Televisión y melodrama: Géneros y lecturas de la telenovela en Colombia* (Bogotá, Colombia: Tercer Mundo Editores, 1992), pp. 123–124.
16 "My Top 27 Favorite Colombian Soap Operas," by tbell1826, created October 9, 2011, https://www.imdb.com/list/ls003608937/.
17 Alanna Nunez and Alex Brady, https://www.cosmopolitan.com/entertainment/tv/news/a31651/10-best-novelas-of-all-time/.
18 "Colombian TV Viewers Obsessed With Fate of 'Betty the Ugly One,'" *Arizona Daily Star* (Tucson), April 25, 2001.
19 Tulane University's library holds a massive collection of these radionovelas – more than 9,000 reel-to-reel tapes – that is named after Bujones and her husband, Louis Boeri, an Italian-born American businessman who founded America's Productions Incorporated.
20 Thompkins, "Massive Digitization Effort."
21 For the summary and other details, see https://en.wikipedia.org/wiki/La_usurpadora_(2019_Mexican_TV_series).

Additional Resources

Reading

Gabriela Jonas Aharoni, *Argentinian Telenovelas: Southern Sagas Rewrite Social and Political Reality* (Eastbourne: Sussex Academic Press, 2015).
O. Hugo Benavides, *Drugs, Thugs, and Divas: Telenovelas and Narco-Dramas in Latin America* (Austin: University of Texas Press, 2008).
Ilan Stavans, *Telenovelas* (Santa Barbara: Greenwood, 2010).

6

Ugh! Soup!

Daniel Garcia/Getty Images.

Mafalda remains the most popular cartoon character of all time among Latin America's extensive cartoon and comic strip characters. These comics represent the humorous media tradition that appeared in the first decade of the twentieth century. Comics, through satire, offered if only superficially relevance, humor, and refining influence in

Latin American Cultural Objects and Episodes, First Edition. William H. Beezley.

table manners, clothing, and conversation. Mafalda and other comic personalities provide commentary on everyday life, challenge middle-class values, offer guidance by example for living in the burgeoning cities, and have become, as iconic figures, national symbols.

Soup – Mafalda detests it. So does the majority of the region's children ages 7 to 11, according to one survey that showed their distaste for soup and their regard for Mafalda.

Frequency of reading Mafalda	*% who said soup is a favorite food*
Always	4.2%
Often	28.6%
Sometimes	47.9%
Not within the last year	55.0%

The statistics should not be exaggerated. The data shows a correlation between reading *Mafalda* and eating soup, but this does not indicate causality, neither that reading *Mafalda* causes young people to dislike soup, nor that disliking soup causes youngsters to read *Mafalda*. The study shows simply that a majority of children surveyed do not like soup and do like Mafalda.[1]

Mafalda speaks not only for Argentine children but also for adults and many Latin Americans. The feisty, precocious girl was the creation of Joaquín Salvador Lavado, better known by his pen name Quino. His parents, Spanish Republicans, had fled to Argentina before the Spanish Civil War. Quino was born in Mendoza in 1932 and grew up in the San Telmo neighborhood of Buenos Aires among other Andalusian immigrants. When he began school, he once said, his Andalusian accent was so heavy his teachers had a difficult time understanding him.

Quino first drew Mafalda and some friends when an advertising manager developing a campaign for the Siam Di Tella company commissioned him to draw cartoons that promoted Mansfield home appliances. The company wanted cartoons that featured children similar to Charles Schultz's Peanuts Gang whose names all began with an M and who used the products. Quino said he bought all the Peanuts books he could get to develop his cartoons. He called the main character Mafalda, because he liked the name when he saw it used for a baby in the 1962 Argentine film *Dar la cara*, which portrayed the challenges of three friends (a cyclist, a filmmaker, and a student), who after military service struggle to develop their careers in the 1960s.[2] The magazine editor liked the cartoons but rejected them because the advertising of the appliances was too blatant. Quino put the cartoons away for a year, until the editor of another magazine, *Primera Plana*, showed interest in them if Quino removed the Mansfield references. Following the changes, Mafalda appeared in print.[3]

Immediately successful, the outspoken six-year-old Mafalda challenged adults, ignored conventions, identified sanctimony, and recognized contractions. Her actions showed that she cared deeply about humanity, loved the Beatles, and had quirky friends. Throughout these early cartoons, Mafalda explored the generational and gender rigidities of the middle class and the significance of irony in its humor in the 1960s.[4] Mafalda achieved popularity because Quino drew on middle-class customs and the comic character also influenced the patterns of society. The difference in this approach to middle-class values was starkly evident when compared to the popular telenovela of middle-class life, *La Familia Falcón*. The comic strip above all used irony and other comedic descriptions to define the emergent middle class, with its conflictive values.[5] The diverse character of the middle class is expressed through the interests and activities of Mafalda and her friends Felipe, Manolito, Susanita, Libertad, and Miguelito, in what has been called "a choral depiction of the ideology of the middle class."[6]

Mafalda soon appeared in South America's major periodicals and other major Spanish-language newspapers. In Spain, ruled by the dictator General Francisco Franco, censors required editors to place a "for adults" notice on the cover of Mafalda comic books. Other countries in the beginning censored the cartoon as well. In Bolivia, Chile, and Brazil, censors, according to Quino, told him, "Pal, jokes against the family no; against military officers no, and nudes no." He concluded, "I was born with self-censorship."[7] Self-censorship or not,

Quino mastered subtleties of critical humor. For example, Mafalda asks her dad for some help with a word. "I'll explain: millibars are a pressure measure. Depending on the atmosphere, it is said that there is a pressure of so many mili…" "Sorry Dad, I asked you about millibars, not the military."[8]

Many of the cartoons considered the life and interests of children – Mafalda and her friends. The comic strip used humor to discuss the participation of people of all ages and to examine the status in society of justice and human dignity.[9] In several cartoons, Mafalda expresses her eagerness for children to have a say in their national society and politics. In several, she declares that children are citizens and should have the right to vote.

The cartoons represented the way many adolescents distanced themselves from their parents' life experience. In particular they showed the distance between women who were full-time housewives or mothers, as seen in the Mafalda comic strips, and rebellious young girls like the cartoon character and most of her friends. Other young working-class girls affirmed their decision to work, and to do so after marriage, based on their experience with working mothers and grandmothers.[10] More generally, the cartoon displayed characters who laughed at their parents and their generation.[11]

Mafalda dominated newspaper funnies from 1962 to 1973, when Quino stopped drawing the cartoon. Afterward the comics continued to be reprinted in books that still sell throughout Latin America and have been translated into 30 foreign languages. Mafalda and her friends have loyal followers and remain so popular that in 2009, a life-sized statue of Mafalda was installed outside the former home of Quino in the San Telmo neighborhood. It immediately became a tourist attraction, and every day people line up to take photographs with her. Also celebrating the cartoon in Buenos Aires, at one subway station Teodolina García Cabo created a ceramic mural, "El Mundo Según Mafalda" (The World According to Mafalda). In Paris, the metro stop Argentina has a mural of famous national figures such as Jorge Luis Borges and Mafalda. Other tributes include a passageway named for her in Angoulême, France, and a street in the city of

Gatineau, Quebec, as part of a project to create a neighborhood featuring famous French-language and other cartoon characters. A statue of Mafalda was installed in 2014 in San Francisco park located in Oviedo, Spain, after Quino received the Princess of Asturias Award in Communications and Humanities.[12]

The popularity of Mafalda notwithstanding, Quino has refused to renew the cartoon, although new stories have appeared. In 1976, he drew some Mafalda cartoons for UNICEF, who selected Mafalda as a spokesperson for the Convention on the Rights of the Child, and he also created some Mafalda cartoons for the fifth anniversary of President Raúl Alfonsín's Argentinian government (1983–1989). He also permits use of the character in some educational cartoons (like the Peanuts television programs) and movies. The popularity of the Mafalda character has made it a significant choice for use in pamphlets and posters to inform schoolchildren of their rights and to encourage them to resist bullying and report violations against them. Quino, for the most part, has also opposed cinema or television adaptations. Nevertheless, two film projects featuring Mafalda have been produced. Daniel Mallo made a series of 260 90-second clips for Argentine television beginning in 1972 that Carlos Márquez adapted into a full-length movie, released in 1981. In 1993, Cuban filmmaker Juan Padrón, a close friend of Quino's, with Spanish financing, produced 104 short animated *Mafalda* films. In none of the cartoons, books, educational announcements or videos does Mafalda willingly or happily eat soup.

What is it about soup? Mafalda comments on it but gives no answer. In one cartoon, she sits at the table facing a bowl and wonders why that "'idiot Fidel Castro' doesn't praise soup, so that Argentines will boycott it." Interesting! But she did not explain her distaste for the liquid meal. Quino once commented that children prefer other foods, especially milanesa (breaded fried chicken in Argentina) – a quick food like a hamburger and fries in the U.S. Quino abandoned Argentina from 1976 to 1983 to escape the heinous repression of the military dictatorship and moved to Italy (he continues to split his time between the two countries today). During this self-imposed exile, in a BBC radio interview with Martín Murphy broadcast August 6, 2004, he remarked about soup, "in reality, this is an allegory for the military regimes we have had to live with here in the Southern Cone. These dictatorships imposed strict rules and forced people to obey them. We had to give up liberty and that is very disagreeable, just as many children find soup."[13]

This anti-authoritarian opinion was clearly articulated in the comic script when Mafalda responded to her mother's insistence that she eat the bowl of soup by saying she was "losing all respect for high-handedness." Soup also had ties to her parents' generation that she recoiled against. In another cartoon, when her father urges her to eat it by saying, "Soup will help you grow up like your mother, like me," she responds, "So, soup, and to top it off…*THAT*." Another critical depiction of soup, from a different political dimension, appeared in another strip: Mafalda's mother, trying to coax her to eat, says that children who do not eat their soup remain little forever. This prompts Mafalda to think, "How peaceful the world would be today if Marx hadn't eaten his soup." Most directly, in a 1971 cartoon that appeared within weeks of General Alejandro Lanusse and the military's seizure of power and the introduction of programs against anyone it considered a leftist opponent or a member of an armed group with torture, murder, and disappearance, a grim Mafalda responds to her mother by giving her a bowl of soup, using a parody of clipped military speech: "If anyone were to rebel deliberately against drinking, eating, swallowing, gobbling and/or sipping this crap, would you beat them?" Sometime later, she summarizes her views in the succinct statement, "soup is to childhood what communism is to democracy."[14]

After Quino stopped drawing Mafalda, the soup kind of subtle subversion became common in popular music during the military dictatorship. The writers and performers of Rock Nacional found ways to express their opposition to the regime.[15]

Mafalda and other cartoons built on the legacy of the last quarter of the nineteenth-century comic strips that appeared in Latin America. Newspapers published both domestic and international cartoons. U.S. examples influenced Latin American editors. In Mexico, for example, comic strip characters appeared soon after they were published around 1892 in the United States. The *San Francisco Examiner* daily printed

Jimmy Swinnerton's "Little Bears and Tigers." Shortly afterward, "Max and Moritz," characters created by German artist Wilhelm Busch and usually credited as the first comic, became popular in the United States. Other comics soon followed as the two giants, Joseph Pulitzer of the *New York World* and William Randolph Hearst of the *Morning Journal* and the *Chicago Daily News,* made comic strips part of their competition for circulation. This inspired new comics such as Richard Outcault's "Katzenjammer Kids" that became famous in the *Journal* and "Mutt and Jeff" in the *San Francisco Examiner.* The popularity of the comics or funnies attracted producers of other media, who from 1910 to 1916 created versions of all the good comic strips as the subject of bad burlesque shows. For Broadway, in 1922, John Alden Carpenter and Adolph Bolm wrote and Bolm choreographed the "Krazy Kat Ballet," a jazz-pantomime of the popular comic strip. With the development of motion pictures, film versions of the comics quickly followed.

In Mexico, Rafael Reyes Spíndola first introduced similar features in *El Mundo* (1894) and *El Imparcial* (1896). During the first decades of the twentieth century, graphic humor in periodicals changed radically with the rise of new mass media that resulted from new technology and marketing. During the disruption of the revolution that began in 1910, two new newspapers appeared. *El Universal* (1916), edited by José Gómez Ugarte, who had worked at *El Imparcial* and *El Excélsior* (1917), whose founder Rafael Alducin was a friend of the Reyes Spíndola family, soon dominated popular circulation. *Universal* began to publish the U.S. comic strip "Happy Hooligan" in 1917, calling it "Adventuras del Papá de Pancholin" (a Mexican comic it had published in a sporadic way for a few months) and changing Happy's name to Pancho. *Excelsiór* introduced "Bringing up Father" initially translated as "Casos y Cosas de Don Folias" to portray the life of this henpecked, unmannered husband. The name tied the cartoon to one of the most famous characters of Mexico's puppet theater. Often the comics had to be dubbed to fit local cultural understandings. For example, instead of the English accent of Irish immigrants, at least in Uruguay, the translators used Spanish accents. In December, often the comics would substitute the name of one of the Wise Men for Santa Claus.

Comic strips that often focused on typical characters and national identity – representing a particular kind of everyday nationalism – soon appeared in Latin American newspapers. The earliest of these characters was the Cuban country worker, Liborio, who quickly became the icon of national culture and a synonym for the common man. Cartoonist Ricardo de la Torriente, the chief editor and owner of *La Política Cómica*, in 1900 created Liborio, based on the guajiro, the Cuban peasant descended from isleño (a native of the Canary Islands) migrants and identified by Victor Patricio Landaluze in his costumbrista painting of Cuban characters. Liborio had a pronounced nose, sideburns, long whiskers, straw hat, red neckerchief, white linen guayabera, leather boots, and a machete. Torriente soon placed Liborio in a weekly comic strip in the newspaper in 1905 where it continued through 1931.

Central Historic Books/Alamy Stock Photo.

Liborio, in the comic strip, experienced all of life's ups and downs, including difficulties with the U.S. (personified as Tio Sam) experienced by the Cuban people during this time. Often, he reacted with no more than a gesture and at others with satirical doggerel. He was passive, usually a victim, although at times he took his machete sheath and beat someone who had exploited an ordinary person. Besides expressing all the joy and sadness of ordinary people, the comic strip character also appeared regularly in locations showing different aspects of the island. He showed up in exile communities, Carnival celebrations, costume parties, and local festivals. Besides cartoons, Liborio appeared in other forms, such as music, and Rodrigo Prats composed "El guanajo de Liborio" (Liborio's Turkey) in December 1941. In the 1950s, updated versions of the figure appeared. One, known as Liborito Liborio Pérez, lacked both sideburns and mustache, and had a chubby face, straw hat, and patriotic guayabera, called a mambí. This new version of Liborio appeared in various publications, including the weekly humor magazine *Zigzag*.[16]

Mexican artists also created original cartoons with nationalistic features. The history of graphic cartoons is sometimes traced back to pre-Columbian codices and to the colonial-era Catholic catechisms with images, although many scholars reject these connections. Following independence, politicians, intellectuals, and artists debated national identity, among other things, with special emphasis on Spanish or indigenous culture as the most important heritage. Political caricatures appeared almost daily in the late nineteenth century. Satirical caricatures developed with the popularity of aleluyas (hallelujahs – Easter strip cartoons with rhyming satirical couplets).

With the turn of the century, a new comic strip character rather than political caricature appeared. Andrés Audiffred created *Don Lupito* in 1903 about a policeman who endured social and economic pressures from his family life, corrupt officials, and local criminals. After 1910, revolutionaries rejected Porfirian cosmopolitanism, which they regarded as a preference for the foreign, and committed to the emergence of popular groups that had moved upward with the rebellion. Newspapers by the 1920s published both national and foreign comic strips rather than political caricatures. Representing a common social type, Don Catarino, the first of these characters, appeared January 1, 1921 in the Sunday supplement of *El Heraldo*. He was a charro, sometimes called in a patronizing way a charrito, a rural individual who had abandoned his milpa (his patch of corn, beans, and chiles) for the adventure of moving to the city. Don Catarino remained a weekly feature until the mid-1950s.

The popularity of comic strips encouraged the newspaper *El Universal* in 1924 to announce a contest for cartoonists. This became an annual event and was just one of the many contests the newspaper sponsored in an effort to increase circulation. These had begun with a sonnet contest in 1917, then popular music compositions, the India bonita, the pleasant woman worker (la obrera simpática), economical clothing (el vestido económico), and oratory, among others.[17] The newspaper announced that it would appoint the winner of a 60-cartoon contest to its staff and would pay the creators of any cartoon published. The editor also declared that the *Universal*'s Sunday comic section after the contest would bring only Mexican cartoons to readers. The new comic strips in some cases reinvented foreign models for Mexican audiences. As part of the contest, the newspaper published one comic strip each day, in addition to about 20 in the pages of the Sunday supplement. At first, the contest included youngsters and amateurs, but quickly became a contest for professionals.

El Universal announced the winner of the comic strip contest Febuary 13, 1927. "Mamerto y sus Conocencias" won out of 300 entries and second place went to "Don Odilón" – a fat office worker – by Andrés Audiffred. The winning cartoon, written by Jesús Acosta and drawn by Hugo Tilghman, portrayed how Mamerto Albondiguilla (the twit called little meat ball) and his wife Ninfa (nymph) arrived in the capital city and had to deal with such urban characters as revolutionary congressional deputy Chicote (whip) and ex-military man Balarassa (worthless). The newspaper described "Mamerto" as a popular charro; Tilghman had drawn him short and chubby with the features of the popular comic Leopoldo Beristáin and dressed in a charro costume of national colors. The contest announcement described him as a "man of great heart, very simple, frank, healthy, talkative, lively, 'with few fleas,' and easy to please." All of Mamerto's adventures were typical experiences of new arrivals in Mexico City at the time.[18]

The immediate and resounding popularity of the character soon created a Mamerto category, the mamertada genre, as he became an important advertising figure for automotive parts and the San Rafael and Alixco Railroad. In 1927, a riding club adopted the name Club Hípico Mamerto and asked permission from *El Universal* to use the character's image. In 1929 El Nuevo Mundo department store organized and held a Mamerto bargain sale, and in the same year the puppeteer Atanasio Velasco created marionettes based on the cartoon characters for a children's show in the Teatro Principal. Mamerto served as the image of Mexico in Czechoslovakia and Japan in the 1930s. Humorist Luis Rojas Feria in 1931 portrayed Mamerto as part of the Independence Day celebration and planned a national and international tour, while others performed as the character in carpa theaters. Mamerto also appeared on the radio, first in a winter program sponsored by *El Universal* with Otilio Gutiérrez doing his voice. Mamerto then received a radio program of 11 weekly one-hour episodes sponsored by Buen Tono cigarettes; Otilio Gutiérrez continued as Mamerto and Elena Ureña provided the voice of his wife. The narrative focused on Mamerto traveling around the world, alternating with musical interludes provided by the Casino Music group. Together the Mamerto character resulted in a conjunction of national symbols, mass media, and retail merchandising. Overall it contributed a commonplace nationalism for ordinary Mexicans.[19]

The basic element of these cartoons was the main character's ignorance of urban life. In the U.S. cartoons, vagrants, immigrants, or blacks did not understand the city and were the target of humor, while in Mexico it was the countryman who served as the object of comic strip humor.[20]

As trivial as they may appear, comic strips became the major daily explication of Mexican popular nationalism. Cartoons featured nationalism through the stereotype of the charro, and xenophobia through the stereotypes of foreigners. *El Universal* provided the major examples, from 1926 (a year before the newspaper's comic strip contest) until 1932, when imported comics again dominated. Nationalism based on the charro stereotype appeared principally in Acosta and Tilghman's "Mamerto y sus Conocencias." The comic showed the charro as the most Mexican of all stereotypes and it also included urban reactions toward rural residents, including the charro who came from the countryside. The strip demonstrated "a utilitarian nationalism" that contains contradictions between the elite discourse of nationalism and its implementation in the press.[21]

The charro – with the wide sombrero, short jacket, and trousers festooned with ostentatious buttons – was slowly established throughout the first half of the twentieth century, not just through comics but also through photographs, movies, and music, as the undisputed representation of Mexico. In 1917, in the midst of revolution, *El Universal* published a gallery of various national types based on verses that had been written in 1905 by Manuel Carpio entitled "Soy Mexicano." The charro was represented with an image drawn by Carlos Alcalde. The charro's lineage drew on the chinacos, guerrilla fighters during independence; plateados, nineteenth-century bandits with silver buttons; los rurales, the constabulary with fancy uniforms; and the common horsemen of the western region. The National Association of Charros also promoted this image and received publicity through a contest in 1926 to select the image to be used on a charro fountain. The contradiction in the image came from the charro's rural character in a nation undergoing urbanization and attempting industrialization. This contradiction reflected the nation with its program of development as a result of the revolution with a primarily rural dimension. The comic strips of the day mocked the rural charros as chief among the rural immigrants coming to the city. Charros appeared in parades celebrating Independence Day and other holidays. Mexico sent a group of national types to Seville's 1929 World's Fair; one charro appeared with national stereotyped women that included three indigenous, a mestiza from Yucatan, four Tehuanas, and four China Poblanas.

The battle over the theme of revolutionary national identity was especially vehement in literature. The argument focused on the revolution's social commitment to the indigenous or mestizos, and the preservation of traditional expressions, especially local costumbrismo. The revolutionary canon shaped music, theater, dance, and photography, including advertising and design. Part of this was the search for national iconic stereotypes.

El Universal with the Asociación Nacional de Publicistas sponsored another contest in 1926 to present the symbol of Mexico with a 1,000 pesos prize and designation as the official symbol of the nation by both the publicists and the newspaper. As part of the promotion of the contest, articles discussed various images that needed to be eradicated and none was more notorious than the lazy Mexican with the frayed sombrero, cigarette glued to his lips, and wrapped in a sarape. The charro, on the other hand, in theory represented criollo culture, mestizo heritage, hacienda owners, and disinherited villagers. The symbol's ability to represent all these groups made it especially appropriate. The *Universal* contest for the national symbol was declared void in early 1927 because the judges – Ricardo Pérez Taylor, director of the department of Bellas Artes, Rafael López, author, Gerardo Murillo (Dr. Atl), painter, José Gómez Ugarte, editor of *El Universal*, and José R. Pulido, from the Asociación de los Publicistas – declared the entries did not meet the standards they wanted for a national symbol.[22]

Next to charros, a favorite narrative in the comic strips concerned foreigners, especially Spaniards, U.S. citizens, and blacks, a category that included African Americans, Cubans, and African individuals. This xenophobia received graphic disparaging explication through comic strip caricatures, movies, and literature. The illustrators portrayed foreign stereotypes in graphic images, speech patterns, occupations, and the customs attributed to them. Spaniards always had a boina (beret), bigotes (mustache), and the shadow of a beard and practiced greedy business habits, while U.S. citizens often appeared in tourist clothes with a camera bag, curiosity about the culture, and interest in investments. Blacks, sometimes speaking with Cuban accents, were described in racist and nationalist terms, and Middle Eastern street vendors showed shrewd bargaining skills. For the latter, newspaper readers viewed Manuel Montalvo Solis and Hugo Tilghman's comic strip "Nagulás y Laburio," about an unemployed Mexican and an Arab street vendor.[23]

A major anti-Chinese theme appeared in comics and popular culture in general. Especially in the North, specifically in Sonora, there were anti-Chinese campaigns that forced Chinese people to flee to other states less opposed to them, or to the U.S., or to return to China during the period 1929 to 1935. The anti-Chinese humor in comic strips focused on physical appearance, poor ability to pronouce Spanish (especially using l in place of r), unhealthy conditions in their kitchens, and their identity as unwanted foreigners.

By 1931, U.S. comic strips reappeared with Felix the Cat and Laura, and a year later with two Disney strips, Micky Mouse (el ratón tripitas) and Bucky Bug. In 1933, new cartoons included Just Kids (Chiquilladas), Nicodamus O'Malley, and Popeye. Mamerto continued until 1942, but in the last year it appeared only in one black-and-white panel. Comic strips, as the principal nationalistic medium in the 1920s, were overtaken by the radio and the movies in the 1930s.[24]

Argentine and Brazilian newspapers began publishing both original and translated cartoons by 1912. Newspapers sought to develop original comic strips in part because sometimes the foreign ones did not arrive by press time and, of course, editors wanted to feature national characters.[25] During the 1930s, a burst of comic books hit the market, including Mexico's *Paquín* and Argentina's *Patorugú* by Dante Quintero. Brazil's *A Nação* newspaper began publishing a weekly supplement with color cartoons called *Suplemento Juvenil* in 1935. A Chilean comic book became regionally popular. René "Pepo" Ríos in 1949 debuted his character Condorito, the little condor, in the comic publication *Okey*, and six years later issued it as a comic book. Condorito used humor in the form of stories as short as one page that usually concluded with an embarrassed character falling backward with the classic *¡Plop!* or shouting *¡Exijo una explicación!* ("I demand an explanation!"). Condorito remains popular and still appears in 105 newspapers in 19 Hispanic countries as well as in Canada, the United States, Italy, and Japan.[26]

Condorito's origin came in response to the U.S. Inter-American campaign during World War II when Walt Disney produced the animated film *Saludos Amigos* in 1942 featuring Donald Duck and a cast of characters representing various nations of the Americas. In the film, Disney depicted Chile as Pedro, a small airplane engaged in his first flight over the Andes to pick up mail from Mendoza, Argentina. Pepo, using the pseudonym Fola, created Condorito in response to what he thought was disrespect for the image of Chile. Over the years, Condorito, as a comic strip and comic book, has become increasingly popular, second only to Mafalda.

Another popular comic strip, "Oily Boogie" ("Boogie el Aceitoso"), appeared in Argentina. Roberto Fontanarrosa in 1972 created this parody of Dirty Harry. Boogie, a Vietnam veteran and later bounty hunter, had exaggerated character traits of racism, violence, sexism, and nationalism. The comic strips, after appearing in newspapers, were collected in 10 books and an anthology, *Todo Boogie* ("The Complete Boogie").[27] He appeared in an animated film, Argentina's first 3-D cinema, in 2009, directed by Gustavo Cova. Boogie's and Marcia's voices were performed by Pablo Echarri and Nancy Duplaá. Echarri had a television and movie career from the 1998 thriller, *El desvío*. He received the Best Actor award at the Havana Film Festival for his role in *Sólo gente*. Later he was honored in Spain and in Argentina. He married fellow Argentine actress Nancy Duplaá. For Spanish-speaking audiences beyond the Southern Cone, Mexicans Jesús Ochoa and Susana Zabaleta, with experience in television and movies, provided the voices and Diego Monk wrote and conducted the soundtrack.[28]

Beyond Oily Boogie in Argentina, other Latin American cartoonists have created well-known fictional personalities besides Mafalda, Condorito, and Mamerto. Others include Atila (by Gosso) and Tío Barbas in Colombia by Geoffrey Edward Foladori, a Uruguayan artist popular in Colombia.[29]

Comic books from the U.S. reestablished a strong relationship with Latin American audiences in the 1960s, especially with the popularity of Marvel Comics superheroes. All the characters remained popular until 1973, when fans reacted with anger toward Spider-Man (el Hombre Araña) after his girlfriend, Gwen Stacy, was thrown to her death off a New York bridge. For probably the first time a comic series killed off a major supporting character. Responding to the hostile audience reaction, the management at *La Prensa*, Spider-Man's Mexican translator, publisher, and distributor to Argentina, Chile, Uruguay, and Peru as well as Spanish-speaking communities in California and Florida, decided to make a change. *La Prensa* had obtained a license for original storylines the year before and decided to hire illustrator José Luis González Durán to draw alternative Spider-Man strips. The alternative Spider-Man lasted for 45 monthly issues in which Gwen does not die but marries Peter Parker and lives happily ever after. Chris Ryall, president of the U.S. comics company IDW, discovered the alternative Spider-Man had never been translated and published in English.[30]

Comic strips serve as a significant synecdoche for many cultural expressions. Argentina has a solid reputation for children's and young adult television, including telenovelas, so animated films had a strong market. The voices belonged to well-known actors. This reflected the overlapping of music, film, television, and newspaper cartoons. The voice artists, with television, film, or music credentials, demonstrated the significant cultural and linguistic differences in Latin America. Voiceovers used the speech patterns common for Argentina and the Southern Cone, and for the rest of Spanish America used Mexican accents. This became the typical pattern that developed early in the sound or talking movie industry to dub English- and other foreign-language films for Latin America and to provide voices for well-known radio programs.

Producing voiceovers became a significant industry beginning in the 1930s. Sound films caused Hollywood to lose audiences in non-English-speaking countries and communities. At first movie moguls remade a film with foreign actors for each of several different languages. Subtitles did not provide a realistic solution because of widespread illiteracy among moviegoers and the distraction that reading caused among literate viewers. The first picture dubbed was Universal Pictures' first talking film (with color sequences), the 1929 *Broadway*. It premiered in Mexico the same year. The dubbing was an isolated effort, because government and film officials in Latin America saw dubbed films as competitors for national film industries. The Mexican government prohibited the showing of dubbed films in early 1940.

Nevertheless in 1944, Metro Goldwyn Mayer decided on a major translation effort and sent two representatives to Mexico to recruit bilingual actors. They contacted Luis de Llano Palmer, who selected actors mainly with radio experience using voice inflections, to learn dubbing. MGM brought 17 actors to its New York City studios. Notable individuals in the group included Edmundo García (announcer for radio station XEW), Miguel Ángel Ferriz (movie actor), and Matilde Palou (wife of Miguel Ángel Ferriz). MGM hired Carlos Montalbán, the brother of actor Ricardo, to train the Mexicans. The first dubbed MGM film, completed in 1944, was *Luz que Agoniza* (*Gaslight*), with the following voices for the stars:

Ingrid Bergman	Blanca Estela Pavón
Charles Boyer	Guillermo Portillo Acosta
Joseph Cotten	Víctor Alcocer
Gregory Peck	Carlos David Ortigosa

They were almost all Mexicans from New York between 1947 and 1948 because both Mexico and Argentina prohibited the showing of dubbed movies. In Mexico, a decision was reached allowing for dubbed animated cartoons. Rapid dubbing became professional by the end of the decade when a dubbing room was established in the Rivatón de América Studios. Churusbusco studios also began dubbing, especially working with Walt Disney films. This pattern continued until nearly the end of the twentieth century.

Television brought about a change in the dubbing industry, not just for TV series, but also more importantly for cartoon programs. The dramatic introduction of the Cartoon Network Latin and Brazil, abbreviated CN LA (Spanish: Cartoon Network Latinoamérica y Brasil, Portuguese: Cartoon Network América Latina e Brasil), became a specialty cable television channel as part of the Time Warner-owned Cartoon Network (United States) and started broadcasting on April 30, 1993. Originating from Atlanta, Georgia, Turner Broadcasting Latin America used four feeds – three in Spanish (one each for Mexico, Argentina, and the rest of Latin America and as an associate member of the Caribbean Cable Cooperative) and one for Brazil in Portuguese – and presented primarily shows and animated material for children and teens.

Most of the programming are original productions produced by the Cartoon Network Station Studios in the United States, which produces both news and specialized adaptations for living in Latin

America. The network since its inception has combined all-time favorite cartoons from the library of the world's largest animation studio and cartoons with original, innovative, award-winning new productions.[31]

Nevertheless, considering the history of comic books, comic strips, movies, and television in Latin America, when all is said and done, the most iconic feature comes from the most famous of all the characters, Mafalda, and her struggle with soup. As she defiantly declares when her mother tries to serve her a bowl of chicken soup, "What did the chickens ever do to you? Nothing! What are they guilty of? Nothing! Your hands, Mother, are stained with the broth of the innocent!!!"[32]

Notes

1 Zona Latina, http://www.zonalatina.com/zldata02.htm.This short report in the *Pan-Latin American Kids Study*, in which children between the ages of 7 and 11 expressed their opinions on Mafalda and soup, appeared in 1996 on the website Zona Latina and it has remained a popular page.

2 The movie was based on the 1962 novel of the same name by David Viñas; https://www.imdb.com/title/tt0121184/.

3 https://en.wikipedia.org/wiki/Mafalda; Lucia Iglesias Kuntz, "Quino on the Funny Side of Freedom," *UNESCO Courier* (July/August 2000), p. 72.

4 This is the major argument of Isabella Cosse, *Mafalda: A Social and Political History of Latin America's Global Comic*, translated by Laura Pérez Carrara (Durham, NC: Duke University Press, 2019), p. 7.

5 Cosse, *Mafalda*, pp. 15, 29, 30–37.

6 Cosse, *Mafalda*, p. 44.

7 Ignacio de los Reyes, "Cinco cosas que probablemente no sabías de Mafalda," BBC Mundo, Buenos Aires (September 29, 2014), https://www.bbc.com/mundo/noticias/2014/09/140929_cultura_cinco_curiosidades_mafalda_ch.

8 Ibid.

9 Tim Shenk, "Quino, creator of 'Mafalda,' keeps it light while inspiring generations," *Justicia Globa* (July 17, 2011), https://enjusticiaglobal.wordpress.com/2011/07/17/quino-creator-of-mafalda-keeps-it-light-while-inspiring-generations/. Quino died September 30, 2020, when this book was in the final stages of production.

10 Isabella Cosse, "Everyday Life in Argentina in the 1960s," *Oxford Research Encyclopedia for Latin America* (July 27, 2017), https://oxfordre.com/latinamericanhistory/view/10.1093/acrefore/9780199366439.001.0001/acrefore-9780199366439-e-316.

11 Cosse, *Mafalda*, p. 63.

12 https://www.tripadvisor.com/Attraction_Review-g312741-d2136797-Reviews-Mafalda_Statue; https://www.expedia.com/Mafalda-Statue-Oviedo.d553248621594454969.Vacation-Attraction; de los Reyes, "Cinco cosas."

13 Lambiek Comiclopedia, "Quino," https://www.lambiek.net/artists/q/quino.htm.

14 Cosse, *Mafalda*, pp. 45, 73, 83–84, 105.

15 Timothy Wilson and Mara Favoretto, "Rock Nacional in Argentina during the Dictatorship," *Oxford Research Encyclopedia of Latin American History* (August 5, 2016), https://oxfordre.com/latinamericanhistory/view/10.1093/acrefore/9780199366439.001.0001/acrefore-9780199366439-e-368.

16 https://www.thecubanhistory.com/2012/01/que-significa-liborio-para-los-cubanos/. The musical score of "El guanajo de Liborio" is in the Cuban Heritage Collection, the University of Miami.

17 Manuel Aurreocoechea, *El Universal: Espejo de Nuestro Tiempo. 90 años del El Gran Diario de México* (México: MVS Editorial, 2006), pp. 41, 47, 71–80.

18 Annalisa Fiorito, "Il Fumetto Messicano negli anni del Nazionalismo Culturale. Studio di un caso: *Mamerto y sus Conocencias*, 1927–1943" (dissertation, Università degli Studi Torino, 2002), pp. 50–52, 67, 68, 71. The announcement of the winner came February 13, 1927, section 2a, p. 4.

19 Fiorito, "Il Fumetto Messicano," pp. 102, 103, 108, 112–114.

20 Aurreocoechea, *El Universal*, p. 85.

21 Daniel Efraín Navarro Granados, "Charros, Chinos y Aboneros. Estereotipos, Nacionalismo y Xenofobia en el Humorismo Gráfico de El Universal" (dissertation, Universidad Nacional Autónoma de México, 2013), p. 8. This is Navarro's term and he says it allowed for an in-depth study.

22 Navarro Granados, "Charros," pp. 53–55, 58, 59, 65–66.

23 Navarro Granados, "Charros," pp. 131–133, 135. This includes a discussion of Max Eastman's 1936 "Enjoyment of Laughter."

24 Fiorito, "Il Fumetto Messicano," pp. 137, 150, 197, 200.

25 Ana Merino, "Veritable Identities in the Mexican Comic Strip: Don Catrarino in the Stereotypical Space of the Cannibals," *International Journal of Comic Art*, 8, no. 1 (Spring/Summer 2006), p. 365.

26 "7 Spanish Comic Book Characters from Latin America," http://www.speakinglatino.com/spanish-comic-book-characters/.

27 https://en.wikipedia.org/wiki/Boogie,_el_aceitoso.
28 https://es.wikipedia.org/wiki/Boogie,_el_aceitoso_(pel%C3%ADcula).
29 "Tras las Huellas del Tío Barbas," eltiempo.com (November 5, 1995), https://www.eltiempo.com/archivo/documento/MAM-446712.
30 David Barnett, "El Hombre Araña! Why Mexico Created an Alternate Spider-Man in the 70s," *The Guardian* (March 5, 2019), https://www.theguardian.com/books/2019/mar/05/el-hombre-arana-why-mexico-created-an-alternate-spider-man-in-the-70s.
31 https://cartoonnetwork.fandom.com/wiki/Cartoon_Network_(Latin_America).
32 Cosse, *Mafalda*, p. 84.

Additional Resources

Reading

Jorge L Catalá-Carrasco, Paulo Drinot, and James Scorer, eds., *Comics and Memory in Latin America* (Pittsburgh: University of Pittsburgh Press, 2017).

Isabella Cosse, Mafalda: *A Social and Political History of Latin America's Global Comic, translated by Laura Pérez Carrara* (Durham, NC: Duke University Press, 2019).

Anne Rubenstein, Bad Language, *Naked Ladies, and Other Threats to the Nation: A Political History of Comic Books in Mexico* (Durham, NC: Duke University Press, 1998).

7

Holy Wurlitzer

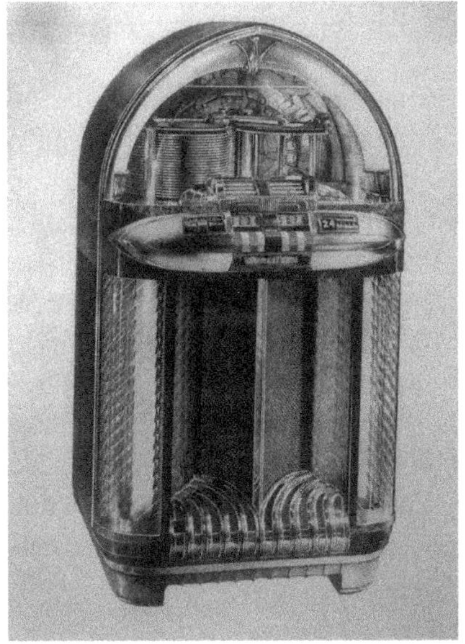

Bettmann/Getty Images.

Latin American Cultural Objects and Episodes, First Edition. William H. Beezley.

Jukeboxes all over Latin America: Where exactly were the Wurlitzers and other brands? Who chose the records, and who distributed them? Most of this story remains untold, although some significant patterns exist.

Popular music flourished with the development of the mass media in the early twentieth century. Records, movies, and radio all contributed to the creation of an expanding audience. Overlooked and perhaps most important in this early period was the jukebox (as it was called beginning in 1939). It soon became standard entertainment in bars, restaurants, and grocery stores. It gave access to music for those who could not afford a record player or records, or a radio, or the electricity to use them, and for those who only occasionally could see films.

What became the jukebox was an invention of Thomas Edison gone wrong; he wanted to create a business recording machine something like a modern dictaphone. Shortly after the invention of recorded sound technology using both cylinders and disks, the jukebox's origin, usually dated as 1889, came when Louis Glass, manager of the Pacific Phonograph Company, introduced the first coin-operated machine with four listening tubes in the Palais Royal Saloon in San Francisco. Reportedly, during its first six months, the machine collected over a thousand dollars in nickels and Glass installed more machines around the city. He soon met Felix Gottschalk of New York, who purchased the rights to its cabinet and combined it with his other plans to produce the machines that he made available nationwide. Before long, he had 750 machines from Maine to Montana that each collected, it was reported, $2 a day.

The machine played cylinders by Columbia Phonograph Company in 1890 and a year later had a catalog with recordings by John Philip Sousa, the whistler Joy Y. Attlee, Shakespeare recitations, Dan Kelly's humor, and others. Reportedly the company shipped 300 to 500 cylinders a day. The popularity of recordings varied in different locations. For example, although the placement of the machines was in taverns in St. Louis, gospel music had the most listeners. Despite its success, the jukebox existed in the shadow of the coin-operated player piano from 1907 to 1933. One of the leaders in this business was the Wurlitzer company that had become the largest provider of band instruments after 1865 and after 1900 had developed a player piano. James Seeburg became another significant figure in the coin-operated piano field and later in the development of jukeboxes.

Radio, movies, and records all contributed to the growing audience for music. Some people listened to the coin-operated box developed with its several listening tubes. Besides music, spoken humor appeared that often focused on satirical recounting of the behavior of foreign and rural migrants to the city. In the U.S., Columbia Phonograph Company had a strongly selling version entitled "Backyard Conversation between two Irish Washerwomen," matched in Argentina by humorous stories of paisanos – rural Argentines – and Italian immigrants for the first time encountering Buenos Aires. In Brazil, recordings looked to the experience of country people, especially from the Northeast, coming to Rio de Janeiro.[1]

The jukebox began to emerge from obscurity in the late 1920s after radio, movies, and Prohibition all had an impact on the coin-operated piano business and individuals sought a machine with vocals that they heard on the radio and in the movies. Five companies came to dominate the new field, Seeburg, Capehart Automatic Phonograph Company (with various names), the Mills Novelty Company, Wurlitzer, and Rock-Ola. Radio provided free music, but it played little country and no rhythm and blues – called race records – and this encouraged jukeboxes.

These patterns in the U.S. during the 1930s indicated probable developments in Latin America. For example, record sales increased in the U.S., but this is misleading because as the term was used, it suggested sales of records to consumers. In fact, during these years of the Depression, over-the-counter sales remained low. The largest number of records were sold not to consumers but to jukebox operators. These sales were as high as 60 percent overall, according to estimates of the U.S. trade press, and likely indicated a much higher number for pop and particularly for race records, both overwhelmingly aimed at the jukebox market. Decca Record Company's success, for example, was built on Louis Jordan, who became known as the King of the Jukebox. A decline in all pop record sales took place during the early 1930s before the jukebox market became a factor (about 1933–1934, with the end of Prohibition). Trying to attract consumers, Decca offered cut-rate releases and some department stores put together labels like the ARC family, but this did not close the gap. Compared to mainstream pop, blues records in particular continued to do relatively well. Leroy Carr and Josh White, among others, steadily recorded songs in the early and mid-1930s. Today's availability of these records for collectors suggests that sales were good. Carr became another jukebox artist, as there seems to have been a continuing market for styles that could not be heard on radio (which had pretty much replaced phonographs as the main home listening device by this period), and for the blues market in the rural South. In particular, there were still to some extent rural consumers who had wind-up Victrolas so the lack of electricity was not an issue.[2]

The single most important event for the jukebox was the repeal of Prohibition, December 5, 1933. Bars spread all over the country and they became the primary location for the jukeboxes that played music not available on the radio or in the movies. By the middle of 1933, 25,000 were in operation across the U.S.

Certainly, this became a pattern as jukeboxes spread across Latin America. Music, both rather tawdry songs and the more plebeian music associated with taverns and bars, did not get airtime on the radio or appear on the soundtracks of movies. Rather, it was recorded for jukeboxes played especially in bars, but also in some countries, in particular the Dominican Republic, in small grocery stores. Government officials developed an aversion to, if not a fear of, this taste in music which was making foreign music popular, a situation that could be called the tango crisis and the foxtrot crisis of the 1920s and 1930s. A different kind of crisis occurred in Cuba with the shortage of vinyl needed for producing the records to place in jukeboxes.

Mexico during the 1920s and 1930s saw the return of major U.S. record companies, who had come to the country at the beginning of the twentieth century and had left during the decade of revolutionary fighting beginning in 1910. Edison, Victor, and Brunswick returned in 1921 and dominated the enterprise until 1936, when the first Mexican-owned record company, Discos Peerless, was founded. LeRoy Shield was RCA-Victor musical director in 1928 and 1929 in Mexico City. In 1930, he left to become composer and musical director for Hal Roach motion picture productions. Also working for Victor was Ralph Peer, who made his first trip to Mexico in 1928. While there he met and signed a publishing contract with Agustin Lara in a Mexico City bar. These two U.S. citizens demonstrated two dimensions of the music business, the sale of records and the sale of sheet music. In fact, Peer soon became the most successful sheet music entrepreneur in the world through his Southern Music Company. The Mexican market, the whole Latin American market, had been quite undeveloped. Most Latin American songs known by North Americans, Europeans, and Asians were published by Peer. For example, "Bésame Mucho" was a hit in Russia in the middle of World War II based on Peer's sheet music. His music from Latin America included translated or new lyrics. The massive U.S. interest for Latin American music – at least, certain genres of it – resulted from the combination of the records made in Mexico and sold there and abroad and, above all, the sheet music.

In other parts of Latin America, jukeboxes began arriving primarily as exports from the U.S., made by Wurlitzer and the four other companies. A German model was briefly imported between the world wars, especially in the Southern Cone. The machine was known by various names. In Ecuador it was called the rocola, after the U.S. jukebox brand, where it popularized the 45 rpm record. Elsewhere in Latin America it was called the traganíqueles, vellonera, sinfonola, vitrola, or Wurlitzer.[3] The U.S. Department of Commerce, Bureau of Foreign and Domestic Commerce began to keep statistics on the export of the coin-operated machines in 1939 when the machines were sent to 34 different countries.

Statistics do not exist for the jukeboxes in Mexico before 1936, but with a domestic recording company producing songs from the successful comedia ranchera films of the late 1930s and early 1940s, mariachi music was pushed to surprising heights of popularity. The singing charro, a national stereotype of machismo and virility, emerged through the songs; audiences wanted to hear them again and again, leading to record sales and purchases through coin-operated machines of the songs by Jorge Negrete and others. The result was an expanded market for jukeboxes.[4]

Mexicans bought the largest number from the U.S., 1,665 boxes in 1939, and again the next year took an additional 1,676. Canada, then Central and South America followed, and the low prices suggested that likely the machines were used ones. Mexico was an attractive market because it used the same electrical current as the U.S. and had low import costs. By 1940, an estimated 3,000 boxes imported from the U.S. were played in Mexico, with 1,000 to 1,500 in the capital city. Favorite singers from the U.S. were Bing Crosby and the Andrews Sisters, but Mexican records by Agustin Lara and the charro vocalists, mariachi bands, and Cuban mambo groups were much more popular.

After World War II, Mexico prohibited the importation of complete – fully assembled – jukeboxes and required the production of the console housing in Mexico. The number of sales was also smaller than expected because of the low value of the peso and because the music was played as loudly as possible, causing constant complaints against the machines. The government gave the jukebox operators six months to solve the problem.[5] Sales remained minimal or about the same in 1945 (799), 1946 (1,792), 1947 (2,320), 1948 (175), 1949 (value $29,954), 1950 (value $21,094), 1951 (1,047), and 1952 (1,967). Even with limited sales, opposition to the coin-operated machines existed as well in different parts of the country. Over 10,000 workers marched, many with signs, in the May Day parade in Ciudad Juárez in 1953. One sign told the governor of Chihuahua: "Two thousand musicians support your administration. Keep jukeboxes out of Mexico."[6]

During these years from 1946 to 1952, the largest number of jukeboxes went to Canada and Central and South America. The leading purchases for the Latin American import were made, in descending order, by Venezuela, Mexico, Colombia, Cuba, Guatemala,

Panama, and El Salvador. Venezuela in 1952 purchased 1,592 jukeboxes valued at over a million dollars, roughly one fourth of all those sold, and continued to buy the U.S. machines as well as reported acquisitions, at least in 1956, from six German producers. A reporter speculated that this resulted because Venezuelan society was the closest to the U.S., and was especially fun loving.[7]

In Colombian music and culture, mass acceptance of popular music came in the 1930s after the Great Depression. Music, including Mexican mariachi and Cuban boleros, reached across the nation because of movies and radio. An overlooked and perhaps the most important source was the jukebox, which provided music to those who could not afford a radio or a record player. The jukebox soon became common in bars and restaurants and gave access to music from Colombia and other locations. Popular taste in music resulted in the fear of government officials of various foreign styles.

Rural-to-urban migration responding to similar processes of city life resulted in popular so-called carrilera music in Colombia, with similar developments in Latin America, which was associated often with the jukebox. For example, musical expressions emerged such as rocolera in Ecuador, bachata (for many years excluded from radio and television) in the Dominican Republic in the 1970s and 1980s, and similar song genres, cebollera in Peru, vellonera in Puerto Rico, and cantinera in Chile. National elites denounced these styles for their association with drunkenness, episodes of violence, and life in shantytowns. The music, on the other hand, provided solace, a refuge for urban lower classes from their social and economic problems and gave them a sense of stability and identity. The lyrics portrayed the victim, usually male, brought low by a bad woman[8] or other tribulations of life, drowning his sorrows in drink.

The experiences of those new to urban life were sometimes expressed as humor and appeared on records that made it to the jukeboxes. Like the early records in Argentina and Brazil, in Colombia, humor was also used to help build an audience. Political satire, in particular, became standard on the radio. Popular programming on commercial radio was directed, as explained by Mary Roldan, toward the significant growing rural migrant community coming to the cities in the 1930s and 1940s. They were attracted especially to Medellín and Bogotá by education and employment opportunities not available in the countryside. In some instances, the radio humor built on the recorded programming, but in other cases it was live radio broadcasts. The program "La Media Hora del Pueblo," broadcast by Ecos de la Montaña in Medellín (the city's second most important radio station), had a 20-year existence from 1937 to 1957. It offered a kind of conservative, anti-elite, Catholic populism through commentary and was well received among recently arrived rural migrants.[9] Mario Jaramillo became a well-known humorist with a popular program that began in the 1950s and continued into the 1970s. Known as "Montecristo Radio Programs," they emerged to address questions of interest among the working and lower-middle classes of recent rural residents new to the city and the pressures of urban life. The program through humor examined living costs, barrio development, basic education, loan-sharking, urban challenges, and limited access to public services.

Music appeared on the radio, but the popular raucous carrilera style was almost exclusively available in the bars on the jukeboxes. (Annual importation of jukeboxes for 1939 and 1940 was 23 and 109.) This provided circulation of recorded music, even more widespread than the radio, and included foreign musicians but also domestic recordings. The latter songs often came from everyday life. Elite efforts to control working-class behavior kept the music off the radio and included a short-lived ordinance in Bogotá in 1956 that banned the playing of the city's 3,000 jukeboxes in bars, cafés, and other public places between the hours of 6 p.m. and 6 a.m. daily.[10]

In a similar decision, Peruvian officials tried to regulate the rocola in Lima bars and night spots. The restriction prohibited playing jukeboxes after 11 p.m. For each song, customers had to place 50 centavos (about U.S. 2 ½ cents) in the slot. For the bar owner or distributor, locally produced records sold for 65 cents and a $1 and imported 45 rpm records sold for $1.25. This was done to encourage the national music and record industry.[11]

Jukeboxes became an accessory to evening life in the Dominican Republic during this time – the era of Rafael Trujillo's dictatorship (1930–1961). Trujillo, as was his practice, gave a monopoly to a family member, in this case his brother-in-law, Francisco Martínez de Alba. After Dominicans imported only 111 boxes from the U.S. in the three years previous, Martínez de Alba, between 1947 and 1952, imported 86,572 jukeboxes and placed them in neighborhood grocery and variety stores called *colmados*, free of charge. He required 50 percent of the earnings. It was a highly successful arrangement because the owner of the colmado only had to buy the records.[12] The colmados with their jukeboxes served, in other words, as decisive locations for the cultivation and dissemination of the bachata music.

The jukebox appeared in the 1940s and 1950s as technology for a modernizing society rather than radio. New styles of popular music became characteristic of Ecuador. The coin-operated jukebox called the "rocola" (from the name of the company owner David Rockola, not for rock music as people tend to think) appeared and during these decades two working-class styles of music – chichera and rocolera – emerged, concurrently but independently, as mestizo expressions of a rural population that was entering a new social environment and forging new urban social identities.

By the 1970s this music known as "rocolera" had become lower class in character. Jukeboxes were confined to lower-class bars and restaurants and an urban style of popular music associated with the cantina and drunkards developed in this decade. Rocola music initially featured as stars Puerto Rican singer Daniel Santos and Ecuadorian singer Julio Jaramillo in the 1960s. They were singers associated with the rocola because of the songs they sang together. Basically, the songs involved boleros antillanos (not the romantic ones), valses del pueblo, and pasillos rocoleros. Rocolera became synonymous with popular or people's music. The singers developed fans across Latin America who were lower and working class and identified with their songs. Their records were played on rocolas in cantinas and gave a name to a style of music. Santos became famous for romantic Antillan boleros, especially "Dos Gardenias." Jaramillo became famous for his song "Nuestro Juramento," and he became known as the ruiseñor de América, the nightingale of America. Like Carlos Gardel in Argentina and Pedro Infante in Mexico, he is considered Ecuador's iconic singer and his songs played on the rocola created his great popularity. The lyrics describe a promise made between a man and a woman in the event one of them dies. If the man dies first, the woman will let her tears drop on his corpse so that everyone will see how much she loved him. If she dies first, the man will write their love story using blood from his heart as ink.

Rocolera music was distinguished from other countries' working-class repertoires, such as the ranchero music in Mexico, as the pasillos composed in the 1970s and 1980s are also considered rocolera music, not música nacional. Because the pasillo is regarded as Ecuador's musical symbol, calling the pasillo rocolera music suggests a class-based struggle over the nature and meaning of an established symbol of national identity. Both rocolera and chichera expressed various Ecuadorian and non-Ecuadorian musical genres and acquired different functions and meanings for their listeners over time. Rocolera became the style of urban popular music meant for listening and coping with heartbreaks caused by feelings of despair and betrayal while chichera expressed the happy, modern, and danceable music.[13]

Jukebox importation remained quite low in numbers for several countries. Chile, for example, purchased surprisingly few of the machines, beginning with none in 1939, 40 the next year, none until 1946, no number given but at a value of about $2,800, which probably meant three or four machines, then probably one or two (value $1,460 in 1950), and a few more in 1951 and 1952 at a value of $6,383 and $16,694. The situation changed in 1961, after almost a decade of no imports, when Chileans bought 213 new and four used machines. They imported no others during the rest of the decade. The absence of jukebox importation raises interesting questions, with perhaps imports from Europe before the war, or a preference for live performers. Uruguay only appears in the statistics for U.S. jukebox exports from 1939 to 1967, four times. In 1940, the Uruguayans imported 14 and then, in a three-year period, 1950 to 1952, imported perhaps 50, with values by year at $2,527, $21,659, and $24,831. Bolivia appeared in these statistics only for the same years 1950 and 1951, with imports valued at $1,935 and $1,003.[14]

A much different pattern appeared in Panama, Costa Rica, Guatemala, and, especially, Cuba. Panamanians purchased large numbers of the jukeboxes throughout the statistical period, beginning in 1939. The statistics record both the Canal Zone and the republic until 1952, although it was not until 1977 when President Jimmy Carter began the return of the canal to Panama. In the two years before World War II, for example, the sales for the Canal Zone numbered three and seven, and individuals in the republic bought 25 and 121. The same disparity continued after the war; in 1945 and 1946, the Canal Zone ordered two the first year and none the second; the republic imported none the first year, then the next year ordered several valued at $22,400 (likely 21 or 22). The Canal Zone, between 1947 and 1951, had annual numbers of perhaps two (value $675), 35 units, perhaps three (value $933), zero, and perhaps two (value $532). During the same years, in the republic, individuals imported 88, perhaps 90 (value $5,960), perhaps 40 (value $30,858), 67, and 168. In the following years, the imports continued to Panama, 141 in 1952, 99 in 1962, and sales for the next three years valued at $112,219, $115,879, and $188,675.

Costa Rican statistics record jukebox imports of seven (1939), four (1940), 10 (1945), perhaps four (value $1,910) (1946), perhaps 30 (value $8,062) (1947), 44 (1948), with imports of three or four between 1949 and 1951, and then none reported until 1963 with 51. During the last three years of these statistics (1965–1967), Costa Ricans purchased imports valued $103,933, $40,455, and $47,879.

Guatemala had a similar pattern, with imports in 1939 and 1940 of 13 and 18. Following World War II, 18 (1945), likely 90 (value $19,086) (1946), perhaps 130 (value $109,936) (1947), 48 (1948), 120 (1949), estimated 240 (1950), estimated 200 (1951), 20 (1952), and an estimated 180 (1953), and none afterwards until the 1960s with the U.S. Central Intelligence Agency-inspired coup against the regime in 1954.

The jukebox import statistics appear high in those countries – Panama, Guatemala, Nicaragua, and other places – that had experienced U.S. military occupation or close commercial relations. Haiti, with its poor economy and meager development, provides an exception, importing a few each year, but never more than a dozen jukeboxes. Perhaps the U.S. Marines had brought some with them for the military clubs on the bases.

Cuba's political and economic dependence created by the United States was reflected in the importation of jukeboxes as well. The statistics before Fidel Castro's revolution clearly revealed the significance of the machine on the island, especially, it can be imagined, in the bars and taverns most frequented by tourists. The total sales for the years 1939 to 1954 numbered 9,261. Only once in 1945 with the end of World War II did the numbers dip below three digits. The imports over these years were as follows: 1939, 280; 1940, 100; 1945, 29; 1946, 844; 1947, 1,128; 1948, 739; 1949, 496; 1950, 885; 1951, 1,210; 1952, 1,580; 1953, 818; and 1954, 1,152. These reveal the cultural ties between Cuba and the U.S. in terms of the music played, and this fits with the larger patterns of sport, especially baseball and boxing, live music performances, and prevalence of dance styles.

Efforts to encourage local recording companies resulted in cheaper costs to provide the records for the jukeboxes and promoted local working- or lower-class culture. Perhaps the most iconic local recording celebrated peanut vendors in Havana, who for decades, especially after the end of the Spanish-American War (1898–1899), sold peanuts to strollers and idlers along the embarcadero and the plazas in the city. The roasted nuts became emblematic of Cuban culture through the 1920s. As a consequence, a song called "El Manisero," the peanut vendor, became the first example of Latin American recorded music to become popular throughout the Americas including the U.S. It sold for the first time one million records for both individual and jukebox play in Latin America. This caused a crisis in Cuba because of the shortage of vinyl needed for producing records to place in jukeboxes. The song also sold well in the U.S. with translated lyrics and sold over a million copies of the sheet music. It popularized the mambo that soon became a craze in the U.S. and prompted musical exchanges between musicians and fans especially in the U.S. and Cuba, but also Latin America in general throughout the 1950s. Recordings were made by various promoters and sold as individual records, but more commonly the audience was built through the ubiquitous jukebox.

Sheet music for "The Peanut Vendor" ("El Manisero") credited as writer Moisés Simons (1889–1945),[15] the Cuban-born son of a Basque musician. The lyrics drew on the cries of a street vendor, called a pregón, and the rhythm was the common son. This song and "Guantanamera" (the 1929 song with its first verse based on a poem by José Martí) became the two most famous pieces of music written by Cuban musicians. The National Recording Preservation Board included "El Manisero" in the United States National Recording Registry, with the notation that it was the first American recording of an authentic Latin dance style. The recording launched a decade of "rumbamania," introducing U.S. listeners to Cuban rhythms based especially on a variety of drums.

The vedette Rita Montaner made the first recording of "El Manisero" in 1928 for Colombia Records. Much bigger sales came when Don Azpiazú and his Havana Casino Orchestra, with stars Julio Cueva (trumpet), Mario Bauza (saxophone), and singer Antonio Machín, recorded it again in New York in 1930 for Victor Records. It became the first million-selling 78 rpm record of Cuban music, selling over a million copies and a million copies of the sheet music for the Edward B. Marks Company that had paid the composer $100,000 in royalties by 1943. In cultural terms, "The Peanut Vendor's" success caused what was called a rumba rage and created the popularity of Cuban drums and rhythms throughout the Caribbean, Mexico, the U.S. and Europe that continued through the 1940s. Rumba became the general label for Cuban music.

Cubans, U.S., and other Latin American musicians recorded it more than 160 times. Among others, it was recorded in the U.S. by Louis Armstrong and his Sebastian New Cotton Club Orchestra, Django Reinhardt, Chet Atkins, and especially Stan Kenton, who recorded two instrumental versions with his band and another recording alone at the piano. Several Hollywood producers used versions of it in the soundtracks of their films. It appeared in MGM's 1931 *The Cuban Love Song*; Groucho Marx whistled the tune in the 1933 film *Duck Soup*; Cary Grant sang it in the 1939 film *Only Angels Have Wings*; and Judy Garland sang a fragment in the 1954 film *A Star is Born*. Recent examples include the Carnival scene in José Luis Cuerda's *La Lengua de las Mariposas* (*Butterfly*, 1999). Ska legend Tommy McCook played "The Peanut Vendor" used for classic reggae songs such as "Top Ten" by Gregory Isaacs. The Alvin "Red" Tyler instrumental was in an episode of the TV series *Breaking Bad*.

The sheet music identified Simons as the author of both music and lyrics, but Gonzalo G. de Mello in Havana claimed he had written it. Others argued it was a traditional song that had been created by an unknown peanut vendor late in the nineteenth century. "El Manisero" was one of those rare cases in popular music where an author received immediate and substantial financial benefits. The English lyrics are by L. Wolfe Gilbert and Marion Sunshine, Azpiazú's sister-in-law, who toured with the band in the U.S. as a singer. The English lyrics are regarded by some to be of almost unsurpassed banality. The song was inducted into the Latin Grammy Hall of Fame in 2001.

Latin America's national recording industries experienced bonanzas in the 1960s and 1970s when several governments adopted the industrial development program known as import substitution. Basically, governments support domestic manufacture, where possible, of items that were being imported, because a market already existed. This campaign received encouragement from the Economic Commission for Latin America (CEPAL), which promoted the industrial development of Latin America. In Ecuador, for example, both IFESA and FEDISCOS were licensed to release records of international music because foreign-record imports were prohibited. As a result, this generated national economic activity through the local production of phonograph records, along with other goods. This also reduced the cost of records of international music for jukeboxes and especially for individual customers.[16]

This latter change affected jukebox use across Latin America, and they began to decline dramatically. More people had home record players, and soon individuals, as in the U.S., turned from single-play records to long-playing albums, then adopted new forms of replay such as tape and later cassettes. Taverns purchased televisions to entertain customers and TVs appeared in private residences, with shows featuring musical performances that eventually resulted in the MTV channel in the U.S., followed in 1993 by the creation of MTV-América Latina as a pay channel that reached throughout the region. Moreover, video games became more significant as coin-operated entertainment in shops and bars, so the years of the jukebox drew to a close.

One feature of jukeboxes, only studied in Jamaica but quite likely similar throughout the Caribbean and across mainland Latin America, was that they became the music teacher and practice band for aspiring musicians. Jukeboxes as a common feature in rum bars, pastry shops, and truck stops had become ubiquitous throughout Kingston by the beginning of the 1960s. The selections generally included music not regarded as suitable for radio. Therefore, jukeboxes had ska, rock steady, reggae, dub and dancehall, and even risqué *mento* records supplemented by foreign discs of country and western, gospel, rock and roll, and pop. Listeners in this popular music university had the opportunity for appropriation of music styles, permitting hybridity and development of cosmopolitan musical taste among regular Jamaicans.

Any aspiring musician with a guitar or other instrument, or just a voice, could play the jukebox and accompany the record as a way of learning to play or sing a popular song. Even if a musician could afford the sheet music, he or she might not be able to read music, but hearing the different parts on jukeboxes was a great teacher. These jukeboxes, especially when they were on a porch, allowed a group to practice with the record. This became a significant dimension of popular music for mastering instruments and singing that created knowledgeable musicians. Youngsters with the desire to learn used the jukebox to hone skills by imitating Jamaican or foreign stars such as Fats Domino, Tom Jones, Jim Reeves, and the Impressions. This has been termed "ghetto karaoke" and existed well before the Japanese invented the technology.[17]

Jukeboxes across Latin America appeared in cantinas and taverns, the businesses that have offered a salve for those suffering heartbreak, shelter for others lost in the city, and comfort for still others in despair. In a bar with a drink in hand, customers often turned to the jukebox as a close and unconditional friend. As Ketty Wong has discussed, the jukebox not only expressed the feelings of an individual suffering love gone wrong or lost, it also talked about the situation to him or her and to others. Or it played lyrics to weave nostalgia for home or family, and to encourage those in despair to persevere. For a few, they may even have danced to the music, but more often they would sing along or just listen. This has been described by Aaron Fox in his study of Texas country music as the jukebox's ventriloquism and the fascination of country music listeners with the "poetic figure of an inanimate object that speaks with a human voice." For example, in the Ecuadorian song "Rocolita de mis penas" ("Little Jukebox of My Sorrows"), as Ketty Wong explains, a man speaks directly to the rocola and asks it to intercede with the woman he loves.[18] Indeed, the jukebox, even though it was a machine that worked on coins, across Latin America offered, as in this song, a voice that spoke to individuals in lyrical sounds or words to capture their feelings.

Notes

1 Barry Mazor, *Ralph Peer and the Making of Popular Roots Music* (Chicago: Chicago Review Press, 2015), p. 18.

2 "I have never come up with good numbers, but my impression is that if we leave jukebox sales out of the picture, the decline in race sales (though large) was probably proportionately less than the decline in mainstream pop sales." Elijah Wald, *How the Beatles Destroyed Rock 'n' Roll: An Alternative History of American Popular Music* (New York: Oxford University Press, 2011).

3 Ketty Wong, *Whose National Music? Identity, Mestizaje, and Migration in Ecuador* (Philadelphia: Temple University Press, 2012), p. 98.
4 Donald Andrew Henriques, "Performing Nationalism: Mariachi, Media and the Transformation of a Tradition (1920–1942)" (thesis, University of Texas, 2006), p. ix.
5 Kerry Segrave, *Jukeboxes: An American Social History* (Jefferson, NC: McFarland, 2002), pp. 3–19, 109, 159.
6 Segrave, *Jukeboxes*, p. 251.
7 Segrave, *Jukeboxes*, pp. 255, 327–330.
8 Wong, *Whose National Music?*, p. 97.
9 Mary Roldan, Professor of Latin American History, Hunter College, CUNY/Graduate Center, to the author.
10 Segrave, *Jukeboxes*, pp. 253–254.
11 Segrave, *Jukeboxes*, pp. 253–254, 327.
12 Christian Krohn-Hansen, *The Dominican Colmado from Santo Domingo to New York* (New York: Oxford University Press, 2016); Segrave, *Jukeboxes*, pp. 327–331.
13 Wong, *Whose National Music?*, p. 98.
14 The statistics used in this chapter come from Segrave, *Jukeboxes*, pp. 327–334.
15 Helio Orovio, *Cuban Music from A to Z* (Durham, NC: Duke University Press, 2004), p. 202.
16 Wong, *Whose National Music?*, p. 55.
17 Dennis Howard, "Punching for Recognition: The Jukebox as a Key Instrument in the Development of Popular Jamaican Music," *Caribbean Quarterly*, 53, no. 4 (December 2007), pp. 32–46.
18 Wong, *Whose National Music?*, pp. 37, 47; Aaron A. Fox, *Real Country: Music and Language in Working-Class Culture* (Durham, NC: Duke University Press, 2004).

Additional Resources

Readings

Carol A. Hess, *Representing the Good Neighbor: Music, Difference, and the Pan American Dream* (New York: Oxford University Press, 2014).

Malena Kuss, ed., *Music in Latin America and the Caribbean: An Encyclopedic History, Volume 1. Performing Beliefs: Indigenous Peoples of South America, Central America, and Mexico* (Austin: University of Texas Press, 2004).

Robin Moore et al., *Musics of Latin America* (New York : W. W. Norton, 2012).

Recorded Music

101 Clásicos De La Música Tropical Colombiana. Various artists.

El Gran Barroco: Latin American Baroque Music. Maria Felicia Perez.

Le Grand Tango: Music of Latin America. Carter Brey and Christopher Orile.

Brazil Classics 3: Forro. Various artists.

8

Mapuche Flag and Rap

Sudowoodo/Shutterstock.com.

The Mapuche people occupy the historic territory of Wallmapu, reaching from the Atlantic across the Andes to the Pacific Coast in southern South America. The Spaniards called the region Araucanía and Alonso de Ercilla wrote a classic epic poem, *La Araucana* (1569, 1578, 1589), praised in *Don Quijote*,[1] about the courageous indigenous resistance against the Spanish conquistadors that serves as a fundamental text for the history of Chile. The Mapuche have been divided by national boundaries since the independence of Chile in 1810 and Argentina in 1819; nevertheless, *Mapudungun* (language)

Latin American Cultural Objects and Episodes, First Edition. William H. Beezley.

and *ülkantun* (song) have preserved cultural identity and shaped social and political attitudes. One of the ways in which the Mapuche preserve their identity is through these cultural expressions.

The Mapuche for centuries have earned a reputation for their continued resistance to foreign ("*wingka*") invasion, having repelled first the Incas and later the Spanish conquistadors from their territory.[2] Although the Chilean government militarily defeated the Mapuche in 1883 and, in theory, incorporated them into the nation, they have maintained their legacy of resistance through opposition to government policies, their efforts to maintain their cultural and linguistic traditions, and their perseverance as a separate people with a distinct history, collective memory, and cultural identity.

The most successful recent Mapuche cultural collaboration has occurred among young people, through a shared interest in hip-hop, mainly rap music. Binational musical festivals have led to a rap group that includes both Chilean and Argentinian members. The Mapuche have a heritage of defending their culture. This struggle has become particularly intense since the 1980s and especially in the last two decades as they have made efforts to promote ethnic identity and to reunite their shared culture with various linguistic, educational, and civic symbols, including a flag created in 1991.

Moreover, they have continued their defense of their culture, land, and territories. Recent forms of resistance have varied beyond general cooperation. In Argentina, they have been battling for lands in Patagonia, and in Chile the struggle has been primarily for cultural expression. Nevertheless, the flag offers hope for the future for their shared culture.

The Conquest of the Desert was Argentina's campaign against the Mapuche, who had lived in Patagonia since 11,000 BCE. The Argentine government sent troops, commanded by future president Julio Argentino Roca, against them from 1878 to 1885. The Conquest of the Desert expelled some 15,000 indigenous people from their lands. The ironic name ignored that the land was both fertile and populated; the goal was to convert the territory to Argentine agricultural production. The troops used British-made rifles and the campaign was largely financed by British funds. Once successful, much of the land was given in 1889 to the Argentine Southern Land Company Ltd, based in London. The company remained in existence until 1982, when it was nationalized and renamed Compañía de Tierras del Sud Argentino S.A. (CTSA). President Carlos Menem soon undertook a neoliberal overhaul of the economy. In 1991, his government encouraged foreigners to buy cheap Patagonian land. Among the purchasers were Sylvester Stallone, Ted Turner, Jerry Lewis, and George Soros. The largest sale was to CTSA, and its 2.2 million acres, an area the size of Puerto Rico, made it the largest private landowner in the country. The buyer, Edizone Holding International, a company owned by the Italian clothing corporation Benetton, paid U.S. $80 million, a fraction of its value. The Italians used the land for livestock, farming, fuel, and logging.

The company clashed with residents who claimed rights as indigenous peoples. These rights are included in an amendment of the Argentine constitution protecting indigenous ancestral properties or providing access to lands that are not being put to use. In 2002, two Mapuches, Atilio Curiñanco and Rosa Nahuelquir, married and requested the Chubut agency to help them occupy 951 acres of undeveloped, former Mapuche land now owned by Benetton. The Chubut agent encouraged them to settle the land and they occupied it with their four children. Benetton then filed suit against the family, and they were evicted and their plow and oxen seized. This resulted in a complex controversy involving the constitution, an international corporation, museum exhibits, and indigenous rights.[3]

The national constitution's provisions on indigenous land rights and protection from eviction are rarely respected. In part this results from the court's demand for land titles, which are not available for traditionally held properties, so it concerned public land. Benetton attempted to prosecute the indigenous family for their occupation of the unused land, although it later offered to drop charges on the condition that the family relinquish their ancestral claims to the land. Acquitted in 2004, the Curiñanco-Nahuelquir family, accompanied by Argentine Nobel Peace Prize Winner Adolfo Pérez Esquivel, traveled to Rome to petition Luciano Benetton to allow them to reclaim their ancestral lands. Benetton refused, but in response to international denouncements against the company, it offered the province of Chubut around 18,500 acres for the Mapuche community. The National Institute of Agricultural Technology recommended that the governor reject the offer, which he did, because of the high cost of making the property workable.

Benetton also took a subtle step with a thought toward future lawsuits. The company owns the museum in the nearest town of Leleque and the museum presents the Mapuche as invaders from Chile. This discredits their claims about ancestral lands.

The Mapuche in the region organized as the Mapuche Ancestral Resistance or RAM in March 2015, occupying some Benetton land and creating a Pu Lof (community). The local police constantly harassed the indigenous community and in January 2017, 200 Argentine gendarmes (a federal security force) attacked it. The local police raided the community for allegedly stealing animals and the following day, police attacked another nearby Mapuche community. On August 1, the gendarmerie raided the Pu Lof again. Benetton has continued to insist on the company's right to private ownership of the land.

Governor Mario Das Neves, who received large amounts of taxes from Benetton, described the Mapuche as "delinquents," compared the RAM to the FARC in Colombia, and attempted to make links to Mapuche acts of sabotage in Chile. The Minister of Security, Patricia Bullrich, explained the violent actions, saying the government would not "allow an autonomous Mapuche Republic in the middle of the Argentine State." The Mapuche have received support from the Association of Lawyers for Indigenous Law, the Provincial Commission for Memory, the National Aboriginal Pastoral Team, and the Center of Legal and Social Studies against the official violence they have endured. Others who have spoken out in support of the Mapuche include Hebe de Bonafini, one of the founders of the *Madres de la Plaza de Mayo* (Mothers of the Plaza de Mayo), as well as the Front for Victory. Despite this support and official requests to the government from both the United Nations and Amnesty International reporters, the Mapuche's desire to regain control of their ancestral lands seems unlikely to be fulfilled.[4]

In Chile, the 2012 census reported that the Mapuche number 1.5 million persons recognized by the United Nations Declaration on the Rights of Indigenous Peoples and the International Labor Organization's Convention No. 169 as a distinct people. Four regional groups, the Huilliche (people of the south), the Puelche (people of the mountains), the Lafkenche (people of the coast), and the Pehuenche (people of the north) compose the Mapuche, who share a common worldview, language (Mapudungun), and most traditions, but they do not constitute a homogeneous people. Distinctions in some cultural practices, vocabulary, and traditional diet differentiate these four populations. Moreover, class, urban versus rural location, and political affiliation further divide them.

Since the end of the Pinochet dictatorship, mainstream media report the Mapuche indigenous movement as illegal in its actions, with images of land occupations and retaliation against police officers, and argue in favor of the antiterrorism law used against them because the Mapuche refuse to negotiate with the government.[5]

Cultural efforts have become as significant as political actions among the Mapuche and throughout the Americas. This reflects the global pattern in which culture has been adopted as an expedient by marginal groups.[6] Mapuche Cultural Centers (CCM) founded in 1978 hosted cultural events including *palin* (a game similar to hockey), *gillatun* (ritual religious ceremony), storytelling contests, and traditional cooking competitions aimed to promote the rediscovery of Mapuche roots, encourage the revival of indigenous culture, and unify the Mapuche against the repression of the Pinochet regime.[7] Ceremonies and marches of remembrance have created martyrs of Mapuche activists killed since democratization.[8]

Major cultural opportunities have been provided by theater, literature, wall painting as murals and graffiti, and music, most dramatically rap. Hip-hop's popularity and its use to mobilize young Mapuche generally toward ethnic solidarity was not surprising.

Hip-hop affected indigenous music, art, fashion, and youth culture in the United States, Canada, and Latin America. Artists have joined electronic rhythms with ancestral drumbeats and used lyrics to talk about their history and processes of assimilation and migration.[9]

Following the disco craze, three anti-commercial genres of popular music emerged: reggae from Jamaica, punk from Great Britain, and hip-hop, whose performances began in the 1970s in the Bronx, New York, with the adaptation of Jamaican outdoor dance parties as an "outsiders' protest" among African American, Caribbean, especially Jamaican, and Hispanic youth and shortly afterwards in Los Angeles, California to describe the violence and marginalization in black neighborhoods.[10] The young inner-city artists drew on the African American Muslim tradition most powerfully represented by Malcolm X in protest against predominant United States culture and authority.[11] Hip-hop included breakdancing, DJing (turntables), MCing (rap), and graffiti and developed meanings that resonated with global youth.[12] Artists adopted rigs of two turntables, a mixer, and an amplifier that they illegally plugged into outdoor lighting systems. The disc jockeys manipulated the turntables to highlight the point where singers stopped for music; these periods, called breaks, were used for a new form of dancing. This became known as break dancing or b-boying. At this point, DJs began hiring a master of ceremony to engage the audiences even more. These MCs began memorizing or improvising doggerel to engage the audience. The MC began "riding the riddims" with words, that is to say, they began rapping about violence and marginalization in their neighborhoods.[13] Graffiti artists became an additional component of hip-hop at the same time in New York. The artists focused on subways that traveled into the centers of the dominant culture and the tags made a response to President Ronald Reagan's attack on the welfare state. Developments in Los Angeles received international recognition in the album *Straight Outta Compton*, the response through rage at riots, crime, gangs, and police repression in gansta rap. Mapuche youngsters heard music that expressed opposition to the official society from indigenous groups and other minorities.

In Canada, the Elsipogtog First Nation's anti-fracking protests, the Idle No More movement, and Attawapiskat Chief Teresa Spence's hunger strike made headlines, as did the Canadian government's arrests and monitoring of First Nations activists.[14] Hip-hop became a form of resistance and influence among First Nations peoples. This resulted in an exhibit entitled "Beat Nation" in Vancouver, British Columbia which traveled across the nation.[15]

In Latin America, the Ecuadorian government of Rafael Correa limited freedom of speech and charged dozens of indigenous protesters with acts of terrorism, sabotage, and road blocking.[16] Ecuadorians responded with music to preserve indigenous community practices. Afro-Brazilians, for example through events in Mato Grosso, have created international attention[17] and Afro-Colombians have performed rap as part of efforts to preserve their cultures.

Hip-hop culture reached the Mapuche region through Temuco, Chile with break dancers called the Pirañas (Piranhas).[18] Johnny Silva founded the Brocas de las Naquis (Kids on the Corner, in *coa*, a Temuco street dialect) in 1986 with about 60 young people as a community organization in Lanín, Araucanía's oldest and largest *campamento* (Mapuche neighborhood) in the roughest section of Temuco. The Brocas practiced traditional *artesanía*, ecological conservation, *palín* (Mapuche hockey), and music.

Jano Weichafe (Jano the Warrior) participated in the Brocas from the beginning. In 1989, he promoted the idea of hip-hop to provide cultural projects designed for Mapuche youth as an alternative to discrimination, drugs, and alcoholism in the city. Participants called their group Weichafe Newen (Force of the Warrior in Mapudungun). Alongside his activities with the Brocas de las Naquis, Jano also gave folkloric stage performances called *peñas*, and had success with his song "Hip-Hop Alternativo" ("Alternative Hip-Hop," 1989).

Rap began in 1992 in Temuco, inspired by the visit of the Santiago hip-hop pioneers, the Panteras Negras (Black Panthers). The Brocas turned to rap and developed homegrown lyrics to give voice to political mobilization and cultural challenges of city life. They received national attention two years later, when the talk show *Venga Conmigo* (Come With Me) traveled to Temuco to broadcast a special episode featuring interviews and live hip-hop performances. Unfortunately, local groups did not take full advantage of hip-hop's early role as a positive community force in Lanín, nor did they capitalize on the temporary limelight of prime-time television. Regional hip-hop instead suffered from weak relationships between rap artists and public institutions, such as the Consejo Nacional de la Cultura (National Cultural Council) that frequently sponsored folkloric, classical, jazz, and some popular music as well as theater and poetry events.

Nevertheless, Mapuche rappers continued to perform. Some described their music as a kind of electroacoustic *artesanía*, asserting cultural identity, rustic production, and economic independence that allowed freedom of expression and promoted development of indigenous identities. Well-known rappers Jano Weichafe, Danko Marimán, and Fabian Marin used hip-hop to describe conditions in Araucanía's interethnic neighborhoods. Jano, for example, composed "Ñi Pullu Weichafe" ("Espíritu Guerrero," or "Warrior Spirit," 1997) in an effort to create consciousness about the demand for territorial recovery. He fused rock, cumbia, and hip-hop in a song that called for mobilization, both within and outside of Araucanía, and has become a classic of Mapuche identity. He followed it with "¿Hasta Cuándo Más Vamos a Soportar?" ("How Much Longer Will We Tolerate This?" 1999). He performed these and other rap songs, sometimes with Mapuche instruments such as the *pifilka* (a short, wooden flute with one opening), the *kultrún* (a ceremonial drum), and the *trompe* (a mouth harp). In recent years he has continued to combine rap and cumbia. Encouraged by this music, Mapuche inner-city youth organizations have utilized hip-hop to promote indigenous ceremonies in urban settings and to involve at-risk kids in constructive activities.

Danko Marimán started with rap in the mid-1990s in the hip-hop scene at the *triángulo*, a crossroads formed by local streets with the Pan American Highway in a neighborhood of Padre las Casas.

He achieved popular success in 2005 with his recording of *V.I.D.A. D.E. A.R.A.U.K.A.N.O.* (L.I.F.E. O.F. A.N. A.R.A.U.C.A.N.I.A.N.) using the name the *Gran Massay*, because his height recalled a Maasai tribesman. His album proposed peaceful interculturalism between Mapuche and non-Mapuche individuals, regional indigenous autonomy, and "Mapuchifying" hip-hop and poetry to express personal and collective struggles. Connecting the violence of the democratic presidencies to that of the Pinochet dictatorship, the song argues that the Mapuche have endured centuries of repression, and they will persist until they achieve autonomy and territory. Also in 2005, Danko, along with Fabian Marin, poet Kvyen Tranamil, and several other artists and activists, formed Kolectivo We Newen (New Strength Collective), originally focused on hip-hop and documentary filmmaking, as a social movement favoring autonomy. The Collective's rap singers (Wenu Mapu, Weichafe Newen, and Gran Massay/Danko Marimán) used themes of victimization, suffering, and retribution as common lyrics in their raps. The same year, the founders of the political party Wallmapuwen expressed coincidental goals as Danko's album, saying they aimed at uniting regional voices and votes behind an agenda of increased autonomy and self-governance.

In 2009 and 2010, Kolectivo We Newen hosted music festivals in Temuco called We Rakizuam (New Wisdom). In 2010, the festival disparaged the celebration of the Chilean bicentennial of independence with the slogan "*nada que celebrar*" (nothing to celebrate). Santiago rapper Minuto Soler, in "Mapuche Anti-bicentenario," protested the celebration:

> Bicentenario es expresión de represión a mi cultura,
> Mi pueblo mapuche ha vivido siempre en dictadura.[19]
> (The Bicentennial is an expression of the repression of my culture
> My Mapuche People have always lived in a dictatorship.)

In another song "Pei Katrileo," the Kolectivo We Newen rapped about the violence of the conflict between the Mapuche and international forestry companies allowed by the government in historical Mapuche territory:

> ¿Usted quiere saber por qué es la lucha de nuestro pueblo mapuche?
> Pues ponga atención a esta rima y escuche...
> Las tierras son tomadas porque fueron robadas
> Por las latifundistas, extranjeros, forestales y transnacionales[20]
> (You want to know why our Mapuche people fight?
> Well pay attention and listen...
> Our lands were taken, stolen
> By landlords, foreigners, forestry companies, and transnationals)

Other hip-hop artists tried to raise awareness about other political protests such as the 82-day hunger strike by Mapuche prisoners facing trial without due process under the government's antiterrorist law.

In Santiago's neighborhood of La Florida, Mapuche youth founded Wechekeche Ñi Trawün as a group that uses its music to face the challenges of urban life. Their performances combine *ranchera*, hip-hop, rap, and reggae styles using words in both Spanish and Mapudungun to address ethnic identity, self-discovery, and Mapuche nationalism.[21] Because of their urban origins, its participants wanted to create music that would speak to others unfamiliar with their heritage and culture and that would promote their Mapuche identity.[22]

As part of growing political and musical mobilization to reinforce binational ethnic identity and politics, the Mapuche hip-hop organizations have become more active. The song "Ñi Pullu Weichafe" has become something of an anthem. Jano performed it in 2009 with the rock group La Mano Ajena in Santiago's Galpón Víctor Jara, where it generated interest in the Mapuche cause among audience members, and Mapuche rappers have become more popular in general.

Hip-hop, along with rap, break dancing, and DJing, includes graffiti as a performance. Artists paint walls to mark community identity and defy political authority. In Chile, the graffiti built on a tradition from the 1950s and 1960s in Santiago, when both Communist and Christian Democrat party members painted political messages with their identifying symbols as propaganda in public spaces. The Pinochet dictatorship repressed all wall painting and other forms of resistance, so that only jokes and *arpilleras* (paintings done with scraps of cloth) remained as subversive cultural opposition. In the mid-1980s, despite the dictatorship, muralists reappeared and began creating *papelógrafos* (temporary paper murals).

With the end of Pinochet's regime in 1990, Mapuche murals and graffiti seized public space[23] as hip-hoppers in poor neighborhoods once again painted walls. Street art in marginalized urban neighborhoods with large Mapuche populations announced their presence. Paintings in Valparaiso, Santiago, and other northern cities outside of historical Mapuche territory gave identity to Mapuche and the urban transformations of their culture, language, and traditions. Painting in southern cities such as Temuco and Valdivia symbolized the recovery of ancestral territory lost during and following the "Pacification" campaigns of the 1880s and defied government authority. The murals and graffiti make a statement of ethnic solidarity, economic injustice, and state repression that forms the collective memory.[24]

The graffiti and murals in the Santiago neighborhood of La Victoria, for example, often depicted Mapuche land conflicts in the south. One mural featured the plight of political prisoners under the antiterrorism law; in the words of its caption: "The *kultrún* [traditional drum] is calling the earth's children to recover the territories held by forestry companies. Liberty to Mapuche political prisoners! Now!" Another mural in La Legua neighborhood portrayed the hunger strikes of activists Jaime Marileo, Patricia Troncoso, Juan Huenulao, and Patricio Marileo, imprisoned for 10 years in 2001 for the arson of a pine plantation.[25]

Other murals in Santiago and Tamuco depicted Mapuche activists killed in recent years. These often have incorporated traditional symbols, such as the *machi* (female shaman) and the *kultrún* (ceremonial drum), and revolved around political themes, such as the construction of hydroelectric dams, the deaths of activists, and the demand for constitutional recognition of the Mapuche. The Brigada

Territorio pal' Arte painted murals in Temuco and other communities in conflict with forestry companies, using Mapudungun and culturally significant colors (for example, blue, the color of cosmic force) in their work. Another group, La Casa de Arte Mapuche, formed in 1989, painted 32 murals in Temuco and other rural communities between 1990 and 2005 with similar themes.[26]

Beyond hip-hop, the Mapuche in both Chile and Argentina have organized theater companies to express their culture and challenge government policies, display their values and knowledge, and teach their history to the public. These include El Teatro Kimen (Chile), Newen Mapu (Argentina), el Centro de Desarrollo Humano Karukinká (Argentina), Proyecto Guluche (Argentina), la Compañía de Teatro Mapuche Püllü Mapu (affiliated with la Universidad de la Frontera, Chile), la Compañía La Maestranza (Chile), Meli Wixan Mapu (Chile), and el Conjunto Artístico Mapuche Llufquehueno (Chile). Their productions have worked to revive collective memories and describe the experience of migration, marginalization, and alienation.[27]

In 1981, the Mapuche theater in Chile got a boost as several authors wrote protest plays against national repression by adapting classic dramas. Isadora Aguirre, for example, wrote *Lautaro! Epopeya del Pueblo Mapuche* (Lautaro! Epic Poem of the Mapuche People), drawing on Ercilla's *Araucana*; the play's subtle undertones defied the Pinochet dictatorship's land division law. Theater groups became more active after 2001 in a cultural response to government repression, especially through the application of the antiterrorism law.

Two Mapuche theater companies and an acting collective in Santiago have been especially active. OOMM's productions incorporated traditional instruments, contemporary dance, and ritual gestures of ceremonial dance. The production *Vivencias Mapuches* (Mapuche Experiences, 2001) addressed the experiences of OOMM's director as an urban youth and his process of indigenous identity formation. A second production, *Cuatro Guardianes de la Tierra* (Four Guardians of the Earth, 2007), proposed an alternative to ecological destruction through references to Mapuche poetry and mythology. Teatro de Mujeres' two most notable productions – *Awkinko Mapu* (2005) and *Malen Weichafe* (Warrior Princess, 2007) – likewise aimed to educate the public about government mistreatment of indigenous peoples and give value to Mapuche culture and traditions through dance, poetry, and traditional instruments. The Colectivo Rumel Mülen performed *Awkarayen* for a month in 2013. The play, dedicated to Mapuche communities in resistance, showcased contemporary conflicts between the Mapuche and the forestry companies supported by the government in southern Chile. Shifting between scenes of Mapuche life and police activities, the production focused on a Mapuche family that suffered the deaths of two of its members and other acts of violence.[28]

Ironically, the Mapuche have both protested and used globalization to their advantage. They have appropriated hip-hop as a means of communication and expression, especially within urban areas. They have used YouTube, Facebook, blogs, and their own websites to spread alternative news about police raids and repression, imprisoned activists, and conflicts with developers or forestry companies, and to raise awareness of upcoming events. They have appealed to international human rights organizations to advertise their movement and to gain support. These means of communicating and sharing the Mapuche's struggles are recent phenomena of globalization, a process that the Mapuche have often opposed due to its negative environmental, cultural, and economic consequences.[29]

Reviewing Mapuche hip-hop's class and ethnic meanings, they derived largely from the manner in which multinational entertainment corporations marketed the street and ethnic themes of U.S. rap. In the late 1980s and early 1990s, all five major labels (Warner Music, EMI group, Sony Music, Universal Music Group, and BMG) decided to cash in on world interest in hip-hop and rap through music markets, radio, television, and cinema. In the 1990s, hip-hop videos arrived in Latin America with the creation of MTV Latino (based in Miami and Brazil) and the production of Yo! MTV Raps, a daily one-hour program dedicated to U.S. videos.[30] Today's Latin American hip-hop artists come from a generation that has been inundated by mass-mediated, racialized, and gendered messages of African American commodified resistance.[31]

Nevertheless, youth from all over Latin America are now practicing hip-hop as a cultural and musical medium for voicing their concerns on social issues. Brazil, for example, has the third largest urban poor population in the world and, along with it, a robust hip-hop movement. Hip-hop culture, Buarque de Hollanda proposes, can serve as an effective response to the government's withdrawal from social life. She examines the efforts of the Grupo Cultural AfroReggae, an NGO dedicated to getting youth off the streets and out of drug trafficking, and the literary works of writers such as Ferréz ("marginal" literature), Sergio Vaz, and Alessandro Buzo, who have integrated literature into the Brazilian hip-hop movement as a way to mobilize youth on behalf of their cultural rights.[32]

In Colombia, Afro-Colombians have developed a collective memory called cimarronismo, by using the images of both the Cimarrón (runaway slave) and the palenque (runaway slave community) as Latin American and Colombian symbols of resistance and black identity. Cimarronismo has been promoted through rap. The common story says hip-hop arrived in Colombia through the port of Buenaventura as stowaways brought cassettes, magazines, and urban styles and fashions, especially the music such as the Fat Boys and Run DMC, from the U.S. This is presented in Tom Feiling's documentary *Resistencia: Hip Hop in Colombia* (2002). Hip-hop, especially rap, quickly moved to nearby Cali, especially Aguablanca neighborhood, one of the largest invasion neighborhoods with 400,000 residents. It resulted in early short-lived groups such as Los Generales R & R from Buenaventura in the late 1980s, and in the early 1990s Gotas de Rap. In general, the musicians share a poor background, but some have high school and even some college degrees, and there are few females. Others, who are not from the Pacific coast, argue that hip-hop came through the ports of Cartagena and Barranquilla or was brought by travelers and tourists to Bogotá and through the influence of hip-hop movies such as *Breakin'*, *Breakin' 2*, and *Beat Street* (all from 1984).[33]

Guatemalan Lucio Yaxon has become the Kaqchikel rapper, with the name Nim Alae. He took part in efforts to rescue the secret police archives and appears in the documentary film *La Isla* about the records.

In a remarkable reversal, the United States Department of State adopted what could be called hip-hop diplomacy, especially in Europe and the Middle East, to reach out to young people. This program began in 2005, when riots raged through the Paris suburbs. The State Department started sending hip-hop envoys – rappers, dancers, DJs – to perform and speak in Europe, and followed with missions to Africa, Asia, and the Middle East. The success of the program has resulted in criticism from hip-hop artists, who contend that those who make "protest music" should not work with governments or accept invitations from embassies. London rapper Lowkey said, "Hip-hop at its best has exposed power, challenged power, it hasn't served power." Despite the disdain of both leftist rappers and conservative European journalists and politicians, the Muslim youth in Europe and other locations appreciate the performances, with the result they have created more positive impressions of the United States. In France, in particular, positive opinion of the U.S. has risen sharply since 2008 among young Muslims.[34] Curiously, the program has not been extended to Latin America.

The Mapuche cultural programs, including rap, provide unification among the members of this indigenous group, especially the youth, in particular in Chile but also in Argentina. Moreover, they provide a cultural connection to other Latin American youth and to global fans and performers of the music. They share a connection through videos and other media available to them all.

Notes

1 Miguel de Cervantes, *Don Quijote*, translated by Burton Raffel and edited by Diana de Armas Wilson (New York: W. W. Norton, 1999), p. 39 and n. 4.

2 The term *wingka*, which is often applied to talk about non-Mapuche people, is a product of the word Inca, used to describe foreign invaders

during the Incan conquest. Doris Sommer, "Introduction: Wiggle Room," in Doris Sommer, ed., *Cultural Agency in the Americas* (Durham, NC: Duke University Press, 2006), p. 11.

3 Jack Pannell, "Benetton in Patagonia: The Oppression of Mapuche in the Argentine South," *Council on Hemispheric Affairs*, https://dbn.f1b.myftpupload.com/wp-content/uploads/2017/08/Benetton-and-Mapuche-1.pdf.

4 Pannell, "Benetton in Patagonia."

5 Mackenzie Rachel Mann, "*Armas de Cultura*: Manifestations of Mapuche Resistance in Chile" (senior thesis, Elon University, 2014), pp. 3–4, 26.

6 George Yúdice, cited in Christopher Dennis, *Afro-Colombian Hip-Hop: Globalization, Transcultural Music, and Ethnic Identities* (Lanham, MD: Lexington Books, 2012), p. 126.

7 Rosa Isolde Reuque Paillalef, *When a Flower is Reborn: The Life and Times of a Mapuche Feminist*, edited and translated by Florencia E. Mallon (Durham, NC: Duke University Press, 2002), p. 113.

8 Mann, "*Armas de Cultura*," p. 48.

9 NPR, "Hip-Hop's Aboriginal Connection," *Oregon Public Broadcasting* (January 4, 2014), https://text.npr.org/s.php?sId=259428743.

10 Robin D. G. Kelley, "OGS in Postindustrial Los Angeles: Evolution of a Style," in Stephen Duncombe, ed., *Cultural Resistance Reader* (New York: Verso, 2002), pp. 153–155.

11 Christopher Dennis, *Afro-Colombian Hip-Hop: Globalization, Transcultural Music, and Ethnic Identities* (Lanham, MD: Lexington Books, 2012), p. 2.

12 Kristina Nelson and Cynthia P. Schneider, "Mightier than the Sword: Arts and Culture in the U.S.-Muslim World Relationship," Brookings Paper (June 30, 2008), https://www.brookings.edu/research/mightier-than-the-sword-arts-and-culture-in-the-u-s-muslim-world-relationship/.

13 Jeff Chang, "Born in Fire: A Hip-Hop Odyssey," *UNESCO Courier* (July/August 2000), p. 23; Kelley, "OGS in Postindustrial Los Angeles," pp. 153–155.

14 "Top Five Aboriginal Stories of 2013," *CBC News* (December 30, 2013), https://www.cbc.ca/news/aboriginal/top-5-aboriginal-stories-of-2013-1.2477363.

15 "Beat Nation: Art, Hip Hop and Aboriginal Culture," Vancouver Art Gallery, https://canadianart.ca/reviews/beat-nation/.

16 "Ecuador: Authorities Misuse Judicial System to Stop Protests," *Amnesty International* (July 17, 2012), https://www.amnesty.org/en/press-releases/2012/07/ecuador-authorities-misuse-judicial-system-stop-protests-2012-07-17-0/.

17 "Brazil National Force Sent to Land Dispute Region," *BBC News* (November 29, 2013), https://www.bbc.co.uk/news/world-latin-america-25161541; "Brazilian Indigenous Man Shot Dead in Mato Grosso do Sol," *BBC News* (June 13, 2013), https://www.bbc.co.uk/news/world-latin-america-22896256; João Fellet, "Indigenous Brazilians Use Web to Fight for Rights," *BBC News* (June 5, 2013), https://www.bbc.co.uk/news/world-latin-america-22787583.

18 Discussion of events in Tamuco, Chile relies on the article Jacob Rekedal, "Hip-Hop Mapuche on the Araucanian Frontera," *Alter/nativas: Latin American Cultural Studies Journal*, https://alternativas.osu.edu/en/issues/spring-2014/essays1/rekedal.html.

19 Minuto Soler, "Mapuche Anti-bicentenario," on Inche Ta Luanko, home recording, 2012, CD. Translated from Mapudungun to Spanish by Mackenzie Rachel Mann in "*Armas de Cultura*."

20 Subverso and Portavoz, "Lo Que No Voy a Decir" (music video), posted January 22, 2013, https://www.youtube.com/watch?v=1Lm00GF5Faw.

21 Walter Alejandro and Imilan Ojeda, "Urban Ethnicity in Santiago de Chile: Mapuche Migration and Urban Space" (dissertation, Technical University of Berlin, 2009), p. 204; "Radio Revista No. 52," *Radio Matraca desde Berlín* (October 31, 2007).

22 "Radio Revista No. 52," *Radio Matraca desde Berlín* (October 31, 2007).

23 Mabel García Barrera and Verónica Contreras Hauser, "La Resistencia Cultural en el Mural," in Mabel García Barrera, Hugo Carrasco Muñoz, and Verónica Contreras Hauser, eds., *Crítica Situada: El Estado Actual del Arte y la Poesía Mapuche* (Temuco, Chile: Editorial Florencia, 2005), p. 155.

24 Bill Rolston, "¡Hasta La Victoria! Murals and Resistance in Santiago, Chile," *Identities: Global Studies in Culture and Power*, 18, no. 2 (2011), p. 115.

25 Rolston, "¡Hasta La Victoria!" pp. 132, 134–135.

26 García and Contreras, "La Resistencia Cultural en el Mural," pp. 146–147.

27 Mann, "*Armas de Cultura*," p. 55, citing Araceli Mariel Arreche, "Teatro Mapuche: Acercamiento a Una *Teatralidad Subyugada*," *Revista Afuera: Estudios de Crítica Cultural*, 4, no. 7 (November 2009), p. 1; Francisco

Sánchez Brick, *Buscando a Kay Kay y Xeng Xeng Vilu* (Santiago, Chile: Tyro Teatro Banda, 2009), pp. 80, 100; "Trilogía Sobre Problemáticas Mapuches Inicia Itinerancia en la Capital," *Santi Teatro y Danza: Crítica de Teatro y Danza/Reseñas/Entrevistas*, 2013, http://santi.cl/dev/index.php/resenas/565-trilogia-sobre-problematicas-mapuches-inicia-itinerancia-en-la-capital.

28 Mann, "*Armas de Cultura*," pp. 50–55; Araceli Mariel Arreche, "Teatro Mapuche: Notas Sobre una Teatralidad ¿Invisible?," *Revista del Centro Cultural de la Cooperación*, 2, no. 1 (April 2008); Araceli Mariel Arreche, Karina Beatriz Giberti, and Andrés Pereira Covarrubias, "Teatro Mapuche: Prácticas de Identidad y Resistencia," *Espacios de crítica y producción*, 39, pp. 21–26, 23.

29 Mann, "*Armas de Cultura*," p. 113.

30 Dennis, *Afro-Colombian Hip-Hop*, pp. 26–27.

31 Christopher Dennis, "Locating Hip-Hop's Place within Latin American Cultural Studies," *Alter/nativas: Latin American Cultural Studies Journal* (Spring 2014), https://alternativas.osu.edu/en/issues/spring-2014/essays1/dennis.html.

32 Dennis, "Locating Hip-Hop's Place within Latin American Cultural Studies," 23; A. J. Samuels, "The AfroReggae Cultural Group: A Rebirth Of Hope Within Rio De Janeiro's Favelas," Culture Trip (January 24, 2018), https://theculturetrip.com/south-america/brazil/articles/the-afroreggae-cultural-group-a-rebirth-of-hope-within-rio-s-favelas/; Silvia Ramos, "Brazilian responses to violence and new forms of mediation: the case of the Grupo Cultural AfroReggae and the experience of the project 'Youth and the Police,'" https://www.scielosp.org/article/csc/2006.v11n2/419-428/en/.

33 Dennis, *Afro-Colombian Hip-Hop*, pp. 5, 21–23, 29, 32, 40, n. 38.

34 Hisham Aidi, "Hip-Hop Diplomacy: U.S. Cultural Diplomacy Enters a New Era," *Foreign Affairs* (April 16, 2014), https://www.foreignaffairs.com/articles/united-states/2014-04-16/hip-hop-diplomacy.

Additional Resources

Discography

Blow, Kuris. *Kuris Blow*. 1980.

Choc Quib Town, *Oro*. Peer Music Compact Disc. 2008.

Choc Quib Town, *Somos Pacífico*. Polen. Compact Disc. 2007.

Gran Massay, *Ayudando a fortalecer una fuerte Identidad Regional en territorio Mapuche*. Futuro Rauko, n.y.

Gran Massay, *V.I.D.A. D.E. A.R.A.U.K.A.N.O.* Futuro Rauko, n.y.

Kolectivo We Newen. *Raizes*. Futuro Rauko. 2007.

N.W.A. *Straight Outta Compton.* Ruthless Records. 1988.

Weichafe, Jano. "Hip-hop alternativo." n.p., 1989.

Weichafe, Jano, and La Mano Ajena. "Ñi Pullu Weichafe." n.p., 2009.

9

Eye Patch Laughs and Bubble Gum Wraps

Source: 2020 Bazooka Candy Brands.

Bazooka Bubble Gum had its largest sales for Latin America in Argentina. The Topps company in Brooklyn, New York created Bazooka after World War II, and in 1957 the company permitted the

Latin American Cultural Objects and Episodes, First Edition. William H. Beezley.

Argentinian candy company Stani to make Bazooka and sell it there, in Chile, Paraguay, and Uruguay. Despite its longtime availability in South America, Bazooka found a major market only in Argentina.[1]

Bazooka delivered an ignored, or at least underappreciated, form of cartoon art. The gum wrappers represented comic mundane art. Jean-Siméon Cardin, an eighteenth-century French painter, it has been said, believed "God was to be found in the mundane life before his eyes, in the domesticity of his own kitchen. He never looked for God anywhere else, just painted again and again, the same ledge and still life in the kitchen of his home."[2] Cardin likely would have approved of the gum wrappers and various forms of advertising and popular art, often taken for granted, that appeared on everyday packages and boxes. Baseball cards are the best known,[3] but popular art forms included, for example, the images contained in cigarette packages and on match boxes. In Cuba, typical images came on cigar and cigarette wrappers. In Mexico, Jorge Cázares (1937–2020) painted landscapes for the common packages of La Central matches. He gave over 200 exhibitions of his landscape paintings throughout Latin America, Europe, the U.S., and Australia and the match company began printing his painting on its packages in the 1970s.[4] Common as well after World War II was the appearance, usually anonymous, of graffiti on city walls and train cars. Often humorous, at times the graffiti formed political statements and social demands. A remarkable example of this practice was the rebellious graffiti that resulted from the anti-government demonstrations in 2019 in Santiago, Chile.[5]

This prosaic humor came from the comics contained with chewing gum that after 1906 included the first bubble-producing product.[6] The best known and most common cartoons came with each piece of Bazooka bubble gum. Topps in 1949 adopted as its logo "Bazooka, the Atom-Bubble Boy." The character chewed gum and blew bubbles large enough to carry him aloft on daring flights. Despite Atom-Bubble Boy's adventures, the gum did not sell well. Perhaps the nickel price for a package of six pieces of gum could not compete with other companies that sold single pieces for a penny. Or perhaps the Cold War had caused what Argentina's famous cartoon character Mafalda called "mass hysteria"[7] about the prospect of a nuclear apocalypse, an association that came with any mention of atoms.

Topps development office director Woody Gelman, a one-time movie animator and co-creator of the advertising symbol Popsicle Pete, decided to try another emblematic character for the gum. In 1954 he contracted cartoonist Wesley Morse (well known in New York City for his drawings on menus, programs for the Ziegfeld Follies, the Cotton Club, and above all the Latin Quarter and Copacabana, amusing advertisements in *Life* and *Collier's* magazines, and several pornographic comic pamphlets known as "Tijuana bibles"). Accounts vary as to whether Gelman or Morse drew the prototype of the new bubble-gum character, but the evidence suggests Morse drew a typical looking boy, with a beanie and a baseball bat.

Topps officials wanted a figure both distinctive and recognizable to the public. After looking at the first sketch, they told Morse they wanted a blonde-haired boy with a baseball cap and an eye patch. At that time, Hathaway shirts had a sensational merchandising campaign, promoted by a model who wore an eye patch. The success of these advertisements caused discussion in *Time*, *Life*, and *Fortune* magazines and quickly had imitators who ran ads featuring eye patches on babies, dogs, and even cows. A *New Yorker* cartoon captured the phenomenon with three men in the first panel viewing a display window of a shirt store; in the second panel, they come out of the store with eye patches. The rage continued as Brenda Starr in the daily newspaper comics encountered the mysterious Basil St. John with an eye patch, TV singer Sammy Davis Junior, who had lost an eye, rather than an artificial replacement wore a patch, and popular mystery writer Steve Harragan's book covers always featured him with an eye patch.[8]

Once they had the sketch they wanted, the Topps managers named their new character Bazooka Joe; the first name demonstrated cultural appropriation and post-World War II playfulness and the second was the name of the Topps owner's son. Moreover, as has been cryptically noted, change two letters and it became the name of one of the most successful comic characters of the 1940s and 1950s, Joe Palooka.[9]

Following these directions, Bazooka Joe along with his eye patch and a gang of friends soon appeared on wrappers used on individual pieces of gum selling for one cent. Morse compensated for the small size of the comics by giving Joe's cronies easily distinguished clothes and haircuts, notably Mort's turtleneck. The rest of the original gang included overweight Hungry Herman, Janet (later Jane), Joe's girlfriend, and Toughie, the nickname for George Washington Abraham Lincoln Jones, a rough-looking kid with a sailor hat. Over the years, the group added Gloomy Gus, Boastful Billy, Silent Cy, and Sam the Stutterer. The production schedule called for about 50 wrappers to be printed three times a year with Bazooka Joe cartoons, a horoscope, and an announcement of a toy premium available for saved wrappers and postage costs. The company decided to recycle some of the cartoons after seven years, when youngsters, managers thought, were likely to outgrow the gum. Morse drew the series (each containing 40 to 50 different gags) three times a year until shortly before his death in 1963. Len Brown, the assistant to Gelman, recalled that for the early cartoons, his job was to read old issues of *Boys' Life* magazine's last page where readers submitted jokes to find ones that could be revised and used for Bazooka Joe. This remained the practice for many years. The jokes, as someone said, were often puns much like a Bennett Cerf joke book. Topps also included baseball cards and disaster scenes in their other candy products.[10]

The Topps gum and candy company reached an agreement just as it was doing in other parts of the world to allow the Stani company to produce and market Bazooka bubble gum. As a result of these international efforts, the company at its high point had trademarks for Bazooka Joe in 30 countries and sold the bubble gum in 55 nations including 10 with licensed manufacturers. Joe and his gang spoke Spanish, French, German, and Hebrew. An African Bazooka Joe told Nigerian jokes in that country. In 1972, Topps even issued bilingual comics in the U.S., "Learn Spanish with Bazooka Joe" and "Learn French with Bazooka Joe," using dialog balloons that contained English and translations.[11]

In 1958, the Argentines initially received coils of the printed wrappers from the United States that needed to be translated into Spanish. The company kept Bazooka Joe's name in English with translations of the comics and horoscopes included on the gum wrappers. Soon, Marcelo Siano, the Stani manager, decided many of the cartoons and fortunes should be replaced with original ones that reflected Argentine local reality. Deciding which jokes to keep and recycle in Spanish and which to replace became the job of a young cartoonist, Carlos Nine. He was the first of several illustrators who worked with Bazooka Joe and then went on to successful careers. Some 20 years later, Nine achieved prominence when he joined the staff of magazine *Fierro* and created popular characters Magician Keko and Saubón the Duck. He also drew some of the front pages of *Humor* magazine with satires of the Argentine transition to democracy.

Once the company committed to producing its own jokes with more culturally appropriate humor and fortunes, the main individual, Bazooka Joe, remained the same, but his friends became more Argentine. Siano asked his acquaintance and sometime business associate, public relations and marketing expert and aspiring author Rodolfo Enrique Fogwill, to write some cartoons and perhaps some horoscopes as well for the gum wrappers.[12] At the time Bazooka first arrived in Argentina, Fogwill worked in advertising and commercial promotional campaigns for cigarettes, whiskeys, and chocolates; later he achieved literary fame with his now classic novel of the Malvinas War entitled *Los pichiciegos* (*Malvinas Requiem* in translation, 2010) about young Argentine troops, metaphorically the endangered species of mole of the title. He had one question for Siano about writing for the gum wrappers: What does it pay? When he learned it was 50 dollars a joke and 30 for each horoscope, he said in an interview, he quickly pulled out his typewriter and went to work.

Siano once guessed that Fogwill did more than a hundred cartoons for the company. He wrote alongside Pablo Dreizik. According to Dreizik, they adopted a madcap writing process that might include "Dadaist exercises" with the artist and inspiration from Vogelmann's translation of the *I Ching*, the Séfer Yetzirá, the Kabbalah, and Sanskrit texts translated by Francisco García Bazán, all balanced by copies of the Chilean comic book *Condorito* that Dreizik brought with him. Fogwill also paid attention to the graffiti of Los Vergara, a countercultural collective that with the Korol Brothers achieved notoriety after 1982 for its absurd and grotesque messages written on the public walls of Buenos Aires. Perhaps they served as a reference for the tight structure of the Bazooka jokes.[13] Dreizik's commentary showed clearly the authors' zany casualness in writing the comics. It is not known which wrappers Fogwill or Dreizik authored but their individual contributions are recognized, even if they were published anonymously.

Others who wrote at least some of the Bazooka Joe comics who then achieved later recognition include Marcelo Birmajer, author and screenwriter of the 2004 film *El abrazo partido*. He wrote often about the Porteño neighborhood of Once and its colorful, often Jewish inhabitants. Other cartoonists who also wrote jokes included Pablo Parés, now recognized as a director and actor for *Daemonium: Underground Soldier* and *Plaga Zombie* (*Zombie Plague*); Gustavo Sala, who after the Bazooka experience became a successful graphic humorist for *Page 12*, *Rolling Stone*, *Inrockuptibles*, and *The Hand*, and now with his own podcast "Sonido Bragueta"; and el Niño Rodríguez, an illustrator of comics and children's books.

The wrapper comics offered a different dimension of humor, society, and young people. Although the inserts contained pictures, usually of the main character (Bazooka Joe in the comics and, at first, the Oriental wizard in the fortunes), the humor and information came in written and visual form. Literacy was paramount to enjoy them. What became immediately apparent was that the humor was literal – the reader needed an understanding of the character of everyday Argentine society and culture. Fogwill once said there had been three generations of Bazooka Joe wrappers. These were "Bazooka Joe & His Gang," and then later when the U.S. company changed the characters, in Argentina the switch became "Bazooka Joe & His Society," and later a more motley group of wrappers that in Argentina offered "Bazooka Joe presents Mysterius," "Humorzooka," "Bazooka Joe – Kabala," "Bazooka Chinese Horoscope," and "Bazooka Joe Fantasy."

From the first generation, a typical early example of "Bazooka Joe & His Gang"[14] (in the U.S. cartoons it is Bazooka Joe and his gang, but in a slang sort of way, gang had no criminal allusion; it was not directly translated into Spanish) was written by Fogwill:

> "I have a very rare boomerang. It doesn't come back."
> "Ah, what do you call it?"
> "A stick."

In another cartoon, when Bazooka Joe and his friends are looking at a mummy with an unwrapped head, Bazooka Joe says,

> "This skull ought to belong to one of you."
> "Why, for its bigness?" asks one of his buddies.
> "No," says Bazooka Joe, "for its emptiness."

Another wrapper shows practical, literal knowledge:

Friend:	"Yesterday I went to a very expensive restaurant."
Bazooka Joe:	"How expensive?"
Friend:	"It had meals for 25 and 35 pesos per person."
Bazooka Joe:	"And what's the difference?"
Friend:	"10 pesos."
Bazooka Joe:	"?"

The three-panel page has color images: Bazooka Joe's friend has a flat-top haircut and wears a t-shirt. Just as in the U.S. wrappers, Bazooka Joe has a standard haircut, wears a baseball cap, and has an eye patch.

Another example from Bazooka Joe & His Gang includes his girlfriend and her little brother:

Bazooka Joe:	"What a cold your brother has, Sol."
Sol (Blonde girl with sunglasses on head):	"Yes, true."
Pitu (in kid's overalls):	"SNIFF, SNIFF."
Bazooka Joe to kid:	"Pitu, don't you have a handkerchief?"
Pitu:	"Sniff, sniff; yes, but my mama tells me not to lend it to anyone."

The brother's name, Pitu, is typical, but one associated with several soccer players.

The humor uses a literal statement, but in combination with more figurative meanings so that the reader knows the character understands the cultural dimension of the statement. In this way, the humor reminds the reader of both the literal meaning of the comment and the broader social character of the words. In the latter case, it reinforces social understanding, everyday experiences, and proper etiquette.

The wrappers also made an effort to appeal to primary school children, with brain teasers that pictured a group of them engaged in typical activities while chewing gum. Bazooka Joe asked the reader to determine how many kids were blowing "maxiglobos" – big bubbles – including Pibe Bazooka – Bazooka Joe himself. Cartoons pictured kids playing soccer with others watching, at recess around the Argentine flag, on a playground, at a school dance, at the beach, and on a picnic. The cartoons showed kids doing things that were familiar activities and provided a chance to count the bubbles.

In the U.S., after Morse's death, Topps used cartoons he had completed and then recycled others. In 1983, the management decided to hire a group of cartoonists to update the gang as teenagers with interests in rock music and video games.[15] The Topps creative director Len Brown, who had hired Art Spiegelman, Jay Lynch, and other underground comic artists to work on Bazooka Joe, in 1983 asked Howard Cruse, associated with Gay Comix, to recreate Bazooka Joe, Mort, and some new characters as teenagers. To Bazooka Joe's crowd, Cruse added wise-cracking Shades, lovesick Val, pretty Robin, and Mr. Martin, the strip's first black character. The jokes, nevertheless, remained dependably predictable.

The Argentine company followed Topps in the U.S. and made Bazooka Joe a teenager and gave him and his friends new adolescent interests.[16] Beside the teenage Bazooka Joe, with some of his now teenage friends like Sol, new characters included Patovica (a muscular, athletic guy nicknamed Bouncer), Javi Metal (a musician), the Professor, and Bobby (the excellent student). The group, now called

Bazooka Joe and his Society, also had contemporary interests, reflected for example in the horoscope, "You will demonstrate your ability in video games" and the career prediction, "You will be the leader of a campaign to heal the environment."

Cartoons in this category showed the teenagers busy with their lives. In one cartoon, Bazooka Joe asks:

> "Javi Metal, why are you so tired?"
> "The teacher asked if any of the students liked music."
> "And?"
> "It was to have them help her move the piano."

Another solo cartoon shows Javi Metal's literal approach to information. In the bathroom at the sink with wet hands, Javi sees the sign on the paper towel dispenser that reads: "Pull down." He pulls the dispenser off the wall, takes a towel to dry his hands, and walks away whistling.

Another wrapper from the same group includes Bazooka Joe and a friend after a soccer match:

Bazooka Joe (holding a soccer ball):	"How is it possible that you play so badly, Grafo?"
Grafo:	"I asked to borrow some boots from my cousin."
Bazooka Joe:	"And, so what?"
Grafo:	"He's 7 years old with a size 29 shoe."

The joke has undeniable Argentine character. The kids had been playing the national sport of soccer. Bazooka Joe, perhaps ironically, calls his friend by a nickname. Using creative nicknames is almost an Argentine sport in itself, especially involving soccer players. Argentines have the reputation in Latin America for their common use of nicknames and nearly all professional, especially national, team players have them, as do Brazilians. Here the name may be a reference to the web-based comic Sr. Grafo, the online name of the Argentine cartoonist Andre Rojas.[17] The joke, of course, hinges on borrowing a cousin's boots, likely a play on words, that are booties in size (given in European measurement). The question of equipment shows the middle-class character of the game in Argentina; in other countries, especially Brazil, children play without shoes – for example, the great Pelé – and a player's performance does not depend on equipment, as the friend suggests here.

Bobby, a new character, appeared in several cartoons. Here Bazooka Joe and Bobby appear on one wrapper, and Bazooka Joe asks:

> "Did you know Patovica went to the stadium and fell from the upper deck?"
> Bobby: "My goodness! What a calamity!"
> "Yes ... and they charged him the difference between upper and lower deck."

Patovica demonstrates his love for soccer in another cartoon, when he tells his friends:

Patovica:	"In this book, it tells what Maradona said in 1986" [his handball goal in the semifinals of the World Cup].
Bobby:	"That's nice."
Bazooka Joe:	"What'd he say? What'd he say?"
Patovica:	"He said, 'Ayoooooooo!'" [exclamation of joy and excitement].

Bazooka Joe and Patovica in another cartoon have the following exchange:

Bazooka Joe:	"Patovica, what do you get if you cross a peacock with chicken?"
Patovica:	"Let me think... Ahhh, I know. An Easter egg."

And showing adolescent interest in the future, one of his girlfriends says to Bazooka Joe:

Girlfriend:	"Consulting the Future Machine, I learned that I will have 11 daughters."
Bazooka Joe:	"11 eat."
Girlfriend:	"No, at 11:30."

This joke does not translate well because it relies on the Spanish-language pun of feeding 11 (a las 11) and saying 11 o'clock (a las 11).

In another exchange, a friend asks Bazooka Joe:

Friend:	"Why has Dany stopped in the bank on the corner?"
Bazooka Joe:	"To be with his impossible love."
Friend:	"His impossible love?"
Bazooka Joe:	"Yes, the computer [feminine noun like a clerk] in the bank on the corner."

The fortunes given in the wrappers also varied. The new version changed from the predictions of an Oriental sage to Bazooka Joe's comments. Such as they were, there appeared a prediction for the future: "Today they're going to tell you a very funny joke." Another of Joe's horoscopes said: "They will reveal a mystery to you that has long since unfolded" – a sort of riddle wrapped in an enigma. Other horoscopes contained prosaic humor. This example features a sketch of a black cat and says:

> Bad luck: You are going to fall in front of everyone.
> Laugh even if you have just a few teeth.

Another example of the black cat bad luck fortune said: "Two commitments at the same time will force you to make a difficult decision. One friend will be angry at you for that."

Other so-called horoscopes were little more than aphorisms typical of middle-class advice: "Help your mother with errands" and respectable behavior: "Accept the advice that friends give you." The horoscopes at this point were largely replaced with clichés for middle-class teenagers: "Someone with a good heart is better than someone intelligent," "Reading a good book enriches your knowledge,"

"Compete with good intentions and you will be able to enjoy your success," and "Take the test that has you worried." And ordinary commentary, such as: "You will receive a birthday invitation that you will not remember," "You will meet a friend you have not seen in a long time," "You will receive a surprise visit," "Try not to run risks," and "Today is a good day to meditate."

Topps made another effort in 1989 to create greater interest in the cartoons with new categories and activities for Bazooka Joe and his friends. The cartoons shifted to new categories. Topps's new themes influenced the Argentine comics that included "Bazooka Joe Fantasies," which depicted the gang in fanciful and future situations. For example, Bazooka Joe talks to Cervantes. He says to the great author, "Tell me, Cervantes, did you lose your left arm at the Battle of Lepanto because there was a sign that said, 'Keep your right?'" The obvious street sign for drivers provides an anachronistic punchline.

In another of these fantasy comics, both Javi Metal and Bazooka Joe are wearing space uniforms, and Javi Metal asks:

Javi Metal: "What did you think of my concert of Galactic Rock?"
Bazooka Joe: "Barbaric. Your style is like that of Borges."
Javi Metal: "But Borges was not a musician."
Bazooka Joe: "Neither are you!"

Javi Metal and music provided a rather common theme. On another wrapper, holding his guitar, he says:

Javi Metal: "I am happy that this past Saturday, I was able show I can move the public."
Bazooka Joe: "Yes, because they could not catch up with you when they started running."

In another script, Bazooka Joe and Patovica relax in togas and eat grapes.

Patovica: "Joe, what emperor came after Julio?"
Bazooka Joe: "Augusto."

Patovica: "Then I already know who came after Augusto."
Bazooka Joe: "Who?"
Patovica: "Septembro."

A final example from this category features Bobby.

Bazooka Joe: "What are you doing, Bobby?"
Bobby: "I am programming the computer to tell me what came first, the chicken or the egg."
Patovica: "The chicken is first. Because the chicken lays eggs and the eggs do not lay chickens."

As painfully humorous as Patovica's answer is, from another vantage point, Bobby's belief that he can program the computer to provide an answer to this age-old question reflects the faith in the magic of computers at this time. These comics show the growing significance of computers in daily life and the lingering importance of the cultural legacy built on, among others, Borges and Cervantes. Obviously, they were aimed at the attitudes and information of middle-class teenagers still in school.

In the U.S., "Bazooka Joe: Mystic Master of Space and Time" created adventures in the past and future; and "Bazooka Joe Raps" tried to give the cartoon a connection to popular music. For example, a new character rapped:

"I'm Zena! I'm hot!
And I love to shop
Give me credit cards
And I can't stop!)."[18]

Steni followed with new Bazooka adventures that served as what Fogwill called the third generation of Bazooka Joe cartoons. Joe's friends introduced themselves on new wrappers that featured the "Bazooka Joe Raps."

Bazooka's onetime girlfriend had grown into a teenager. Sol, whose name resonates with the G (musical note), so or sol note of the solfege music scale and is a nickname for Soledad, Solange, Isolde, and Sole, identified herself in a rap:

My name is Sol. I am very pretty.
I make the boys sigh
My vibe has no equal
The crowd always envies me
And that is so good
It only bothers me
when some guy doesn't know me.

More than any other character, Sol changed the most in the cartoons. She became in this cartoon the equivalent of an Argentine version of a U.S. Valley Girl or Mexico City Fresa. A stereotypical blonde,[19] for example, she says to one of her friends:

Sol: "Ay, Flopi, you knew that blabla blab la in the beauty shop blabla blabla and later I went to Blabla and then I left and blablabla blabla because I told you that blabla…"
Flopi: "Yes, and besides you have a pimple here" (pointing to Sol's forehead).
Sol: runs off, shouting "No-o-o-o-o!"
Flopi: "The pimple trick never fails to send her away."

Sol appeared in other cartoons, especially as the girl Bobby aspired to date. In one, Bazooka Joe said to his friends:

Bazooka Joe: "I am sure that Sol is coming behind us."
Patovica: "Hey, Professor, how do you know?"
Bazooka Joe: "Because I was looking at Bobby's [star-struck] face and knew she was on the way."

Another one of Bazooka Joe's friends in these later wrappers was Javi Metal. He had long, mullet-like hair, a t-shirt and vest, ripped jeans, and, on his bicep, a fishhook tattoo. In his rap he says:

These are my cords
I want to introduce myself
I am Javi Metal, the unrivaled
Hard Rock fits me
And I make my guitar cry
The public shouts at me
And some ask me to sing
The majority in a hostile way
Say I should be quiet

The professor said about himself, in his rap, that he liked to postpone examinations, so when the students weren't expecting it, he could ask them to take out a sheet of paper for a surprise test. This way the "0" grades come right along.

Another rapping character, studious Bobby, with red bushy hair, glasses, of course, a collared shirt, and colorful shorts, declares:

I am the Ace of computers.
There is nothing that I don't know.
And in the classroom, I am the best
And in love, I don't decide
And I share with passion
On one side Sol and on the other my computer.

All these characters were urban and at least middle class, with goals of future success. On one wrapper, for example, Bazooka Joe tells Bobby and Patovino:

Bazooka Joe:	"It's tough to achieve success. Right, guys?"
Bobby:	"Not earlier. My grandfather started with ripped pants and now he has millions."
Patovino:	"Why does your grandfather want millions of ripped pants?"

Topps made another change in the 1990s and brought in more new characters (grunge-rocker AJ) and gag types ("Tao of Mort" and

"Meet the Gang"). In Argentina, Bazooka Joe faced new cartoon styles and competition from another Argentine gum company that offered Mafalda cartoons with the slogan "Finally, gum that makes you think!"[20] The Bazooka change came with miscellaneous comic wrappers such as "Humorzooka" (Father: "Carlos, if you don't stop playing the drums, I am going to go crazy." Carlos: "You're too late, Dad. I stopped an hour ago.") and a return to horoscopes with "Horóscopo Chino – Bazooka" and "Bazooka Joe – and Chip."

Chip, with red hair and glasses, had earlier been the character Bobby. Perhaps the nickname alludes to computers. He is introduced with the wrapper "What Chip has in his head," with balloons indicating 25 percent software, 18 percent navigating the internet, 5 percent worry about his cranium, 5 percent to do homework, 5 percent to do other people's homework, 25 percent hardware, 13 percent inventions, 1 percent learning to play soccer, and 33 percent extra brain space. The panel includes a sketch of him thinking about the formula for $E = MC^2 + 32$ and other numbers.

In another cartoon in the Chip category, the scientist tells Bazooka Joe and Chip:

Scientist:	"Today I am going to test my new time capsule."
Bazooka Joe:	"Great!"
Chip:	"I'm first."
Scientist, with Chip in the machine:	"Now you are going to go back a million years." *BZARP!*

The machine opens again. Bazooka Joe and the scientist see a red-haired ape with glasses.

In this same era of miscellaneous wrappers, a Bazooka coded message appeared that required a secret decoder. Anyone who solved it could redeem it at a kiosk, or save 10 secret messages and send them to an address in Buenos Aires or Montevideo to participate in a super Bazooka drawing.

Bazooka Joe produced another popular scientific genre called Mystoríus, focused on the production of clones and the use of ultraviolet light. Here the evildoer, who produces clones of prehistoric flying creatures that look like dragons, is the mysterious Tony Caro. Dr. Mystoríus works to save society and creates a being to battle those of Caro that is nearly invisible because of its ultraviolet color produced by thousands of pieces of violet gum. Along with flying saucers, monster clones, and ultraviolet gum-producing monsters to save society, there were fascinating stories reminiscent of *Dr. Who* episodes on television and sci-fi movies, especially *Attack of the Clones* in the Star Wars series, which brought Bazooka bubble gum and Bazooka Joe up to date with the popular culture of the time.

The effort in the U.S. did not help with sales. Bazooka Candy brands announced in the *New York Times* that in January 2013, they would no longer include Bazooka Joe comics in gum packages, replacing them with brain teasers.[21] He and Mort (the friend with the high turtleneck sweater) were not scheduled to disappear completely but would show up occasionally and also appear at BazookaJoe.com, a marketing site with games and videos for kids to purchase.

What enter do bubblegum wrapper jokes and fortunes explain? First, we see that in Argentina as in the rest of the Americas, an Oriental man or woman, the medium, has access presumably to occult knowledge of the future. Rather than use this capability to gain control over others, acquire fortune or receive fame, it is shared for only enough to cover the seer's food and shelter. In this there is a sense of responsibility to others, but it cannot just be given or it will be mistrusted and misused. For kids, perhaps knowing a corner of the future somewhat leveled the field with knowledgeable teachers, parents, priests, and even older children. Or maybe fortunes did nothing as direct as this, but only provided something to tell friends, who were often just as baffled by the aphorisms that served as fortunes.

Laughter gives life rhyme if not reason. Laughing we know disarms fears, reduces dangers, negates sadness, and prevents worry. It helps make the day pleasurable, work less onerous, and people more friendly. It serves as an audio image, a sound picture of joyful recognition of others, objects, and aphorisms that provide a small book of advice to live by. No one normally shared gum, but the wrappers could be passed around for others to read the joke and to consider the fortune. Who was the seer, beyond being Oriental, who delivered the encouragement or the caution?

Bazooka Joe stood out as a role model to his bunch of friends and offered an image for readers to emulate. His eye covered with an eye patch implied that visual or other impairments should not limit anyone. Meanwhile, the Argentines who bought Bazooka, read the sappy cartoons, and blew bubbles joined the purchasers of a billion pieces worldwide each year – the true meaning, one might say, of globalization.

Notes

1 Jennifer P. Mathews, author of *Chicle: The Chewing Gum of the Americas, From the Ancient Maya to William Wrigley* (Tucson: University of Arizona Press, 2009), to author (June 28, 2019). The Stani company was sold in 1994 to Cadbury, then Kraft, and later to Mondelez. None of these companies have preserved any original Bazooka cartoons.

2 Quoted in Richard C. Morais, *The Hundred-Foot Journey* (New York: Scribner, 2010), p. 47.

3 Josh Wilker, *Cardboard Gods: An All-American Tale Told Through Baseball Cards: With 1 Stick Bubble Gum* (New York: Seven Footer Press, 2010).

4 "Murió Jorge Cázares, el pintor de los paisajes de las cajas de cerillos," https://www.milenio.com/cultura/jorge-cazares-muere-autor-pinturas-cajas-cerillos?fbclid=IwAR0_yBKEnVonqnezk0XEzjbvjBjjreXNkEABsENwkMNlI-WQT3F7GfqdM9U.

5 See both examples of the images and discussion by Terri Gordon-Zolov and Eric Zolov, "The Walls of Chile Speak of a Suppressed Rage," https://www.thenation.com/article/archive/chile-protest-art/.

6 *Bazooka Joe and his Gang* (New York: Abrams ComicArts, 2013), p. 42.

7 Isabella Cosse, *Mafalda: A Social and Political History of Latin America's Global Comic*, translated by Laura Pérez Carrara (Durham, NC: Duke University Press, 2019), p. 30.

8 Mark Morgan Ford, "The Man in the Hathaway Shirt" (November 19, 2015), https://www.earlytorise.com/the-man-in-the-hathaway-shirt/; *Bazooka Joe and his Gang*, p. 210.

9 *Bazooka Joe and his Gang*, p. 129.

10 *Bazooka Joe and his Gang*, pp. 54–56.

11 *Bazooka Joe and his Gang*, pp. 109, 111.

12 "Author of Some of Bazooka Gum's Jokes Finally Revealed in Argentina," *Latin American News Digest* (June 12–20, 2019), https://latinamerican-newsdigest.com/author-bazooka-gums-jokes-finally-revealed-argentina/.

13 Mariano Vespa, "Las globolocuras de Fogwill," *La Agenda Revista* (June 23, 2015), https://laagenda.buenosaires.gob.ar/post/122207613355/las-globolocuras-de-fogwill.

14 This analysis of the gum wrappers results from the collection of 103 Bazooka wrappers from Argentina in the Champion Folk Collection, Raleigh, North Carolina. The collection resulted from the assistance of Ernesto Semán, University of Bergen, Norway, and Viviana Grieco, University of Missouri-Kansas City, and her family in Buenos Aires.

15 *Bazooka Joe and his Gang*, p. 125.

16 Glen Weldon, "Bazooka Joe Has Been Honorably Discharged," *New Republic Digital Edition* (December 7, 2012), https://newrepublic.com/article/110868/bazooka-joe-comics-pulled-bubble-gum-after-58-years.

17 https://www.reddit.com/r/SrGrafo/comments/evtxs7/; Daiana Halac, "What's in an Argentine Nickname?" (December 7, 2014), https://fusion.tv/story/68349/whats-in-an-argentine-nickname/; "Argentines: The Past Masters of Nicknames," https://www.gringoinbuenosaires.com/argentines-masters-nicknames/.

18 Weldon, "Bazooka Joe."

19 Blonde jokes are a longstanding category in the U.S. See for example https://thoughtcatalog.com/melanie-berliet/2015/11/30-dumb-blonde-jokes-that-will-actually-make-you-lol/.

20 Cosse, *Mafalda*, p. 188.

21 Weldon, "Bazooka Joe."

Additional Resources

Reading

Guido Indij, *Sin Palabras: Gestiario Argentino – Speechless: A Dictionary of Argentine Gestures* (Buenos Aires: La Marca editora, 2007).

Quino, *Si, cariño/Yes, Dear* (Buenos Aires: Ediciones de la Flor, 2016).

Video

T4Tango. Humorous documentary of tango championships held in San Francisco. 2012.

10

Ski Masks

Jorge Uzon/Getty Images.

On January 1, 1994, the Zapatista National Liberation Army (EZLN) – almost exclusively indigenous Mexicans wearing *pasamontañas* (or ski masks) – seized a military base and five main towns of the municipalities of San Cristóbal de las Casas, Ocosingo, Chanal, Altamirano, and Las Margaritas in the state of Chiapas. The rebellion coincided with the implementation of the North American Free Trade Agreement (NAFTA). The 2,000 or so Zapatistas were led

Latin American Cultural Objects and Episodes, First Edition. William H. Beezley.

by Subcomandante Marcos, who also wore a ski mask, and did so whenever he appeared in public or on the internet, and still does. As their mark of identification, EZLN members claimed the black balaclava or ski mask.

The EZLN was not the first group to wear the ski mask. It has symbolized insurrection, revolution, and terrorism. It received its English name, balaclava, in the 1854–1855 siege at the town of the same name near Sevastopol during the Crimean War. British troops wore the woolen hat and mask because their supplies of warm clothing had not yet arrived. Later the troops called it the "balaclava helmet." More recently, it became a mask to conceal the identities of criminals, terrorists, and revolutionaries as well as paramilitary and special forces personnel. The Provisional Irish Republican Army (IRA) used them from 1969 until 1997 in their guerrilla war against England and Northern Ireland. During the 1972 Munich Olympic Games, terrorists wore them when they attacked and murdered Israeli team members. Marxist guerrillas in El Salvador, Tupamaro rebels in Peru, and bank robbers in the U.S. wore them in the 1970s and 1980s. In the Soviet Union, as early as perestroika during the 1980s, the OMON (special police task force) adopted the balaclava as part of its uniform to protect the identity of officers battling Russian criminals because the raids often appeared on TV news. Russian police who conducted raids of white-collar premises, especially in Moscow, wore them and their raids came to be known as "maski shows," an allusion to a popular comedy group on TV in the 1990s.[1] The ski masks also became objects of intimidation as much as protection of identity, as they hid the faces of the enforcement agents. English police officers in Kent confiscated the board game "War on Terror" in part because it included a balaclava that they claimed "could be used to conceal someone's identity or could be used in the course of a criminal act."[2] The mask became well known in fiction through the terrorist who hid his identity with a ski mask in the 1971 Frederick Forsyth novel *The Day of the Jackal.* The Venezuela media nicknamed the renowned terrorist Ilich Ramirez Sanchez, who used the ski mask, Carlos the Jackal.[3] Recently, in La Paz, Bolivia, an indigenous group of shoe shiners began wearing ski masks to keep their identities secret and to avoid discrimination.[4] It also became featured in advertisements. The ski mask sometime around the 1980s became associated with Mexico's EZLN, so that it now expresses rebellion like other symbolic clothing and objects, including Castro's cigar and Sandino's hat.[5] The ski mask has multiple purposes that often overlap. It serves from hiding individual identity to creating a common, anonymous identity as soldier, rebel, or terrorist. During the Covid-19 pandemic of 2020, face masks provided health protection and gave the message that everyone faced the disease risk. On close inspection, these masks often showed individual character that never appeared in the ski masks of the EZLN or other groups that sought anonymity.

The ski mask became common garb for revolutionaries when it received widespread publicity as the indigenous peoples of the EZLN rose up in arms in Chiapas against the Mexican government, January 1, 1994.[6] The ski mask and pipe instantly became the trademark visage of the hologram, as he called himself, of Subcomandante Marcos, the face of the EZLN, and it quickly became closely associated with the Zapatista Liberation movement. Marcos's ski mask-clad face adorns handcrafted dolls, t-shirts, posters, and badges. When the EZLN began fighting, the ski mask did more than simply hide the identity of the soldiers. It made a comment on "the indigenous face," and ruptured visual history. Before 1994 in terms of national recognition, the indigenous peoples had no face as they were presented as simple, poor, and happy people who lived passive, silent, and submissive but aesthetic lives. The ski mask rejected this characterization and served as a refusal to act as objects of exoticism. The ski mask constructed a new indigenous face, one linked to aggression, organization, and noise, not silence. Marcos has said he will take his mask off once the conflict is over, because it is crucial to his role in the struggle. "Once the mask is gone, so is Marcos," he declared.

The Subcomandante used the ski mask as a symbol that fused complicated economic and political opinions with a wicked sense of humor. What the Zapatistas demanded, Marcos explained to British

Broadcasting Corporation (BBC) reporter Nathalie Malinarich, was for the constitution to be changed to recognize the rights of indigenous Mexicans. He was recognized as a leader who spoke for the poor and dispossessed. The mask served as a synecdoche of him. His opponents declared that the EZLN and the ski mask represented a demagogue, an irresponsible dreamer, and a blackmailer.

Responding to the ski mask-clad Zapatistas, President Carlos Salinas de Gortari immediately sent troops to Chiapas and they regained control of the region in four days. The president only halted the campaign against the rebels because thousands of demonstrators occupied the Zócalo, the central square in Mexico City, to show their solidarity with the Zapatistas. After the army halted its advance, government officials quickly banned tourism to the state. Nevertheless, many curious travelers, human rights advocates, and foreign journalists ignored the restriction to visit the Zapatistas, who continued to resist from several villages and a base in the Lacandón rainforest. Sporadic rebel–military fighting continued and the last major battle occurred in 1997, although reports of military violence continued.

One Zapatista in a radio interview explained the EZLN. "We are a product of 500 years of struggle," he said, "first against slavery, then during the War of Independence against Spain…then to avoid being absorbed by North American imperialism, then to promulgate our constitution and expel the French empire from our soil…Later the dictatorship of Porfirio Díaz denied us the just application of the Reform laws, and the people rebelled and leaders like Villa and Zapata emerged, poor men just like us." The revolution brought changes to the state with the publication of the "Workers' Law" of 1914 that ended the system of servitude of rural workers on haciendas and the exploitation of workers trapped in contracts and debts. The Agrarian Law of 1915 called for the restoration to indigenous communities of expropriated lands, the granting of *ejido* lands to country people, and the determination of small properties as no more than 50 hectares. This law was expanded as the fundamental article 27 of the 1917 Constitution. The promises of the revolution notwithstanding, the new revolutionary regime did little to change the social and economic hierarchy of the past, even with the creation of the Instituto Nacional Indigenista (INI) that intended to break patterns of discrimination and exploitation and promote customs and cultural uses to nationalize and modernize the indigenous peoples.[7]

Most accounts appropriately focus on the struggle over land reform (between landowning ladinos and landless or small-holding indigenous peoples), but other issues must be included in discussions of the needs of indigenous Chiapanecos, especially the questions of elementary education (in Spanish or native languages?) available to children and, from the 1970s onward, community (that is, municipal) government. The situation worsened in the 1980s with the national economic crisis and the growing rural population that with the division of family or community properties resulted in minifundia (extremely small holdings) for both subsistence agricultural and family coffee production. The 1992 reform of the federal constitution's article 27 ended the agrarian reform and opened the possibility of selling, renting, or mortgaging *ejido* lands in order to obtain credit.[8] Mexico had become a nation importing agricultural products, including corn as a product of neoliberalism. The Federal government under President Salinas also adopted economic programs called PROCAMPO (for the countryside), or PRONASOL (for solidarity), to support the rural population, reduce poverty, and eliminate corruption.

The EZLN uprising focused national attention on the question of the rights of Mexico's 20 million indigenous people. In Chiapas, these people in search of subsistence plots had carried out peaceful occupations of fallow land. Their efforts turned bloody when local coffee barons and cattle ranchers hired pistoleros to attack the settlers. In response, the villagers created self-defense brigades to protect against the gunmen. Soon this resulted in united action. As Subcomandante Marcos said in one interview, the brigades soon learned that they could not defend a single community, they needed alliances to face the paramilitary and later military units arrayed against them.

The necessary alliance came with the EZLN. It developed from the efforts of the Maoist organization Popular Politics (PP) and its chief theoretician, National Autonomous University professor Adolfo Berlinguer. He argued that radical students and intellectuals must live among the masses to organize them. Another account claimed that Father Samuel Ruiz, the Catholic archbishop of Chiapas and proponent of liberation theology, was so impressed with the PP's neighborhood organizing in Torreón that he invited PP activists to Chiapas. Subcomandante Marcos said that he was one of the first 12 members of PP who relocated to Chiapas in 1983 to organize a guerrilla war. These radicals operated under the protection of the church, often accompanying priests on missions into rural areas. They spoke on behalf of the oppressed indigenous peoples and demanded "work, land, housing, food, health, education, independence, freedom, justice and peace" for them and pledged to form a "free and democratic government."

If one single event can be said to have pushed these defense groups to embark on armed insurrection, it came when the Salinas government in 1992 amended article 27 of the federal constitution of 1917. This article, written by the revolutionaries, declared that property ownership was a social responsibility and guaranteed country people the right to petition for unused private land or land held by the state. Over the course of nearly a century since the implementation of the constitution, the quality of land distributed under article 27 had worsened, with only about one fifth of it considered suitable for forestry and tourism but not for agriculture. Changing article 27 closed off the hope that landless rural people might be able to gain a plot of ground to call their own. The government's repeal polarized indigenous communities and organizations between those who supported continued "peaceful" methods and those who chose "armed" struggle. In the debates that broke out over how to respond to the government, the "armed struggle" tendency won out. Long before NAFTA was ratified by Congress in the U.S., the EZLN's leadership had set a date for an uprising.

Once the EZLN rebelled, it achieved global attention from international leftists, who saw the rebellion as the first major blow against the free-market celebration that reigned after the collapse of the Soviet Union in 1991. Moreover, the uprising was the first major guerrilla challenge to the Mexican regime since the 1970s. Twice the government attempted to suppress the EZLN – once in January 1994 and again in February 1995. Both times, the president had government troops stand down because of massive protests in Mexico City, the rest of the country, and around the world. In May 1994, government officials met with Zapatista leaders and offered a series of reforms. These ranged from improved health care and sanitation to increased prices for agricultural produce. The government also agreed to address indigenous issues, such as support for indigenous-language radio stations. The EZLN leaders, arguing that the government's offer was insufficient, rejected it in June 1994. Since then, as many as 25,000 troops have surrounded the Zapatistas in the hills of the Lacandón jungle and conducted a "low-intensity" war against them.

Initially, the Zapatistas announced a march on Mexico City to depose Salinas. Within a few weeks, Subcomandante Marcos revised the statement and insisted the Zapatistas had no desire to "take power," nor to interfere with the elections planned for August 1994. He announced through internet dispatches that the EZLN had embarked on a new kind of revolution that relied on the worldwide web to publicize its activities and to attract supporters in a cultural struggle. This revolution the EZLN considered far more important than traditional battles with military weapons for political control.

After on-again, off-again negotiations, in 1996, the EZLN thought it had reached an agreement known as the San Andrés Accords with representatives of the government of President Ernesto Zedillo. This established local autonomy for indigenous peoples as well as new educational, social, and cultural rights through revised local, state, and federal laws and the constitution. The accords committed the government to eliminating "the poverty, the marginalization and insufficient political participation of millions of indigenous Mexicans." After signing the accords, the Zedillo government reversed itself and refused to implement the agreement. Meanwhile, the army stepped up its war against the civilian population of Chiapas in an attempt to undermine rebel support. The most brutal incident occurred in December 1997, in the village of Acteal, where 45 civilians, including 36 women and children, were murdered by government-backed paramilitaries. The Acteal massacre resulted in the resignations of the government's interior minister and the governor of Chiapas, who was found to have advance knowledge of the killings.

The EZLN responded to the deadlock and the increased violence by trying to mobilize broad support from the public. In 1999, it organized a national *consulta*, or referendum, on the question of indigenous rights and the implementation of the San Andrés Accords. More than 3 million individuals participated in the consulta, 95 percent of them endorsing the EZLN's demands.

Vicente Fox, running as the National Action Party (PAN) presidential candidate of "change" in 2000, pledged to solve the deadlock with the Zapatistas in "15 minutes." Fox defeated the PRI candidate, as the ruling party lost its first presidential election in seven decades. Soon after his inauguration in December 2000, Fox committed himself to submitting the San Andrés Accords to Congress, although PAN did not have a majority there. In an effort to build support for approval of the accords, the Zapatistas and their supporters mounted a 16-day caravan, bringing Marcos and other EZLN comandantes to Mexico City in February and March 2001. At every stop along the way, enthusiastic crowds supporting the EZLN and the accords greeted the caravan. As many as a quarter of a million rallied in the Zócalo in Mexico City in solidarity with the Zapatistas' demands. Yet Congress gutted the accords, and the Zapatistas returned to Chiapas empty-handed. With few exceptions since then, the Zapatistas and Subcomandante Marcos have remained largely aloof from major political developments. At one time, 38 pro-EZLN communities in Chiapas subsisted on support from U.S. and European non-governmental organizations.

In the first two decades since the uprising, as the Zapatistas predicted, real wages of workers have fallen since 1994, while the economy's growth at 1.2 percent per year has been among the lowest in Latin America. As many as 2 million farmers have been driven off their land, and the country now has begun to import corn for tortillas. These conditions brought thousands of farmers into the streets in 2004 and led the major unions to threaten a general strike against Fox's plan to increase taxes on working people's necessities. The protests culminated in the demonstrations that helped to sink the World Trade Organization (WTO) summit meeting in Cancún that year. In 2006, President Vicente Fox reversed the travel ban because his advisors saw the Zapatistas – who had used the internet to create an international following, many of whom had unofficially visited them – had potential as a tourist attraction. This greatly increased the flow of reporters, non-governmental volunteer workers, and sympathetic travelers.

But in the years since, the right-wing PAN, followed by the return to government of the PRI, have continued to privatize and dismantle the state's minimal social provisions. The PRI-dominated Congress voted in 2008 to privatize the national oil company PEMEX.

The publicity campaign reached beyond the internet generation to garner great international attention. It soon included extensive sales of Marcos and Zapatista t-shirts, coffee mugs, and bumper stickers. Some critics assert that the government has been involved in this souvenir business to transform a serious challenge to the regime into kitsch novelties, but this argument repeated a misunderstanding of the EZLN's cultural revolution. Through the internet and other cultural and social media, the rebels gained world renown and support. More significant than military victories, they have created cultural icons and performances through dolls, art, poetry, music, and sport.

The EZLN organized the Mujeres Sembrando la Vida, a Weaving Cooperative. Non-governmental agencies began to support the EZLN, both health (especially water purification) and cultural projects. The U.S. NGO Aid to Artisans Mexico, a subsidiary of Creative Learning in Washington, DC, supported the weaving cooperative SNA Jolobil. The was founded by a prominent ladino within the INI and U.S. citizen Chip Morris, a co-founder and director of Aid to Artisans.[9]

Simultaneous with the military invasion in 1994, markets throughout Chiapas began selling dolls representing rebel leaders. These became increasing a part of the fundraising effort. They originated from the community of San Juan Chamula, where Tzotzil women for years have used ancestral weaving, dying, and wool felting techniques to create cloth dolls (muñecas Chamulitas) wearing traditional clothing. The women modified the dolls to represent leaders of the EZLN by covering their faces with ski masks. Reflecting rebel membership, they made both male and female dolls carrying carved wooden weapons. Some female rebels also carried a masked infant. The women artisans insisted that they are not Zapatistas and their dolls represented for them nothing more than an economic opportunity. They added masks to their traditional "Chamulita" dolls that appealed to international travelers curious about the EZLN rebellion.

This explanation may have represented a sensible precaution against official reprisals. The addition of the ski mask to the dolls according to some commentators signaled a symbolic rebellion among the women against the common trivialization of native cultures. Sharon M. Scott, for example, argued the dolls served as an object of resistance to the systematic global exploitation of indigenous peoples through the metaphor that conveys the message "the other is not a plaything for First World Nations." An unsubstantiated story current among some international observers claimed the rebel dolls developed ideological roots in the 1994 *Caracoles* (community) of San Andrés.[10]

Many radical commentators heralded the Zapatistas as examples of a new kind of left that "changes the world without taking power." Instead of seeking to challenge the power of the regime at a national level, the Zapatistas were supposed to be leading by example from Chiapas. Little was known about how the EZLN actually operated in the autonomous communities and they have remained out of national issues such as the question of oil privatization and international questions such as the struggles of other indigenous peoples in Ecuador and Bolivia. Despite the efforts of the left to claim them, the Zapatistas are not socialists. On the contrary, they place themselves in the revolutionary tradition of Zapata and Villa. Their "First Declaration of the Lacandón Jungle," issued on the eve of their uprising, cited the authority of the constitution to legitimize their insurrection. "We are patriots," they declared, "and our insurgent soldiers love and respect our tricolored flag."[11] The EZLN has made several attempts to establish a support network. It launched the Zapatista National Liberation Front (FZLN) to forge a link with "civil society" – other citizens – in 1995. In 2006, the Zapatistas launched "the other campaign" of rallies against capitalism and racism, and for democracy, during the national presidential campaign.

In 1999, Marcos and the Zapatistas reworked the meaning of the ski mask from "the indigenous face'" to common people in general through popular culture, especially humor and soccer. This occurred through the so-called consulta. By taking the ski mask out of the Lacandón jungle, and disassociating it with guns, and reassociating it with dialog, playing soccer, and walking on the beach, the EZLN tried to demonstrate visually that their battle could be everyone's battle by sharing with as many sectors of society as possible the ski mask symbol. They reminded Mexicans of other masked heroes such as Santo, the movie star, professional wrestlers, and Super Barrio. The Zapatistas created a logo for common people.

Who was the man behind the mask? Many reporters and authorities discovered the guerrilla leader's real name was Rafael Sebastian Guillén, a 43-year-old born in the state of Tamaulipas. They said he had taught philosophy at Mexico City's National Autonomous University and in 1983 he moved to the southern state of Chiapas to work with Indian communities. Marcos revealed he comes from middle-class parents and once lived in Mexico City. He said he did not know if his mother recognized him behind the mask. Showing his renowned sense of humor, he added, "although they say a mother cannot be fooled." Of course, the ski mask did not obscure the fact that he is not an indigenous individual.

Marcos made rebellion an internet phenomenon as he used it to make pronouncements of the EZLN goals. He used the technology to create international connections with sympathetic people and organizations. The mass media also provided opportunities for the EZLN to communicate with the rest of the nation and the wider world. The Los Angeles rap-rock band Rage Against the Machine become well known for its support of the EZLN, using the red star symbol as a backdrop to their live shows and often informing concert crowds of the ongoing situation. This has created situations for Mexico's president, on trips abroad, in which he is routinely confronted by small activist groups protesting "the Chiapas situation." The Zapatistas are featured prominently in Rage Against the Machine's songs, in particular "People of the Sun," "Wind Below," "Zapata's Blood," and "War Within a Breath."[12]

Later, Marcos turned to television in 2001, following President Vicente Fox's announcement that he would withdraw federal troops from Chiapas and meet to discuss a resolution of the differences with the EZLN.[13] The Zapatistas condemned the president's moves as nothing more than publicity stunts. Ski mask, pipe, and automatic rifle in hand, Marcos pondered an appropriate response to the president. He decided on a comedy interlude. He gave a television interview from his jungle hideout in Chiapas with the famous comedian Andrés Bustamente. In the 15-minute exchange of jokes, Marcos explained the ski mask symbolized the rebellion. Bustamente asked, "And can you comb your hair?" He then presented Marcos with what he said was a gift from President Vicente Fox. The Subcomandante asked if it was a letter bomb. It turned out to be an oversized belt buckle spelling out the president's surname.

Humor like that in the interview, Marcos later explained, formed a bond between the EZLN and ordinary people.[14] This demonstrated his training and skills of communication. In his writing, discussions, formal and informal conversation, he used language that combined politics, poetry, images drawn from history, fables, and local customs, and colloquial expressions of the common people and leftist communes where he had lived for 40 years. His language was festooned with phrases that reflected his academic education in communications at UNAM and the double meaning of words, especially in the slang of Mexico City.

In the next major phase, the Subcomandante and the EZLA decided to organize what was called the consulta and go to Mexico City. Shortly before setting out from the jungle for the first time in years, Marcos revealed that he had been married for five years and would like to have a child. Correspondents said the existence of "La Mar" – a nickname for Mariana – came as a surprise to his supporters, most of whom are believed to be women. Marcos and a group of rebels made the 3,000-kilometer 15-day trek from the Lacandón jungle to the presidential office in the heart of Mexico City. Wearing ski masks, the EZLN delegates fanned out across the nation. Newspapers carried many stories as they arrived in busloads in Tijuana, Monterrey, Guadalajara, Mexico City, Acapulco, Oaxaca, and dozens of smaller cities and towns. In Tijuana, the Zapatistas organized a cross-border protest, where they pushed up against the south side of the fence, as supporters (including a few Americans who had been deported by the Mexican government) came down from Los Angeles and San Diego to push against the north side of the fence. In Acapulco, they wandered around on the beach.

Ski-mask-clad Zapatistas arrived in Mexico City and editors spread their images across the newspapers. The front page showed the EZLN playing soccer against a group of ex-professionals. Their custom-made jerseys had a red star and the letters EZLN and they played in their ski masks. They lost 5–3, but declared that because of the publicity of the event, "Even when we lose, we win." Another photograph showed them eating at Sanborn's in a historical pictorial reference to the Zapatistas in 1914 in Sanborn's. The publicity expanded the meaning of the Zapatista logo – the ski mask. The EZLN held its nationwide "Meeting for the Recognition of the Rights of the Indian People and for the End of the War of Extermination." Known as "The Consulta," it brilliantly expanded the ski mask's meaning and its omnipresence. Mexicans recognized the significance of the mask as the symbol of the people's rights. Anyone can see evidence of this in the movies of El Santo, and many other professional wrestlers who champion society. After the earthquake of 1985, another masked spokesman for the people appeared as Super Barrio. The masks were different but related to the ski masks of the EZLN.

Notes

1 Andrew E. Kramer, "Memo to Exxon: Business With Russia May Involve Guns and Balaclavas," *New York Times* (August 31, 2011).
2 https://en. wikipedia.org/wiki/Balaclava_(clothing).
3 Carlos, who may have been the mastermind behind the murder of the Israeli Olympians, and other myths about him are considered in David Yallop, *Tracking the Jackal: The Search for Carlos, the World's Most Wanted Man* (New York: Random House, 1994), which should be matched with the review "The Question of Carlos" by Joseph Finder, *New York Times* (January 2, 1994).
4 "The Masked Shoe Shiners of Bolivia – in pictures," photos by Federico Estol, *Guardian* (September 11, 2019), https://www.theguardian.com/artanddesign/gallery/2019/sep/11/shoe-shiners-la-paz-bolivia-picture-gallery-photography. Thank you to Sally Beezley for the reference.
5 Salman Rushdie, *The Jaguar Smile: A Nicaraguan Journey* (New York: Random House, 1987), pp. 11–12.
6 Nathalie Malinarich, "BBC Profile: The Zapatistas' Mysterious Leader" (March 11, 2001), http://news.bbc.co.uk/1/hi/world/americas/1214676.stm.
7 Antonio García de León, *Fronteras interiores. Chiapas: una modernidad particular* (México: Océano, 2002).
8 Neill Harvey, *Rebellion in Chiapas* (New York: Cambridge University Press, 2000).
9 Email from Michelle Mason, Colorado University-Colorado Springs, to author, March 8, 2019.
10 https://schoolsforchiapas.org/store/artesania/dolls/rebelde-zapatista-doll/.
11 Lance Selfa and Stuart Easterling, "Twenty Years after the Zapatista Uprising," *Socialist Worker* (January 21, 2014), https://socialistworker.org/2014/01/21/twenty-years-after-the-zapatista-uprising.

12 Rosalva Bermudez-Ballin, "Interview with Zach la Rocha (Rage Against The Machine)," Nuevo Amanecer Press (via spunk.org), July 8, 1998.
13 "Zapatista Consulta," Invisible Cinema, http://www.invisibleamerica.com/zapatista.html.
14 "Zapatista Leader Stars as Comedian," BBC News (February 1, 2001), http://news.bbc.co.uk/1/hi/world/americas/1148832.stm.

Additional Resources

Reading

Hilary Klein, *Compañeras: Zapatista Women's Stories* (New York: Seven Stories Press, 2015).

Stephen E. Lewis, *The Ambivalent Revolution: Forging State and Nation in Chiapas, 1910–1945* (Albuquerque: University of New Mexico Press, 2005).

Mihalis Mentinis, *Zapatistas: The Chiapas Revolt and What It Means For Radical Politics* (London: Pluto Press, 2006).

10 Coda

Ski Masks and Soccer

Subcomandante Marcos spoke often about the importance of humor and sport in making the EZLN relevant and accessible to common Mexicans. The EZLN players wore ski masks, and he wanted soccer to connect the Zapatistas to everyday Mexicans. Apart from cheering for the local Chiapas Football (as soccer is called in most of the world) Club before it relocated to Querétaro, Subcomandante Marcos and the EZLN supported the Italian Serie A – the major league – club F.C. Internazionale, located in Milan.

Around 2004 the manager of F.C. Internazionale Milano visited a village in Chiapas, bringing donations from Inter Campus, the club's charity organization, and its owner, Massimo Moratti. During the trip, the manager of Inter, as the team is known, was approached by a Zapatista commander about developing a stronger relationship. Inter agreed to a program in which it funded sports, water, and health projects in Chiapas. The team captain, famed Argentine Javier Zanetti, publicly stated his support for the Zapatista cause.

Contact continued between Inter and the Zapatistas. In 2005, Subcomandante Marcos wrote on May 25, 2005 to Inter president Massimo Moratti with an invitation to play a friendly match, as a gesture of appreciation and solidarity, against the EZLN Football Club.[1] His invitation was filled with irony and emotion and Inter accepted

Latin American Cultural Objects and Episodes, First Edition. William H. Beezley.

the challenge. The Subcomandante acknowledged the relationship between Mexico and Italy and expressed his delight, as the captain of the team's intergalactic relations, with the prospects of the match or perhaps a home series. Overcome with enthusiasm, Marcos suggested several games in Mexico, with the ticket revenue going to the villagers in Chiapas whose towns had been destroyed by the Mexican army and to altermundistas (program for social emancipation) and other social prisoners in Mexican jails. He added that in order to encourage the EZLN squad, they should appeal to the lesbian and transsexual community to provide "ingenious pirouettes" on the sidelines. He predicted this also would provoke TV censorship, scandalize conservatives, and disconcert the Inter players. As referees for the matches, Marcos proposed famous retired Latin American players such as Diego Maradona from Argentina and Sócrates from Brazil. He suggested as announcers the famous authors Eduardo Galeano and Mario Benedetti, for what he called the Zapatista System of Intergalactic Television ("the only television which is read"). Matches would follow in Italy. The winner of the friendly competition would receive a trophy, in Marcos's humorous description of the traditional drink of Chiapas, "The pozol of mud."[2]

The president of Inter responded by expressing his pleasure at the invitation and accepting the challenge of a match. Inter offered to provide the balls if the EZLN would provide the pozol. He concluded that arrangements needed to be made, but wherever the match happened, it would make "all equals. Dreamers all. We imagine great things, and we take pleasure in the small ones: a dribble, a scissors kick, a header, all make us happy."[3]

The soccer matches, unfortunately, were never played. Nevertheless, EZLN's futbol players did find chances to compete on the pitch against international teams. An English team, the Easton Cowboys, in 1999 became the first European football team to travel to Chiapas. The players had anarchist political views and represented the Plough, a neighborhood pub in intercity Bristol. The match resulted from the efforts of Matt Dymond and Yvette McLoughlin, two activists who had visited EZLN base communities in Chiapas as human rights observers in 1997. The Zapatista movement was experiencing one of its most difficult periods with constant pressure and attacks by the army and paramilitary groups. In December, 45 unarmed people – mainly women and children – from the refugee camp in Acteal were murdered by one of these paramilitary groups. Government officials had banned visitors to EZLN-controlled areas of Chiapas, but their regulations allowed visits by sporting teams. Dymond and McLoughlin saw an opportunity to arrange for a soccer team to play the EZLN and in 1998 discussed the idea with the Cowboys. The team liked the idea of a new adventure, but some players hesitated because of EZLN temperance laws in the communities they controlled.[4]

The Cowboys team had begun at the Baptist Mills primary school playing field in Easton where, beginning in the late 1980s, "various punks, hippies and general ne'er do wells (as well as the odd talented youngster) congregated for a regular Sunday afternoon kickaround." The team sign-up sheet said players should bring boots, shin pads, and sideburns. The country music-obsessed secretary suggested the name Cowboys, and other players who were fans of Johnny Cash, Hank Williams, and other country stars supported the suggestion. Others who liked old western movies quickly agreed. The players thought it gave them a kind of swagger.[5]

Twenty-five Cowboys and Cowgirls, including two guest players from Republica and one from the 1 in 12 club, departed on April 30, 1999. When they arrived in San Cristóbal de Las Casas and prepared to go into EZLN territory, they noticed the Zapatista presence through the "cute ski-masked dolls sold by street vendors." Throughout their travels in Chiapas, they had to avoid troops and army check points. They first stopped in Diez de Abril, where they divided up with local players for an impromptu seven-a-side tournament. At the concluding awards ceremony, the locals sang the Zapatista hymn, and the English responded in poor voice, "You'll Never Walk Alone," the Liverpool soccer song, and delighted nearly everyone by dancing the "Hokey Cokey," known in most places as the Hokey Pokey. They next walked, or in the team's lore, made the March of Death, beginning at 2 a.m., to the village of Morelia, where they played a two-day tournament with local teams from the community and the surrounding area. Their final destination was La Garrucha, where they managed to win the tournament. An invitation came to go to another village, Moises Ghandi. Half the group decided to go, and they participated in a basketball tournament of sorts before returning to join their mates. The others returned to San Cristóbal for showers and clean clothes. All told, they played 21 games of futbol and managed a week without alcohol. Team member Jasper Beese said, "while we were there, we had time to try to get our head around what was happening in the Chiapas region, and having played football matches with the indigenous people, when we came home we felt we wanted to do something to help them. So half a dozen of us formed Kiptik – which means "inner strength" in Tzetzal – one of the native languages of the region."[6] The Cowboys continued their support for the EZLN after they played in Chiapas. After the trip, the Cowboys adopted as the team slogan "Freedom through Football." They raised £100,000 in 10 years to initiate clean water projects for Zapatista communities.

The team planned another trip to play matches and to participate in Zapatista solidarity work, an area that has, generally speaking, been led by Italian, Basque, and Catalan groups. The formation of Kiptik was a direct result to help the locals to build clean water systems. In May 2000, the Cowboys organized an event at the club Thekla to raise money for a water project. The campaign caught the attention of an up-and-coming Bristol artist by the name of Banksy. "It's hard to believe, but Banksy actually wasn't that well known back then," Jasper Beese says. "And when we decided to go out for a second football tour later on in 2000, Banksy came out with us to see the situation for himself – and to play in goal… He turned out to be a half-decent goalie, but it was the indigenous community's heritage of painting protest murals that really caught Banksy's attention. In fact, he painted a number of new murals himself while he was over there with us. He's a lovely guy – just a very normal bloke, but clearly with an extraordinary talent."[7]

The first touring team, consisting of some 20 players, arrived in May 1999 and a second squad arrived in November the same year, with another following in January 2001. The Cowboys spent eight days in the communities playing three tournaments, beginning in La Realidad, the Zapatista jungle stronghold. Ten teams took part: the Cowboys and nine Zapatista teams from nearby villages. The rumor spread that "the whitest white people we have ever seen are coming!" This could have provided the distraction needed to take them to a 2–0 victory in the final against the Realidad team. The stadium stood in the rainforest. Corner kicks represented a minor challenge, and knee-high grass tended to obscure the ball entirely. The match organizer kept spirits high with a non-stop barrage of mariachi music, interspersed with Italian-style commentary as the games took place, without a doubt one of most surreal aspects of the tour. The Cowboys argued that the modern professional game often included dirty play and increasing levels of commercialization. They wanted to promote healthy competition and solidarity. At the tournament in La Realidad, no players were sent off, aside from a few stray pigs who were given the red card.

The club went to Mexico again in 2006, but this time turned to basketball, a game popular among men and women in the Chiapan Highlands. The Cowgirls organized a basketball team and, with their height advantage, won two tournaments. The Cowboys, on the other hand, managed to escape the tour without recording a single victory. Each of these tours was a huge success. Many Cowboys and Cowgirls continued to be involved in Zapatista solidarity work and raising money for Kiptik.

Communities throughout Chiapas have no clean drinking water.[8] So the Cowboys soon helped with the design, materials, and work to assist communities to build a water system. They devised gravity-fed systems that avoid using often unreliable pumps that prove expensive to fix. Special concrete holding tanks along the route made it possible for water to be piped directly to each house. The team reported that the average system cost around £4,000/€4,500, took three months to build, and supplied water to communities ranging from 10 to 50 families. "It's hard work, but we all roll our sleeves up and work with the indigenous people to try to get these things working." When they left, the team left a toolbox and spare parts, so the community could maintain the system for an estimated 20 years.

The water system changed the daily lives of women, many of whom had had to walk as much as an hour to fetch and carry fresh water. The system put an end to that by providing clean water. This supply of clean water offered the most important health measure for a community. Kiptik has helped fund and build over 21 water systems in the autonomous communities of Chiapas since 2000. This has brought a clean water supply to an estimated 5,000 people. Almost all the systems continue to work well, with the communities taking care of maintenance.

Beyond water projects, the soccer players led by the Cowboys also provided stoves. The great majority of families in the communities cooked on open wood fires in small smoky huts. This caused continual respiratory diseases for women and children and wasted a large amount of fuel. Although large parts of Chiapas are still forested, due to the increasing demand for fuel and extensive logging the forest cover has reduced dramatically in recent years. Ecological stoves are a major step forward in reducing the health problems associated with cooking on open fires. There are over 200 toxins in smoke produced from burning wet wood, and these stoves release very little smoke into the room. The stoves are also much more efficient, using up to 70 percent less wood, so reduce levels of deforestation. The stoves also have had a major impact on the lives of women in the communities who are almost always the ones who go out to collect wood. The stoves Kiptik helped build are fired clay burners that sit in a cinder block or brick base, surrounded by stones to preserve heat and maximize efficiency. The clay parts are made by women's cooperatives in the communities and almost all the material needed to build the stoves can be obtained locally. They are simple to use and maintain and can last for up to 15 years.

Kiptik's latest tenth anniversary fundraising venture ties in with Jasper Beese's day job, as well as the main source of income for the Zapatistas – growing coffee beans. Beese worked at "a workers' food cooperative, and so I recognized it would be a nice idea if we could sell coffee – one of the region's few exports – to raise cash for

Kiptik... when we sell the Zapatista coffee, 0.40 Euros goes to Kiptik for every kilo of coffee sold. It's just one more way we can help these people – and it just so happens that it's particularly good coffee too."[9]

The second tour included players from both the Antwerp Lunatics and the Leeds La Republica Internationale. Both of these clubs soon made tours of their own to play games and support the EZLN. "Much of 2002 and 2003 were spent raising money for a truly mixed Republica team to go to Chiapas and a film was made to document the trip. This was the first mixed football the Zapatista had ever seen or played. Whatever direct influence this had is difficult to assess but five years later Zapatista women were playing football as a demonstration of their own liberation."[10]

As the Subcomandante hoped, sport, especially soccer, has had a great impact on Chiapas and globally as well.

Notes

1 "Zapatista Rebels Woo Inter Milan," BBC News (May 11, 2005), http://news.bbc.co.uk/2/hi/4537859.stm.

2 http://todochiapas.mx/chiapas/el-pozol-de-chiapas/426. This source provides a discussion of pozol, the tradional drink.

3 "Zapatista Rebels and Inter Milan," November 14, 2012. Originally published in Spanish by F.C. Internazionale Milano, translated by irlandesa, https://footballbar.wordpress.com/2012/11/14/zapatista-rebels-and-inter-milan/.

4 The club was founded in 1992. Will Simpson and Malcolm McMahon, *Freedom through Football: The Story of the Easton Cowboys and Cowgirls* (Bristol: Tangent Books, 2012), pp. 8, 5, 10, 12; "Futbol y Libertad: Banksy, Inter Milan, and the Zapatistas," *The People's Game* (June 24, 2014), http://www.thepeoplesgame.org/2014/06/24/futbol-y-libertad-banksy-inter-milan-and-the-zapatistas/.

5 Easton Cowboys & Cowgirls, https://eastoncowfolk.org.uk/; Jane Onyanga-Omara, "Banksy in Goal: The Story of the Easton Cowboys and Cowgirls," BBC News (September 14, 2012), https://www.bbc.co.uk/news/uk-england-bristol-19410566.

6 Simpson and McMahon, *Freedom through Football*, pp. 87–114; “Futbol y Libertad.”

7 Simpson and McMahon, *Freedom through Football*, p. 114. See “Mural Painting in Chiapas with Banksy: Easton Cowboys,” http://schoolsforchiapas.org/library/mural-painting-chiapas-banksy/, for a pdf of Banksy painting murals in Mexico. For a documentary about Banksy, murals, and graffiti, see *Exit through the Gift Shop* (2010). Banksy’s graffiti can be seen on walls from post-hurricane New Orleans to the separation barrier on the Palestinian West Bank. He fiercely guards his anonymity to avoid prosecution. An eccentric French shopkeeper turned documentary maker attempts to locate and befriend Banksy, only to have the artist turn the camera back on its owner. The film includes footage of Banksy, Shepard Fairey, Invader, and many of the world’s most infamous graffiti artists at work, on walls, and in interviews. As Banksy describes it, “It’s basically the story of how one man set out to film the unfilmable. And failed.” https://en.wikipedia.org/wiki/Exit_Through_the_Gift_Shop.

8 Chiapas has over 30 percent of Mexico’s entire drinking water reserves. Annual rainfall amounts to 14,000 cubic meters per person, the highest figure in the country.

9 Easton Cowboys & Cowgirls, https://eastoncowfolk.org.uk/. For more details about Kiptik, visit the website at https://kiptik.org/. The fundraising coffee is available from https://www.cafe-libertad.de/coffee-and-espresso.

10 Republica team members became more active in domestic protests against the planned war in Iraq, distributing leaflets in local elections against the fascist British National Party, and in 2004 formed a fair trade committee that led boycotts of products from Nike, Coca-Cola, McDonalds to Nestlé. Republica Internationale, https://republica.international/. See also Rosalba Icaza, “Whose Prosperity and Security? Women Citizenships in Age of Neo-liberal Regionalisms” (November 5, 2013), https://www.alternative-regionalisms.org/wp-content/uploads/2009/07/icaza_womencitizenship.pdf; Mick Totten, “Playing Left Wing: From Sunday League Socialism to International Solidarity. A Social History of the Development of Republica Internationale FC,” *Sport in Society*, 18, no. 4 (2015), pp. 477–496; Simpson and McMahon, *Freedom through Football*, pp. 16–17.

Re-Call and Conclusion

Tarzan's signature yell echoed across Latin America in the 1950s as Tarzan movies, radio, and comics continued to circulate widely. The Ape man had enormous popularity in Mexico. Young people read Tarzan comics, saw Tarzan movies, and collected picture cards of Tarzan, Cheetah, Jane (Yein), and other characters, and scenes from their adventures were saved in souvenir albums. "I myself was a great fan of the character," recalls Professor Carmen Nava. "On Sundays after hearing Mass, my brothers and I went to the matinees of the two cinemas that were in Tlalnepantla; in the theaters, the kids shouting and hollering made it difficult to follow the film, but that was part of the fun. My brothers and I would pool our money to buy the comics first thing on Saturdays and, over the next week, we would rent them to our schoolmates for a few cents to thicken our comic book collections and buy the cards to fill the albums."[1] Nava continues, "My grammar school was very near a river and big trees and sometimes we skipped classes and went over there to reenact Tarzan's adventures; instead of monkeys we pretended that our dogs, rabbits, and even chickens were wild animals. It was great fun. Sometimes climbing trees or trying to use ropes to cross the river (actually a small spring), would get us bruised or soaked. Our mothers knew what went on on

Latin American Cultural Objects and Episodes, First Edition. William H. Beezley.

our 'expeditions' but accepted our excuses to justify the bumps on our heads and purple bruises on our arms and legs."[2]

The actor who personified Tarzan, notwithstanding the many who played the jungle hero, was Johnny Weissmuller, who appeared in RKO and MGM films – all widely shown in Latin America. He had won five Olympic gold medals in swimming and, after becoming a movie star, married Mexican beauty queen and singer Lupe Vélez, moving to Acapulco. Some six years after the marriage, Hollywood moguls thought it would be better if Johnny, as a popular star and sex symbol, were single, so they offered Lupe $10,000 to accept a divorce and she did. Weissmuller continued to live off and on in Acapulco until his death. During World War II, one Tarzan film was made without him in Quetzaltenago, Guatemala, creating stories and legends about Tarzan and cultural appropriation and globalization.

Perhaps the most persistent Tarzan in Latin America story concerns Weissmuller playing in a celebrity golf tournament in Havana on New Year's Day, 1959. As his son recounted it, "rebel troops were rounding up and summarily executing anybody who remotely resembled a rich capitalist [this fabricates events], and the golf course was a prime hunting ground for them. They found Johnny Weissmuller there, playing in a foursome on the thirteenth hole." The bearded revolutionaries demanded the golfers identify themselves and "They began to interrogate the[m]. . . one by one. When they came to Weissmuller, he grinned and said, 'Me Tarzan.' Since Dad did not know how to pronounce Tarzan in Spanish ('Tarzaan'), the rebels had no idea what the hell he was talking about, and they began to prod him with their rifles. In desperation, Dad threw back his head and gave out a Tarzan yell while beating his chest. 'Eeee!' shouted the rebel leader. 'Es Tarzan! Tu viste? Es Tarzan de la Jungla!' [It's Tarzan. Do you see? It's Tarzan of the jungle.] They laughed, patted him on the back, and tried to shake his hand all at the same time." One added, "'Tarzan! Welcome to Cuba!'" Johnny and his companions, rather than being kidnapped, were given a rebel escort to the club house. These rebels "might not have recognized the pope, but they sure as hell knew who Tarzan was."[3]

Castro later appropriated Tarzan to use in his propaganda against the United States. In a newsreel critical of racial relations and police policies in the U.S., the news commentator denounced programs of racial discrimination and laws of white supremacy, illustrated with a clip of Johnny Weissmuller as Tarzan killing African tribesmen. A scene followed of contemporary racial conflicts in Southern cities, in which police used dogs, billy clubs, and tear gas to break up Civil Rights demonstrations.[4]

Conclusions

Throughout the text of these chapters, theoretical and methodological approaches to culture have been imbedded, inferred, and suggested. Almost never have they been discussed, preventing the distraction of the narrative away from either the object or the episode of primary concern. These theories and methods do make for intriguing discussion and perhaps might provide deeper understanding of the topics. For example, the chapter on bowler hats refers or alludes to "cargo cults," as developed by Bronislaw Malinowski, Karl Marx's "commodity fetishism" Thorstein Veblen's "conspicuous consumption," and James Scott's "weapons of the weak" –anthropological and economic paradigms of analysis that enrich the discussion of Andean hats. Nevertheless, that these intellectual constructs can be incorporated so easily without comment in the text shows their ready acceptance in descriptive analysis. Yet, each one, if considered in the Andean context, would enliven the discussion and prompt further explication of hats in everyday culture and ordinary life. For some, the entire narrative will suggest comparison with Michel Foucault's *The Order of Things* (1966; translation 1970) and his development of discourse analysis and the episteme. Others will prefer to ignore this rather shopworn approach and to examine the episodes and objects without theoretical interference.

Another dimension of this collection uses narration that may seem to border on stream of consciousness, that is, an object, interesting in itself, may only be stated to initiate improvisation and discussion. This approach resembles, it appears, the software practice of connecting different pieces together so data can flow from one to the next, called a pipeline – a reference to surfing language and music.[5] This relates as well to the internet review called surfing the web. "Red Flags," for example initially ties the location to the Entre Rios region of Argentina, but otherwise results in improvisational themes of folk saints and the ex votos offered to them. In this sense, the material item or object serves the chapter the way a blue note – played lower and flatter than the standard note of a composition to introduce improvisation – occurs in musical performances. The rest of the narrative may prove barely recognizable without close attention to the blue note and handy acknowledgment of the improvised relationships. Carlo Ginzburg once wrote about these kinds of relationships, developed from the smallest and seemingly most irrelevant of clues, using all sorts of analogies such as Mendel's genetic laws that he called an indexical paradigm. Art historian Nicolas Bourriaud described Ginzburg's method as "where one witnesses the practice of the decryption of silent or imperceptible traces" or, in his felicitous phrase, it "can be thought of as 'retrospective prophecies.'"[6] This narrative offers another exercise in this way of applying the same approach. These 10 chapters represent a composite that projects a mosaic, not bound by the geographic boundaries of Latin America, but one that connects global cultures with local communities, and in which appropriation, blending, and re-creation are typical. Overall, they represent a mosaic that offers delight and surprise.

"The Tarzan craze lasted for years," says Carmen Nava. "The hobby was shared by our friends and relatives, even the adults. A good portion of our talks and fantasies was dedicated to commenting on everything we saw, read and invented about Tarzan. Still today [2020], people of my generation cite or evoke sayings, scenarios and attitudes (imitations of the language of Cheetah and Tarzan)."[7]

These objects and episodes, and many others, as a pipeline help define memories for individuals. Often they have outgrown the activity or lost track of objects, but the shadows of them linger.

Notes

1 There are books and articles on the impact of the "Monkey Man" movies and comics in Mexico. Irene Herner (*Tarzan, Man and Myth*) from time to time appears in the second-rate book stalls. Carmen Nava, Professor of History, Universidad Autonoma Metropolitana, to the author, May 25, 2020.

2 Carmen Nava to the author, May 28, 2020.

3 Johnny Weissmuller, William Reed, and W. Craig Reed, *Tarzan, My Father* (Toronto: ECW Press, 2008), p. 101.

4 "Cuba Uses a Tarzan Film For Anti-U.S. Propaganda," *New York Times* (August 16, 1964), https://www.nytimes.com/1964/08/16/archives/cuba-uses-a-tarzan-film-for-antius-propaganda.html.

5 Cliff Cary, software engineer, to author, June 4, 2020. The surf classic is the Chantay's 1963 "Pipeline" on the Lawrence Welk show: https://www.youtube.com/watch?v=j09C8clJaXo.

6 Nicolas Bourriaud, "Refuse – Notes on Artistic Work as Social Waste," https://www.pca-stream.com/en/articles/refuse-notes-on-artistic-work-as-social-waste-47, discussing Carlo Ginzburg's paradigm from *Threads and Traces: True, False, Fictive* (Berkeley: University of California Press, 2012).

7 Carmen Nava to the author, May 25, 2020.

Bibliography

Archives

Archivio Storico Borsalino Indice, Municipal Library, Alexandria, Italy.

Champion Folk Collection, Raleigh, North Carolina. 103 Bazooka wrappers from Argentina.

Cuban Heritage Collection, the University of Miami.

Tulane University Library, Special Collection holds a massive collection of radionovelas – more than 9,000 reel-to-reel.

Online Sources

http://movingtoecuador.blogspot.com/2009/10/ecuadorian-hats.html

http://mundohispanoloscervantinos.blogspot.com/2013/11/las-cholitas-luchadoras.html

http://todochiapas.mx/chiapas/el-pozol-de-chiapas/426

http://www.bloganavazquez.com/2010/02/07/el-sombrero-bombin-borsalinoy-las-mujeres-de-bolivia/

http://www.ecuadortravelsite.org/traditional_costume.html

http://www.hathistory.org/borsalino/

http://www.italianosenchile.cl/documentos/documentos-tacna.html

Latin American Cultural Objects and Episodes, First Edition. William H. Beezley.

http://www.made-in-italy.com/italian-fashion/designers-and-brands/borsalino

https://cartoonnetwork.fandom.com/wiki/Cartoon_Network_(Latin_America)

https://en.wikipedia.org/wiki/Boogie,_el_aceitoso

https://en.wikipedia.org/wiki/Mafalda

https://en.wikipedia.org/wiki/Santa_Muerte

https://kiptik.org/

https://schoolsforchiapas.org/store/artesania/dolls/rebelde-zapatista-doll/

https://www.expedia.com/Mafalda-Statue-Oviedo.d553248621594454969.Vacation-Attraction

https://www.tripadvisor.com/Attraction_Review-g312741-d2136797-Reviews-Mafalda_Statue

"Antonio Gil," documentary by Lía Dansker, premiered at BAFICI (Buenos Aires International Festival of Independent Cinema), 2013, Competencia Argentina; CDROM – Almas Milagrosas, https://www.equiponaya.com.ar/forms/suscripcion_almas.htm.

"Argentines: The Past Masters of Nicknames," https://www.gringoinbuenosaires.com/argentines-masters-nicknames/.

"Author of Some of Bazooka Gum's Jokes Finally Revealed in Argentina," *Latin American News Digest* (June 12–20, 2019), https://latinamericannewsdigest.com/author-bazooka-gums-jokes-finally-revealed-argentina/.

"Beat Nation: Art, Hip Hop and Aboriginal Culture," Vancouver Art Gallery, https://canadianart.ca/reviews/beat-nation/.

"Brazil in the World Cup 1938 – France," http://www.v-brazil.com/world-cup/history/1938-France.php.

"Brazil National Force Sent to Land Dispute Region," *BBC News* (November 29, 2013), https://www.bbc.co.uk/news/world-latin-america-25161541.

"Brazilian Indigenous Man Shot Dead in Mato Grosso do Sol," *BBC News* (June 13, 2013), https://www.bbc.co.uk/news/world-latin-america-22896256.

"Cuba Uses a Tarzan Film For Anti-U.S. Propaganda," *New York Times* (August 16, 1964), https://www.nytimes.com/1964/08/16/archives/cuba-uses-a-tarzan-film-for-antius-propaganda.html.

"Culto al Gauchito Gil," Diccionario de Mitos y Leyendas, https://www.cuco.com.ar/gauchito_gil.htm.

"Día del Pollo a la Brasa: entérate cómo empezó la historia," Peru.com (July 16, 2017),https://peru.com/estilo-de-vida/gastronomia/dia-pollo-brasa-enterate-como-empezo-historia-noticia-523670.

"Ecuador: Authorities Misuse Judicial System to Stop Protests," *Amnesty International* (July 17, 2012), https://www.amnesty.org/en/press-releases/2012/07/ecuador-authorities-misuse-judicial-system-stop-protests-2012-07-17-0/.

"El Gauchito Gil, el santo popular que conquistó la Argentina," https://www.elmundo.es/america/2013/04/17/argentina/1366226839.html.

"Ex Votos – Mexican Folk, Peruvian Milagros," https://marciaweberartobjects.com/artists/ex-votos-mexican-folk-art/.

"Filmmakers search for Montezuma's treasure in Three Lakes Pond," https://whatliesbeyond.boards.net/thread/1160/filmmakers-search-montezumas-treasure-haunted.

"Futbol y Libertad: Banksy, Inter Milan, and the Zapatistas," *The People's Game* (June 24, 2014), http://www.thepeoplesgame.org/2014/06/24/futbol-y-libertad-banksy-inter-milan-and-the-zapatistas/.

"History of Samba Music," https://www.brazilcultureandtravel.com/history-of-samba-music.html.

"Las cholitas luchadores," Mundo Hispano Los Cervantinos, http://mundohispanoloscervantinos.blogspot.com/2013/11/las-cholitas-luchadoras.html.

"Mural Painting in Chiapas with Banksy: Easton Cowboys," http://schoolsforchiapas.org/library/mural-painting-chiapas-banksy/.

"Murió Jorge Cázares, el pintor de los paisajes de las cajas de cerillos," https://www.milenio.com/cultura/jorge-cazares-muere-autor-pinturas-cajas-cerillos?fbclid=IwAR0_yBKEnVonqnezk0XEzjbvjBjjreXNkEABsENwkMNlI-WQT3F7GfqdM9U.

"My Top 27 Favorite Colombian Soap Operas," by tbell1826, created October 9, 2011, https://www.imdb.com/list/ls003608937/.

"Pollo a la brasa . . . divine pleasure!!!!!" Gringo Peru, https://gringoperu.blogspot.com/2016/05/pollo-la-brasa-divine-pleasure.html.

"¿Qué son los Objectos Desobedientes?" (August 9, 2014), http://www.bbc.co.uk/mundo/noticias/2014/08/140801_finde_cultura_objetos_desobedientes_ch.

"*Secret of the Incas* (1954)," Turner Classic Movies, https://www.tcm.com/tcmdb/title/89450/Secret-of-the-Incas/notes.html.

"7 Spanish Comic Book Characters from Latin America," http://www.speakinglatino.com/spanish-comic-book-characters/.

"Sumac, Yma," Encyclopedia.com, https://www.encyclopedia.com/education/news-wires-white-papers-and-books/sumac-yma.

"The Masked Shoe Shiners of Bolivia – in pictures," photos by Federico Estol, *Guardian* (September 11, 2019), https://www.theguardian.com/artanddesign/gallery/2019/sep/11/shoe-shiners-la-paz-bolivia-picture-gallery-photography.

"Top Five Aboriginal Stories of 2013," *CBC News* (December 30, 2013), https://www.cbc.ca/news/aboriginal/top-5-aboriginal-stories-of-2013-1.2477363.

"Tras las Huellas del Tío Barbas," eltiempo.com (November 5, 1995), https://www.eltiempo.com/archivo/documento/MAM-446712.

"Trilogía Sobre Problemáticas Mapuches Inicia Itinerancia en la Capital," *Santi Teatro y Danza: Crítica de Teatro y Danza/Reseñas/Entrevistas*, 2013, http://santi.cl/dev/index.php/resenas/565-trilogia-sobre-problematicas-mapuches-inicia-itinerancia-en-la-capital.

"USDA International Egg and Poultry: Peru Poultry Production to Increase," https://www.themeatsite.com/reports/?id=3751.

"Zapatista Consulta," Invisible Cinema, http://www.invisibleamerica.com/zapatista.html.

"Zapatista Leader Stars as Comedian," BBC News (February 1, 2001), http://news.bbc.co.uk/1/hi/world/americas/1148832.stm.

"Zapatista Rebels and Inter Milan," November 14, 2012. Originally published in Spanish by F.C. Internazionale Milano, translated by irlandesa, https://footballbar.wordpress.com/2012/11/14/zapatista-rebels-and-inter-milan/.

"Zapatista Rebels Woo Inter Milan," BBC News (May 11, 2005), http://news.bbc.co.uk/2/hi/4537859.stm.

A. J. Samuels, "The AfroReggae Cultural Group: A Rebirth Of Hope Within Rio De Janeiro's Favelas," Culture Trip (January 24, 2018), https://theculturetrip.com/south-america/brazil/articles/the-afroreggae-cultural-group-a-rebirth-of-hope-within-rio-s-favelas/.

Alanna Nunez and Alex Brady, "These Are the Absolute Best Telenovelas of All Time," *Cosmopolitan for Latinas* (May 5, 2020), http://www.cosmopolitan.com/entertainment/tv/news/a31651/10-best-novelas-of-all-time/.

Christopher Dennis, "Locating Hip-Hop's Place within Latin American Cultural Studies," *Alter/nativas: Latin American Cultural Studies Journal* (Spring 2014), https://alternativas.osu.edu/en/issues/spring-2014/essays1/dennis.html.

Claudia Looi, "Bowler Hats and the Cholas of Bolivia," http://travelwritingpro.com/bowler-hats-cholas-bolivia/.

Daiana Halac, "What's in an Argentine Nickname?" (December 7, 2014), https://fusion.tv/story/68349/whats-in-an-argentine-nickname/.

David Barnett, "El Hombre Araña! Why Mexico Created an Alternate Spider-Man in the 70s," *The Guardian* (March 5, 2019), https://www.theguardian.com/books/2019/mar/05/el-hombre-arana-why-mexico-created-an-alternate-spider-man-in-the-70s.

Don Anderson, "Bowled over by a hat beloved by Orangemen," *Belfast Telegraph* (March 3, 2015), https://www.belfasttelegraph.co.uk/opinion/columnists/bowled-over-by-the-history-of-a-hat-beloved-by-orangemen-30380950.html.

Easton Cowboys & Cowgirls, https://eastoncowfolk.org.uk/.

Félix B. Caignet, interview with Orlando Castellanos on Radio Havana, Cuba, August 30, 1972, https://en.wikipedia.org/wiki/F%C3%A9lix_B._Caignet.

Glen Weldon, "Bazooka Joe Has Been Honorably Discharged," *New Republic Digital Edition* (December 7, 2012), https://newrepublic.com/article/110868/bazooka-joe-comics-pulled-bubble-gum-after-58-years.

Guillermo Torrejon Nava, "Pollo a la brasa," Sabores de mi Tierra (October 28, 2013), http://amoperusaboresdemitierra.blogspot.com/2013/10/pollo-la-brasa.html.

Gwen Thompkins, "Massive Digitization Effort Is The Latest Plot Twist For Cuban Radio Soap Operas," *Repeating Islands* blog (July 26, 2019), https://repeatingislands.com/2019/07/26/massive-digitization-effort-is-the-latest-plot-twist-for-cuban-radio-soap-operas/.

Haroldo and Flávia de Faria Castro, "Bolívia dos Mil e Um Chapéus," *Revista Geográfica Universal*, no. 44 (May-June, 1978), p. 105, http://unboliviable.tumblr.com/post/11006496682/sombreros-bolivianos.

Hisham Aidi, "Hip-Hop Diplomacy: U.S. Cultural Diplomacy Enters a New Era," *Foreign Affairs* (April 16, 2014), https://www.foreignaffairs.com/articles/united-states/2014-04-16/hip-hop-diplomacy.

Ignacio de los Reyes, "Cinco cosas que probablemente no sabías de Mafalda," BBC Mundo, Buenos Aires (September 29, 2014), https://www.bbc.com/mundo/noticias/2014/09/140929_cultura_cinco_curiosidades_mafalda_ch.

Isabella Cosse, "Everyday Life in Argentina in the 1960s," *Oxford Research Encyclopedia for Latin America* (July 27, 2017), https://oxfordre.com/latinamericanhistory/view/10.1093/acrefore/9780199366439.001.0001/acrefore-9780199366439-e-316.

Jack Pannell, "Benetton in Patagonia: The Oppression of Mapuche in the Argentine South," *Council on Hemispheric Affairs*, https://dbn.f1b.myftpupload.com/wp-content/uploads/2017/08/Benetton-and-Mapuche-1.pdf.

Jacob Rekedal, "Hip-Hop Mapuche on the Araucanian Frontera," *Alter/nativas: Latin American Cultural Studies Journal*, https://alternativas.osu.edu/en/issues/spring-2014/essays1/rekedal.html.

James Owen, "Lost Inca Gold," National Geographic, https://www.nationalgeographic.com/history/archaeology/lost-inca-gold/.

Jane Onyanga-Omara, "Banksy in Goal: The Story of the Easton Cowboys and Cowgirls," BBC News (September 14, 2012), https://www.bbc.co.uk/news/uk-england-bristol-19410566.

João Fellet, "Indigenous Brazilians Use Web to Fight for Rights," *BBC News* (June 5, 2013), https://www.bbc.co.uk/news/world-latin-america-22787583.

John Noble Wilford, "First Chickens in Americas Were Brought From Polynesia," *New York Times* (June 5, 2007), https://www.nytimes.com/2007/06/05/science/05chic.html.

Jorge Yeshayahu Gonzales-Lara, "La historia del pollo a las brasas peruano Patrimonio cultural e identidad gastronómica," Monografias.com, https://www.monografias.com/trabajos82/historia-pollo-brasa-peruano/historia-pollo-brasa-peruano.shtml.

Kew Royal Botanical Gardens, "Conservation, Restoration and Sustainable Management of Dry Forest in Southern Peru: *The Huarango Project*," https://www.kew.org/science/tropamerica/peru/index.htm.

Kew Royal Botanical Gardens, "Working alongside Community: The Huarango Festival," https://www.kew.org/science/tropamerica/peru/activities.html.

Kristina Nelson and Cynthia P. Schneider, "Mightier than the Sword: Arts and Culture in the U.S.-Muslim World Relationship," Brookings Paper (June 30, 2008), https://www.brookings.edu/research/mightier-than-the-sword-arts-and-culture-in-the-u-s-muslim-world-relationship/.

Lance Selfa and Stuart Easterling, "Twenty Years after the Zapatista Uprising," *Socialist Worker* (January 21, 2014), https://socialistworker.org/2014/01/21/twenty-years-after-the-zapatista-uprising.

Lucius Beebe, "The Hat that Won the West," *Deseret News*, Salt Lake City, Utah (October 27, 1957), https://news.google.com/newspapers?nid=336&dat=19571026&id=xQQpAAAAIBAJ&sjid=PkgDAAAAIBAJ&pg=7036,5636283&hl=en.

Mariano Vespa, "Las globolocuras de Fogwill," *La Agenda Revista* (June 23, 2015),https://laagenda.buenosaires.gob.ar/post/122207613355/las-globolocuras-de-fogwill.

Mariolina Rizzi Salvatori, "Understanding Ex Votos," http://www.mariolinasalvatori.com/understanding-ex-votos/.

Mark Morgan Ford, "The Man in the Hathaway Shirt" (November 19, 2015), https://www.earlytorise.com/the-man-in-the-hathaway-shirt/.

Mark Palmer, "InterMat Rewind: 1932 Olympics" (August 11, 2008), http://intermatwrestle.com/articles/3962/Rev-Rewind-1932-Olympics.

Mayra Cue Sierra, "Radionovela 'El derecho de nacer' (Tercera Parte y final)," *el arte de hacer radio* blog (April 27, 2008), https://haciendoradio.blogspot.com/2008/04/radionovela-derecho-de-nacer-tercera.html.

Michael Powell and Jürgen Horn, "A Tour of Sucre's Hat Factory," http://bolivia.for91days.com/2011/06/12/a-tour-of-sucres-hat-factory/.

Nathalie Malinarich, "BBC Profile: The Zapatistas' Mysterious Leader" (March 11, 2001), http://news.bbc.co.uk/1/hi/world/americas/1214676.stm.

NPR, "Hip-Hop's Aboriginal Connection," *Oregon Public Broadcasting* (January 4, 2014), https://text.npr.org/s.php?sId=259428743.

R. Andrew Chesnut, "Jesus Malverde: Not Just a Narcosaint," HuffPost (January 9, 2014, updated March 11, 2014), https://www.huffpost.com.

Republica Internationale, https://republica.international/.

Rosalba Icaza, "Whose Prosperity and Security? Women Citizenships in Age of Neo-liberal Regionalisms" (November 5, 2013), https://www.alternative-regionalisms.org/wp-content/uploads/2009/07/icaza_womencitizenship.pdf.

Rosalva Bermudez-Ballin, "Interview with Zach la Rocha (Rage Against The Machine)," Nuevo Amanecer Press (via spunk.org), July 8, 1998.

Rosamond Purcell, "The Stories of Strangers: Mexican *Ex-Voto* Paintings," *VQR*, 84, no. 2 (2008), https://www.vqronline.org/vqr-gallery/stories-strangers-mexican-ex-voto-paintings.

Sarah Brown, "The Top 15 Brazilian Samba Songs to Add to Your Playlist Right Now" (October 3, 2017), https://theculturetrip.com/south-america/brazil/articles/the-top-15-brazilian-samba-songs-to-add-to-your-playlist-right-now/.

Silvia Ramos, "Brazilian responses to violence and new forms of mediation: the case of the Grupo Cultural AfroReggae and the experience of the project 'Youth and the Police,'" https://www.scielosp.org/article/csc/2006.v11n2/419-428/en/.

Subverso and Portavoz, "Lo Que No Voy a Decir" (music video), posted January 22, 2013, https://www.youtube.com/watch?v=1Lm00GF5Faw.

Terri Gordon-Zolov and Eric Zolov, "The Walls of Chile Speak of a Suppressed Rage," https://www.thenation.com/article/archive/chile-protest-art/.

Tim Shenk, "Quino, creator of 'Mafalda,' keeps it light while inspiring generations," *Justicia Globa* (July 17, 2011), https://enjusticiaglobal.wordpress.com/2011/07/17/quino-creator-of-mafalda-keeps-it-light-while-inspiring-generations/.

Timothy Wilson and Mara Favoretto, "Rock Nacional in Argentina during the Dictatorship," *Oxford Research Encyclopedia of Latin American History* (August 5, 2016), https://oxfordre.com/latinamericanhistory/view/10.1093/acrefore/9780199366439.001.0001/acrefore-9780199366439-e-368.

Zoila Mendoza, "From Folklore to Exotica: Yma Sumac and the Performance of Inca Identity," *The Appendix*, http://theappendix.net/issues/2013/7/from-folklore-to-exotica-yma-sumac-and-inca-identity.

Zona Latina, http://www.zonalatina.com/zldata02.htm.

Books and Articles

Arreche, Araceli Mariel. "Teatro Mapuche: Acercamiento a Una *Teatralidad Subyugada*," *Revista Afuera: Estudios de Crítica Cultural*, 4, no. 7 (November 2009).

Arreche, Araceli Mariel. "Teatro Mapuche: Notas Sobre una Teatralidad ¿Invisible?," *Revista del Centro Cultural de la Cooperación*, 2, no. 1 (April 2008).

Arreche, Araceli Mariel, Giberti, Karina Beatriz, and Pereira Covarrubias, Andrés. "Teatro Mapuche: Prácticas de Identidad y Resistencia," *Espacios de crítica y producción*, 39.

Aurreocoechea, Manuel. *El Universal: Espejo de Nuestro Tiempo. 90 años del El Gran Diario de México* (México: MVS Editorial, 2006).

Bazooka Joe and his Gang (New York: Abrams ComicArts, 2013).

Beezley, William H. and Colin M. MacLachlan, "Profile: Sarita - The People's Saint," in William H. Beezley and Colin M. MacLachlan, *Latin America: The Peoples and their History* (Ft. Worth, TX: Harcourt Brace College Publishers, 2000), pp. 250–251.

Belmonte Pijuán, Mauricio. *Polenta: Familias italianas en Bolivia* (Editorial Gente Común: Ambasciata d'Italia in La Paz, 2009).

Benamou, Catherine L. *It's All True: Orson Welles's Pan-American Odyssey* (Berkeley: University of California Press, 2007).

Blaya Alende, Joaquín. *El Progreso Italiano en Chile* (Santiago: Imprenta La Ilustración, 1921).

Brooklyn Daily Eagle (November 11, 1930), p. 4.

Canavesi de Sahonero, M. Lissette. *El Traje de la Chola Paceña* (La Paz, Bolivia: Editorial Los Amigos del Libro, 1987).

Castellanos, Nelson. "Historia de los medios: *El precio de un pecado*: Oír radionovelas a escondidas," *Signo y Pensamiento*, 48 (January/June 2006).

Castro, Ruy. *Uma biografia de Carmen Miranda* (São Paulo: Companhia das Letreas, 2005).

Cervantes, Miguel de. *Don Quijote*, translated by Burton Raffel and edited by Diana de Armas Wilson (New York: W. W. Norton, 1999).

Chang, Jeff. "Born in Fire: A Hip-Hop Odyssey," *UNESCO Courier* (July/August 2000).

Chesnut, R. Andrew. *Devoted to Death: Santa Muerte, the Skeleton Saint*, 2nd edition (New York: Oxford University Press, 2018).

Chico, Beverley. "South American Headwear," in Margot Blum Shevill, ed., *Berg Encyclopedia of World Dress and Fashion: Latin America and the Caribbean*. Berg Fashion Library, pp. 456–464. eBook.

Cohan, Tony, Levick, Melba, and Takahashi, Masako. *Mexicolor: The Spirit of Mexican Design* (San Francisco: Chronicle Books, 1998).

"Colombian TV Viewers Obsessed With Fate of 'Betty the Ugly One,'" *Arizona Daily Star* (Tucson), April 25, 2001.

Cosse, Isabella. *Mafalda: A Social and Political History of Latin America's Global Comic*, translated by Laura Pérez Carrara (Durham, NC: Duke University Press, 2019).

Cushman, Gregory. *Guano and the Opening of the Pacific World: A Global Ecological History* (New York: Cambridge University Press, 2013).

Davis, Darién J. "Racial Parity and National Humor: Exploring Brazilian Samba from Noel Rosa to Carmen Miranda, 1930–1939," in William H. Beezley and Linda A. Curcio-Nagy, eds., *Latin American Popular Culture: An Introduction* (Wilmington, DE: SR Books, 2003), pp. 183–200.

de Faria Castro, Haroldo and Flávia. "Los Mil y Un Sombreros de la Cultura Boliviana," *Geomunco*, 8, no. 6 (1984), pp. 566–571.

De Ferrari, Gabriella. *Gringa Latina: A Woman of Two Worlds* (Boston: Houghton Mifflin Company, 1995).

Dennis, Christopher. *Afro-Colombian Hip-Hop: Globalization, Transcultural Music, and Ethnic Identities* (Lanham, MD: Lexington Books, 2012).

Dewey, Matías. *Making it at Any Cost: Aspirations and Politics in a Counterfeit Clothing Marketplace* (Austin: University of Texas Press, 2020).

Fernández-Lamarqu, Maia. Foreword by John Stephens. *Variations of the Story as a Socio-Ethical Text* (Jefferson, NC: McFarland & Company, 2019).

Finder, Joseph. "The Question of Carlos," *New York Times* (January 2, 1994).

Fox, Aaron A. *Real Country: Music and Language in Working-Class Culture* (Durham, NC: Duke University Press, 2004).

García Barrera, Mabel and Contreras Hauser, Verónica. "La Resistencia Cultural en el Mural," in Mabel García Barrera, Hugo Carrasco Muñoz, and Verónica Contreras Hauser, eds., *Crítica Situada: El Estado Actual del Arte y la Poesía Mapuche* (Temuco, Chile: Editorial Florencia, 2005).

García de León, Antonio. *Fronteras interiores. Chiapas: una modernidad particular* (México: Océano, 2002).

Gill, Lesley. *Precarious Dependencies: Gender, Class, and Domestic Service in Bolivia* (New York: Columbia University Press, 1994).

Ginzburg, Carlo. *Threads and Traces: True, False, Fictive* (Berkeley: University of California Press, 2012).

Graziano, Frank. *Cultures of Devotion: Folk Saints of Spanish America* (New York: Oxford University Press, 2007).

Guss, David M. *To Weave and Sing: Art, Symbol, and Narrative in the South American Rainforest* (Berkeley: University of California Press, 1990).

Harvey, Neill. *Rebellion in Chiapas* (New York: Cambridge University Press, 2000).

"Hats Off to Bolivians – From Derbies to Helmets, They're Tops," *Los Angeles Times* (January 25, 1987).

Howard, Dennis. "Punching for Recognition: The Jukebox as a Key Instrument in the Development of Popular Jamaican Music," *Caribbean Quarterly*, 53, no. 4 (December 2007), pp. 32–46.

Iglesias Kuntz, Lucia. "Quino on the Funny Side of Freedom," *UNESCO Courier* (July/August 2000).

Kaufman, J. B. *South of the Border with Disney: Walt Disney and the Good Neighbor Program, 1941–1948* (Burbank, CA: Disney Press, 2009).

Kelley, Robin D. G. "OGS in Postindustrial Los Angeles: Evolution of a Style," in Stephen Duncombe, ed., *Cultural Resistance Reader* (New York: Verso, 2002).

Kramer, Andrew E. "Memo to Exxon: Business With Russia May Involve Guns and Balaclavas," *New York Times* (August 31, 2011).

Krohn-Hansen, Christian. *The Dominican Colmado from Santo Domingo to New York* (New York: Oxford University Press, 2016).

La Prensa (Managua), June 1, 1955.

Leite Lopes, José Sergio. "Class and Ethnicity, and Color in the Making of Brazilian Football," *Daedalus* 129, no. 2 (Spring 2000), pp. 239–270.

Lever, Janet. *Soccer Madness: Brazil's Passion for the World's Most Popular Sport* (Long Grove, IL: Waveland Press, 1983).

Lewis, Jerry D. "Brazilian Athletes Perked Up The 1932 Games With Their Coffee Caper," *Sports Illustrated* (August 11, 1980), pp. 11–12.

Limansky, Nicholas E. *Yma Sumac: The Art Behind the Legend* (New York: YBK Publishers, 2009).

Macklin, June. "Two Faces of Sainthood: The Pious and the Popular," *Journal of Latin American Lore*, 14, no. 1 (Summer 1988).

Magdalena, Carlos. *The Plant Messiah: Adventures in Search of the World's Rarest Species* (New York: Doubleday, 2017).

Martín-Barbero, Jesús and Muñoz, Sonia. *Televisión y melodrama: Géneros y lecturas de la telenovela en Colombia* (Bogotá, Colombia: Tercer Mundo Editores, 1992).

Mathews, Jennifer P. *Chicle: The Chewing Gum of the Americas, From the Ancient Maya to William Wrigley* (Tucson: University of Arizona Press, 2009).

Mazor, Barry. *Ralph Peer and the Making of Popular Roots Music* (Chicago: Chicago Review Press, 2015).

Medino Cano, Federico. "La radionovela y el folletín," *Revista Universidad Pontificia Bolivariana*, 47, no. 145 (September 1998).

Merino, Ana. "Veritable Identities in the Mexican Comic Strip: Don Catrarino in the Stereotypical Space of the Cannibals," *International Journal of Comic Art*, 8, no. 1 (Spring/Summer 2006).

Metz, Jr., Jerry D. "Carnival as Brazil's 'Tropical Opera,'" in William H. Beezley, ed., *Cultural Nationalism and Ethnic Music in Latin America* (Albuquerque: University of New Mexico Press, 2018).

Mintz, Sidney. *Sweetness and Power: The Place of Sugar in Modern History* (New York: Penguin Books, 1985).

Morais, Richard C. *The Hundred-Foot Journey* (New York: Scribner, 2010).

Orovio, Helio. *Cuban Music from A to Z* (Durham, NC: Duke University Press, 2004).

Quinones, Sam. *True Tales from Another Mexico: The Lynch Mob, the Popsicle Kings, Chalino and the Bronx* (Albuquerque: University of New Mexico Press, 2001).

"Radio Revista No. 52," *Radio Matraca desde Berlín* (October 31, 2007).

Reuque Paillalef, Rosa Isolde. *When a Flower is Reborn: The Life and Times of a Mapuche Feminist*, edited and translated by Florencia E. Mallon (Durham, NC: Duke University Press, 2002).

Rizzi Salvatori, Mariolina. "Porque no puedo decir mi cuento: Mexican Ex-Votos' Iconographic Literacy," in John Trimbur, ed., *Popular Literacy: Studies in Cultural Practices and Poetics* (Pittsburgh: University of Pittsburgh Press, 2001).

Roberts, Sam. "Object Lessons in History," *New York Times* (September 27, 2014).

Rolston, Bill. "¡Hasta La Victoria! Murals and Resistance in Santiago, Chile," *Identities: Global Studies in Culture and Power*, 18, no. 2 (2011).

Rushdie, Salman. *The Jaguar Smile: A Nicaraguan Journey* (New York: Random House, 1987).

Sánchez Brick, Francisco. *Buscando a Kay Kay y Xeng Xeng Vilu* (Santiago, Chile: Tyro Teatro Banda, 2009).

Segrave, Kerry. *Jukeboxes: An American Social History* (Jefferson, NC: McFarland, 2002).

Seldes, Gilbert. *The 7 Lively Arts: The Classic Appraisal of the Popular Arts: Comic Strips, Movies, Musical Comedy, Vaudeville, Radio, Popular Music, Dance* (Mineola, NY: Dover Publications, 2001; originally published in 1924).

Simpson, Will and McMahon, Malcolm. *Freedom through Football: The Story of the Easton Cowboys and Cowgirls* (Bristol: Tangent Books, 2012).

Smith, Frederick H. *Caribbean Rum: A Social and Economic History* (Gainesville: University Press of Florida, 2008);

Sommer, Doris. "Introduction: Wiggle Room," in Doris Sommer, ed., *Cultural Agency in the Americas* (Durham, NC: Duke University Press, 2006).

Totten, Mick. "Playing Left Wing: From Sunday League Socialism to International Solidarity. A Social History of the Development of Republica Internationale FC," *Sport in Society*, 18, no. 4 (2015), pp. 477–496.

Vanderwood, Paul J. *Juan Soldado: Rapist, Murderer, Martyr, Saint* (Durham, NC: Duke University Press, 2006).

Vanderwood, Paul. *The Power of God Against the Guns of Government: Religious Upheaval in Mexico at the Turn of the Nineteenth Century* (Stanford: Stanford University Press, 1998).

Vilchis Roque, Alfredo. Photography by Pierre Schwartz. Foreword by Victoire and Hervé Di Rosa. *Infinitas Gracias: Contemporary Mexican Votive Painting* (San Francisco: Seuil Chronicle, 2004).

Wald, Elijah. *How the Beatles Destroyed Rock 'n' Roll: An Alternative History of American Popular Music* (New York: Oxford University Press, 2011).

Walker, Charles F. *The Tupac Amaru Rebellion* (Cambridge, MA: Harvard University Press, 2014).

Weissmuller, Johnny, Reed, William, and Reed, W. Craig. *Tarzan, My Father* (Toronto: ECW Press, 2008).

Wilker, Josh. *Cardboard Gods: An All-American Tale Told Through Baseball Cards: With 1 Stick Bubble Gum* (New York: Seven Footer Press, 2010).

Wong, Ketty. *Whose National Music? Identity, Mestizaje, and Migration in Ecuador* (Philadelphia: Temple University Press, 2012).

Yallop, David. *Tracking the Jackal: The Search for Carlos, the World's Most Wanted Man* (New York: Random House, 1994).

Unpublished Materials

Alejandro, Walter and Ojeda, Imilan. "Urban Ethnicity in Santiago de Chile: Mapuche Migration and Urban Space" (dissertation, Technical University of Berlin, 2009).

Díaz Aguad, Alfonso and Elías Pizarro Pizarro. "Algunos Antecedentes de la Presencia Italiana en la Ciudad de Tacna: 1885–1929" (manuscript).

Fiorito, Annalisa. "Il Fumetto Messicano negli anni del Nazionalismo Culturale. Studio di un caso: *Mamerto y sus Conocencias*, 1927–1943" (dissertation, Università degli Studi Torino, 2002).

Henriques, Donald Andrew. "Performing Nationalism: Mariachi, Media and the Transformation of a Tradition (1920–1942)" (thesis, University of Texas, 2006).

Mann, Mackenzie Rachel. "*Armas de Cultura*: Manifestations of Mapuche Resistance in Chile" (senior thesis, Elon University, 2014).

Navarro Granados, Daniel Efraín. "Charros, Chinos y Aboneros. Estereotipos, Nacionalismo y Xenofobia en el Humorismo Gráfico de El Universal" (dissertation, Universidad Nacional Autónoma de México, 2013).

Steiner, Peter. "A Suit Fit for A King: Narratives from a Cultural Empire" (seminar paper, University of Wyoming, 2014).

Correspondence and Interviews

Barickman, Bert, discussion with the author, Tucson, AZ, April 22, 2012.

Cary, Cliff, software engineer, to the author, June 4, 2020.

Galindo, Anabelle, interview with the author, Tucson, AZ, March 22, 2011.

Garcia, Elizabeth, discussion with the author, Tucson, AZ, March 26, 2011.

Gamba, Gian Paolo, Panizza company, email to the author, March 22, 2015.

Mason, Michelle, Colorado University-Colorado Springs, email to the author, March 8, 2019.

Mathews, Jennifer, Trinity University, San Antonio, TX, to the author, June 28, 2019.

Nava, Carmen, Professor of History, Universidad Metropolitana Mexico, to the author, September 2, 2014, May 25 and 28, 2020.

Nemser, Daniel, to the author, February 4, 2019.

Roldan, Mary, Professor of Latin American History, Hunter College, CUNY/ Graduate Center, email to the author, August 11, 2013.

Talamas, Adrienne, Buenos Aires high school teacher, to author, October 30, 2015.

Index